IRISH CHILDREN'S LITERATURE AND THE POETICS OF MEMORY

Bloomsbury Perspectives on Children's Literature

Bloomsbury Perspectives on Children's Literature seeks to expand the range and quality of research in children's literature through publishing innovative monographs by leading and rising scholars in the field. With an emphasis on cross and interdisciplinary studies, this series takes literary approaches as a starting point, drawing on the particular capacity for children's literature to open out into other disciplines.

Series Editor:

Dr Lisa Sainsbury, Director of the National Centre for Research in Children's Literature, Roehampton University, UK

Editorial Board:

Professor M. O. Grenby (Newcastle University, UK), Dr Marah Gubar (University of Pittsburgh, USA), Dr Vanessa Joosen (Tilburg University, The Netherlands)

Titles in the Series:

Adulthood in Children's Literature, Vanessa Joosen
The Courage to Imagine: The Child Hero in Children's Literature, Roni Natov
Ethics in British Children's Literature: Unexamined Life, Lisa Sainsbury
Fashioning Alice: The Career of Lewis Carroll's Icon, 1860–1901, Kiera Vaclavik
From Tongue to Text: A New Reading of Children's Poetry, Debbie Pullinger
Literature's Children: The Critical Child and the Art of Idealisation, Louise Joy
Rereading Childhood Books: A Poetics, Alison Waller
Metaphysics of Children's Literature, Lisa Fitzgerald

Forthcoming Titles:

Children's Literature and Material Culture, Jane Suzanne Carroll
Activist Authors and British Child Readers of Colour, Karen Sands-O'Connor
The Dark Matter of Children's "Fantastika" Literature, Chloé Germaine Buckley
British Children's Literature in Japanese Culture, Catherine Butler

IRISH CHILDREN'S LITERATURE AND THE POETICS OF MEMORY

Rebecca Long

BLOOMSBURY ACADEMIC
LONDON • NEW YORK • OXFORD • NEW DELHI • SYDNEY

BLOOMSBURY ACADEMIC
Bloomsbury Publishing Plc
50 Bedford Square, London, WC1B 3DP, UK
1385 Broadway, New York, NY 10018, USA
29 Earlsfort Terrace, Dublin 2, Ireland

BLOOMSBURY, BLOOMSBURY ACADEMIC and the Diana logo are
trademarks of Bloomsbury Publishing Plc

First published in Great Britain 2021
This paperback edition published 2022

Copyright © Rebecca Long, 2021

Rebecca Long has asserted her right under the Copyright, Designs and Patents
Act, 1988, to be identified as Author of this work.

Cover design by Namkwan Cho
Photograph © DEA / G. DAGLI ORTI / Getty Images

All rights reserved. No part of this publication may be reproduced or
transmitted in any form or by any means, electronic or mechanical,
including photocopying, recording, or any information storage or retrieval
system, without prior permission in writing from the publishers.

Bloomsbury Publishing Plc does not have any control over, or responsibility for, any
third-party websites referred to or in this book. All internet addresses given in this
book were correct at the time of going to press. The author and publisher regret any
inconvenience caused if addresses have changed or sites have ceased to exist, but can
accept no responsibility for any such changes.

A catalogue record for this book is available from the British Library.

A catalog record for this book is available from the Library of Congress.

ISBN: HB: 978-1-3501-6725-4
PB: 978-1-3501-9076-4
ePDF: 978-1-3501-6726-1
eBook: 978-1-3501-6727-8

Series: Bloomsbury Perspectives on Children's Literature

Typeset by Newgen KnowledgeWorks Pvt. Ltd., Chennai, India

To find out more about our authors and books visit www.bloomsbury.com
and sign up for our newsletters.

To Fergal Keyes, my best friend in all the world. He always knew the right questions to ask.

CONTENTS

INTRODUCTION   1

Chapter 1
RETRIEVING: STANDISH O'GRADY, ELEANOR HULL, AUGUSTA GREGORY   17

Chapter 2
RETELLING: ALICE DEASE, ELLA YOUNG, VIOLET RUSSELL, PADRAIC COLUM, JAMES STEPHENS   43

Chapter 3
REMEMBERING: PATRICIA LYNCH, UNA KELLY, EILÍS DILLON, J. S. ANDREWS   75

Chapter 4
REIMAGINING: PAT O'SHEA, ORLA MELLING, JIM O'LEARY, KATE THOMPSON, SIOBHAN DOWD   117

CONCLUSION: DARRAGH MARTIN, PEADAR Ó'GUILIN   157

Notes   169
Works Cited   179
Index   191

INTRODUCTION

Irish children's literature is shaped by a pattern of recurring mythological and folkloric narratives.[1] The narratives in this pattern carry and communicate images of cultural heritage that remain essentially the same, though their manifestations are continuously changing, with archetypes and stereotypes alike available to be reimagined by succeeding generations of authors and readers. This reimagination is discernible in texts that engage with mythological narratives, and with domestic narratives of childhood experience. This book investigates the presence and significance of cultural and mythological heritage in Irish children's literature between 1892 and 2016. It analyses representative works by Standish O'Grady (1894), Eleanor Hull (1898), Augusta Gregory (1906), Alice Dease (1907), Ella Young (1910), Violet Russell (1913), Padraic Colum (1916), James Stephens (1920), Patricia Lynch (1934), Una Kelly (1945), Eilís Dillon (1952), J. S. Andrews (1969), Pat O'Shea (1985), Orla Melling (1986), Jim O'Leary (1993), Kate Thompson (2005), Siobhan Dowd (2008), Darragh Martin (2013) and Peader Ó'Guilín (2016). These texts function as examples of the ways in which Irish children's literature uses myth to engage with issues of landscape, time and identity across the decades of the late nineteenth, twentieth and early twenty-first centuries. The texts are explored within a chronological timeline beginning with the publication of Standish O'Grady's *The Coming of Cuculain* in 1894 and concluding with Peader Ó'Guilín's *The Call* in 2016. The former stands as one of the first retellings of the Cuchulainn myth to both engage with Cuchulainn's childhood experiences and to establish a foundation for the repurposing of that material for reading by contemporary child readers. The latter, published in 2016, the centenary year of the 1916 Easter Rising, stands as another new departure in the treatment of myth in Irish children's literature. Its subversive reimagination of mythological figures offers an appropriate endpoint for this literary timeline, which aims to chart the development of that treatment in the aftermath of the Celtic Revival.

Cultures across the globe are influenced by stories, and Irish culture is markedly shaped by the power of narrative and by the necessity of remembering. The texts analysed here operate at the intersection between Irish children's literature and culture and Irish mythology; this book explores the meaning produced at that intersection and how it evolves from the late nineteenth into the early twenty-first century. While each of the chosen core texts functions within specific social and cultural contexts, to examine them together is to illuminate the thematic reciprocity that exists between them. They share a fundamental concern with issues of myth, time, identity and landscape, which is in turn part of a pattern that incorporates mythological narratives into Irish children's literature. This pattern operates within a cycle of retrieving cultural heritage, retelling the narratives that articulate that heritage, remembering those narratives, and reimagining them. The cycle allows new generations of readers to move towards an interaction with the cultural heritage that these representative texts convey and communicate. These are stories that return to be retold.

Such recurring and returning narratives are also narratives of childhoods lived in the landscapes of Ireland. Childhood experiences, whether domestic or mythic in nature, become the medium through which images of Irish cultural heritage are articulated. Through imaginative engagement with images of landscapes, heroic figures and mythological events, child figures within the texts examined here and child readers outside of those texts reconnect with Ireland's cultural heritage. This book explores the ways in which narratives of childhood experiences function as a medium through which Irish mythological culture is reimagined, marking the first exploration of the recurring patterns of cultural heritage and reimagination in Irish children's literature.

My research is concerned with the ways in which experiences of Irish childhoods are represented through and framed by mythological, folkloric and traditional oral narratives. It explores how attempts by authors to articulate the realities of childhood in Ireland facilitate the reimagination of Irish mythological and folkloric culture.

The reuse of legends, myths, beliefs, folk tales and oral history is common in literary texts created for children, a body of work where traditional narratives and contemporary storytelling trends often intersect.[2] European authors such as Cornelia Funke with her *Reckless* series (2010–), which engages heavily with the fairy tales of the Grimm Brothers, and Jean-Claude Mourlevat with his retelling of the French fairy tale 'Le Petit Poucet', *L'Enfant Océan* (2010) are examples of a contemporary trend towards retelling fairy tales, folk tales and myths for a child audience. Though these three types of narratives are distinctive, they hold in common a connection with oral tradition. Irish children's literature engages with cultural heritage and communal memory through oral tradition. Marina Warner points out that the term 'fairy tale' is often used as an epithet because a text might happen to depend 'on elements of the form's symbolic language' (xviii). In fairy tales 'the necessary presence of the past' emerges through 'combinations … of familiar plots and characters, devices and images' (xviii). Fairy tales, then, are always already associated with the act of retelling. They reside within 'the broader context of the folk tale' (Ellis Davidson and Chaudhri 1) and the presence of magic in such narratives creates the effect of wonder and facilitates acts of symbolic imagination. These are imaginary tales set in imaginary lands.

If fairy tales articulate the symbolic life of a people, folk tales articulate the culture and traditions of those people. Folk tales are traditional prose tales, stories which have been passed on in writing or through oral performance for generations. Folk tales are affected by 'the nature of the land where they are current' and also by 'the linguistic and social contacts of [their] people' (Thompson 13).[3] So if fairy tales are the imagination of a people, and folk tales are the memory, then myths are the beliefs of a people. Myths are essentially sacred narratives that chronicle the foundational moments in a society or community, intimately linked to rituals and to the re-enactment of those rituals. A myth articulates and 'confirms society's religious values and norms' and 'provides a pattern of behaviour to be imitated' (Honko 49) generation after generation.

In her book *Making the Italians: Poetics and Politics of Italian Children's Fantasy* (2012), Lindsay Myers writes about the Compensatory Fantasy of the late twentieth century. These texts include child protagonists who leave recognizable settings and journey into secondary worlds in order to 'compensate for social, environment, or personal short-comings in their own life' (208). In the latter part of the twentieth century, English and Scottish authors have also engaged with oral tradition to retell folk tales for children. Mollie Hunter's *A Stranger Came Ashore* (1975) is a selkie narrative, while Diana Wynne Jones's *Fire and Hemlock* (1985) is a retelling of the Scottish legends of 'Tam Lin' and 'Thomas the Rhymer'. Alan Garner's *The Owl Service* (1967) is a reimagining of Lleu, Blodeuedd and Gronw from the Fourth Branch of the Mabinogion. Irish children's literature is clearly not the only body of national literature produced for children that is shaped by recurring mythological and folkloric narratives.

Critical conceptions

For decades, critics have been exploring the ways in which myths and folk tales have been and are retold. But the connections between cultural heritage, landscape, memory, identity and time in Irish literature produced for children that is influenced by mythology and folklore remain relatively unexamined. In her 1981 article 'Folklore & Children's Books: Bridging the Gap', Agnes Perkins argues that folklorists and retellers of folk tales (two distinct categories) share source material but lack a commonality in perspective. The former are often so concerned with 'local variants and the unusual persistence of motifs' (1) that they often ignore or fail to expand the literary value of the folk tales in question. The latter neglect the 'authenticity of tone and language' (1) that might provide readers with the opportunity to engage further with oral traditions. Jon C. Stott's 1996 article 'The Poetics and Politics of Adaptation: Traditional Tales as Children's Literature' asks whether modern retellers of traditional oral tales are under obligation to remain faithful to the original contexts and tones of those tales or whether they are at liberty to reinterpret or even recreate them. In their critical examination of the notion and practice of retelling, *Retelling Stories, Framing Culture: Traditional Story and Metanarratives in Children's Literature* (1998), John Stephens and Robyn McCallum focus on what happens to traditional stories when they are retold in another cultural context and for a different audience. The text investigates the capacity of stories to carry cultural heritage and to provide child readers with a cultural and social education, and also how the processes of interpretation can influence the retellings that are produced. *Folktales Retold: A Critical Overview of*

Stories Updated for Children from 2006 is an attempt by Amie A. Doughty to address the lack of thoughtful critical examination of contemporary folk tale revisions, particularly those aimed at a child audience. The text examines the 'ways in which contemporary authors of folktale revisions for children and young adults take … the folktale … and rework it into its own distinct form' (xiii). That examination looks at cultural and regional variations, genre and intended audience, asking how each of these ultimately affects the retelling of the tale. Brian Attebery's *Stories about Stories: Fantasy and the Remaking of Myth* (2013) argues for the connection between the timelessness of myth and fantasy as a modern literary mode. Attebery presents fantasy and the modern fantastic as a form through which myth can be understood and interpreted in new and multiple ways. As a text that concerns itself with interpretations, it places an emphasis on the evolving ways in which metafiction can explore mythic constructions and perceptions of reality.

My work explores how Irish mythological and folkloric narrative traditions are reimagined through representations of childhood experiences in Irish children's literature and how the works of these authors provide an access point into Irish culture for a new generation of child readers. The core texts I examine demonstrate the significance of cultural and mythological heritage in Irish children's literature. In this critical context, childhood itself becomes a space, invested with meaning by the manner in which authors chose to represent it.

Time and myth, identity and landscape

Chapter 1 engages with the Celtic Revival as a literary and cultural renaissance beginning in the late nineteenth century in Ireland. As a project focused on reconnecting the Irish nation with its ancient heritage, and on re-envisioning its mythological past, the Revival and its cultural effects shaped the representation of Ireland in contemporary literature for children. Consequently, the Revival is an important and meaningful context for the first chapter, which investigates the imaginative and cultural significance of literature for children in the period, and the degree to which that literature was affected by mythological narratives. Irish children's literature becomes a cultural discourse within which child readers can be encouraged to engage with traditional and cultural narratives, and to reconnect with the notion of a lost mythological past. Through an examination of the child figure and the nature of mythic childhoods in three retellings of the myth of Cuchulainn by Standish O'Grady (1894), Augusta Gregory (1902) and Eleanor Hull (1909), this chapter investigates whether a broader contemporary awareness of the imaginative and cultural significance of literature for children existed in the period, and the extent to which children's literature was perceived as an investment in the cultural future of the nation.

Chapter 2 argues that the cultural project of the Revival influenced the images of cultural heritage transmitted by contemporary narratives for children. This influence provided and provides a relevant model for the processes of retelling which have continued to feature prominently in Irish children's literature. Through the imaginative engagement of successive generations of child readers, these narratives offer opportunities for the retrieval, the retelling and the repurposing of the nation's cultural and mythic pasts. Against the backdrop of the Celtic Revival then, the focus of Chapter 2's investigation is brought to bear on key children's texts from the period: Alice Dease's *Old Time Stories of Erin* (1907), Ella Young's *Celtic Wonder Tales* (1910), Violet Russell's *Heroes of the Dawn* (1913), Pádraic Colum's *The King of Ireland's Son* (1916) and James Stephens's *Irish Fairy Tales* (1920). These texts represent a significant contemporary engagement with Irish mythological heritage during the Celtic Revival, and with the Irish landscape as a setting for the myths they retell.

In order to examine the representation of childhood experiences and the development of selfhood within texts influenced by recurring mythological narratives, Chapter 3 analyses Patricia Lynch's *The Turf-Cutter's Donkey* (1934), Una Kelly's *Cuchulain and the Leprechaun* (1945), Eilís Dillon's *The Lost Island* (1959) and J. S. Andrews's *The Bell of Nendrum* (1959). These texts articulate aspects of the relationship between myth, folklore and history in Irish oral culture and in rural communities. By examining what it means for the child figures at the centre of such narratives to remember and interact with figures from Irish mythology and history, the chapter posits that the themes of memory and identity reside at the core of engagements with mythological narratives in Irish children's literature. Chapter 3 explores the concept of identity and the experiences of childhood in Irish children's literature produced in the middle decades of the twentieth century. It examines how childhood is influenced by the oral culture so prevalent in the communities depicted here, and how the myths of Irish culture are repeated and echoed through the narratives encountered by these child figures. It investigates the connection between narrative constructions of childhood and the development of national and personal identity in Irish children's literature. In doing so, it interrogates how individual identity is constructed within and mediated through a framework of traditional narratives that are themselves being constantly reimagined. The chapter explores how contemporary representations of childhood experiences contribute to the reimagination of cultural heritage, asking how the selected texts interrogate contemporary images and experiences of Ireland, and how they engage with and represent the past. Focusing on the child figures within the selected texts, the chapter assesses their interaction with the mythological narratives of Irish culture.

Chapter 4 continues with a detailed examination of child figures in the literal and metaphoric landscapes of Ireland. Pat O'Shea's *The Hounds of the Morrigan* (1984), Orla Melling's *The Singing Stone* (1986), Jim O'Leary's *The Fuchsia Stone* (1993), Kate Thompson's *The New Policeman* (2005) and Siobhan Dowd's *Bog Child* (2008) engage with the physical and metaphorical landscapes of Ireland through their central figures' experiences of myth, temporality and identity. A particular pattern of reimagination occurs in the landscapes depicted here, where imaginative vision and experiences of emplacement produce instances of 'mythic apprehension' (Von Maltzahn 19). The depth of the narrative engagements explored here reveals the extent to which representations of landscape in Irish children's literature are dominated by images of cultural heritage. These texts are used to explore the potential for reimagined mythological narratives to produce images of cultural heritage and the potential for these images to facilitate reciprocal relationships between tradition and modernity, identity and community, myth and folklore. For the central child figures here, mythic experiences are mediated through time, and through landscape. Knowledge and identity are gained as a result of mythic experiences. The chapter investigates how the child and young adult figures at the centre of these texts move through the landscapes of Ireland, and the extent to which an awareness or knowledge of mythological narratives supports or inhibits their ability to progress through the environments they find themselves in. The chapter examines the degree to which exposure to imagined landscapes informed and shaped by those recurring myths influences the development of identity in Irish children's literature. Through the act of reimagination, and through imaginative reveries into the landscapes of Ireland, child figures are presented with opportunities to reconcile past and present realities, both personal and national, through recurring mythic patterns.

The texts explored here, in both their domestic narratives and the underlying mythological narratives contained within them, are elements in a series of patterns of retelling and reimagination in Irish children's literature that have been occurring and recurring since the Celtic Revival. These patterns continue to influence the narratives produced for children in Ireland in the twenty-first century. In order to engage with these recurring narrative patterns, I propose a poetics of reimagination, and an original analysis of the ways in which mythology permeates the landscapes of Irish children's literature. This marks a new departure in the study of Irish texts produced for children, not only because these particular texts have never been considered collectively before but also because the ways in which Irish children's literature as a body of work uses myth to articulate and interrogate issues of time, place, identity and childhood experience have never been analysed or explored in the manner undertaken here. This analysis is situated within what Geertz calls a system of cultural meaning (312) that individuals can access to shape and interpret their own experiences. Within that system the recurring tendency towards reimagination becomes a cultural pattern in Irish children's literature, made manifest in a collection of images that are continually used and reused.

Culture and heritage

Mircea Eliade writes that 'the symbol, the myth, the rite, express, on different planes ... a complex system of coherent affirmations about the ultimate reality of things' (*Myth and Reality* 3). In the patterns of reimagination that structure Irish children's literature, Eliade's symbol is an image of cultural heritage, his myth is a traditional, recurring narrative and his rite is an act of reimagination. Together, these elements resonate within Eliade's complex system of affirmation, and in the context of Irish children's literature, the reality that is articulated are the collective realities of Ireland, its pasts, presents and futures. At the centre of this system is a mythological inheritance which must be retrieved through acts of reimagination. Such an inheritance 'demands to be passed on' (MacRaois 330) in the form of archetypal images and narratives of Irish culture and heritage. These are archetypal because they are typical and recurring (Frye *Anatomy of Criticism* 99). Archetypal images and symbols connect narratives to each other (99). They operate within exemplary models, where meaning is generated through retrieving, retelling, remembering and reimagining. Even in an imagined or reimagined context, images have the capacity to function as 'summarised knowledge of the real' (Lewis 44). Traditional and recurring narratives structured around such images can be seen as examples of Eliade's ritual ceremonies in that they re-actualize, re-present and re-enact events that occurred in the past. Myths preserve and transmit exemplary paradigmatic models through which the world is structured and reimagined. Myth functions as a form of remembrance, and in the intersection between Irish mythology and Irish children's literature 'the attempt at recollection' (Vernant 134) becomes associated with reimagination and with heritage.

Heritage and its production necessarily '[reflect] inherited and current concerns about the past' (Harrison 14). It is the process of connecting to and preserving narratives of the past. The connections available 'might manifest as a particular set of practices that appear to be separate from material things' or as a 'set of relationships with an object, building or place' (14). The acts of retelling and reimagination that influence certain texts in Irish children's literature are part of these practices. Culture is used by individuals and societies alike to shape experiences of existence, and heritage 'is profoundly associated with the stories we tell about ourselves' (Gillman 3). Heritage and culture can both be defined as interconnected systems of symbols that produce meaning; what may be removed or lost from a nation's culture may be preserved and remembered in its heritage (Sandis 13). Images of cultural heritage are an integral aspect of the patterns of imagination and reimagination which are so prevalent in the chosen core texts, and within Irish children's literature itself.

Mythological narratives are also among 'the practises [*sic*], representations, expressions, knowledge, skills that communities … recognise as part of their cultural heritage'.[4] The community, and indeed the individual, is endowed with the capacity to construct its cultural heritage from the 'instruments, objects, artefacts and cultural spaces' (UNESCO) available to them. This cultural heritage is transmitted from generation to generation, 'constantly recreated by communities and groups in response to their environment, their interaction with nature and their history' (UNESCO). Cultural heritage provides a sense of continuity in time for these communities and groups. In an Irish context, mythological narratives are a vital aspect of this construction process, and in the ongoing retrieval and reimagination of cultural heritage.

In the same way, if heritage not only relates to a nation's, or an individual's, 'relationship to history and history-making' but also to 'the production of the past in the present' (Harrison 5) then the canon of Irish children's literature itself is a repository of cultural history, precisely because it makes a critical contribution to that practice. Heritage is 'that which has been or may be inherited' (Sandis 11). The process of inheritance is one that has occurred in the past, and one which is always occurring in the present; it is the presence of the past in the present. But cultural heritage is not only inherited. It must be constructed and reconstructed, imagined and reimagined using a repository of images and stories that is continuously changing. The processes of retelling and reimagination which shape and influence it bring the past into the present and take the present into the past. These traditional narratives which recur again and again are not only images of cultural heritage; they are also heritage stories in and of themselves that are accessed by child figures in these texts, and child readers outside these texts.

Critical principles: Narratology, imaginative narrative and reverie

The recurring and cyclical pattern of traditional, mythical, historical and social narratives that permeates Irish children's literature offers images of cultural heritage to be retold and reimagined by succeeding generations of readers. My exploration of this thesis is grounded in close textual analysis of the core texts. The fundamental critical principle informing this analysis is that of narratology, defined by Mieke Bal as 'the theory of narratives, narrative texts, images, spectacles, events; cultural artefacts that tell a story' (3). The range and the specificity of this definition supports my textual analysis of the core texts, which are key examples of the primacy of cultural heritage in Irish children's literature. These narratives are Bal's 'cultural artefacts' (3) and do more than tell stories; they promote the acts of retelling and reimagination, presenting cultural, social, historical and mythological images of Ireland through representations of childhood experiences within traditional narrative structures. They are also symbolic artefacts, carriers of meaning, tradition and heritage.

Bal takes her definition further by defining a theory as a 'systematic set of generalised statements about a particular segment of reality' (3). Narratology as a theory or set of statements attempts to engage with a reality that consists of narrative texts of all kinds (3). My analysis focuses on the narrative realities constituted by these texts. If language shapes and articulates both our vision and the ways in which we perceive the world, then narratives contain within them both that vision and that perception, internalized in imaginative and narrative language (19). Narration 'has always implied focalization [sic]' (19). Bal uses the concepts of vision and perception to define focalization as 'the relation between the vision and that which is "seen" [or] perceived' (142). Events are necessarily presented from a chosen point of view, 'from within a certain "vision"' (142). This constitutes a specific way of perceiving the world. Focalization enables authors to put the reader in a particular position in relation to the text. As the relation between the vision and what is perceived then, focalization forms part of the meaning-making process that is integral to the act of storytelling (Maybin 3–4). The vision and perspective of each new generation of readers of Irish children's literature is shaped, not only through the processes of retelling and reimagining that these texts encourage and facilitate but also through focalization and identification with the child figures they encounter in the landscapes of Ireland. Focalization leads to identification. The synergy between focalization and identification produces meaning and facilitates the development of new perspectives. Focalization 'belongs in the story' (Bal 143), specifically in the layer of meaning 'between the linguistic text and the fabula' (143). Focalization, then, is not mediated through the elements of the narrative, but through the language of the narrative.

Storytelling or narration facilitates 'an enlargement of present reality' (Le Guin *Dancing* 48) by reaching back into the past and sending it forward into the future. The past cannot be verified, and the future cannot be predicted but narration centres us in the experience of the present by offering us 'an active encounter with the environment' (48). By narrating our environment and the lives we live within it, we engage with that environment on both a personal and a communal level. By virtue of their movement out of the past towards the present moment, narratives also provide opportunities 'for presentations of the self' (Maybin 97) across temporal, spatial and emotional contexts; narratives provide a framework which supports images of the self, even as they change over time. Given these two functions or uses of narratives, to evaluate and create meaning from experience and to present the self, storytelling is placed 'at the centre of the double-sided process of socialisation and identification' (98). Through telling stories and reading stories, children learn how to be part of the world while simultaneously strengthening their perception of themselves as individuals, narrators and readers. Storytelling and reimagination are the acts around which this process of development turns. In the context of a community which finds its origins in the traditional patterns of storytelling, narrative becomes a 'symbolic resource' (98) which is used to recount and represent experiences of childhood, and to re-present images of cultural heritage. Narration as language and as communication provides an access point 'into a shared world of imagination' (Le Guin 48). The connections between words, the meanings they carry and the sounds they make when spoken aloud combine to create vivid and 'authentic' (197) images.[5] The authenticity of these images is imbued with an intensity that 'may surpass that of most actual experience' (197); through imagination and through narration we participate in a community of understanding. Narration is the sharing of experience and of cultural heritage. It is the collaboration between the writer and the reader, between the teller and the listener that creates the imaginative world. It is in this 'joint creation of the fictive world' (197) that the processes of retelling and reimagining are made manifest.

I employ Le Guin's theory of imaginative narrative as the basis for a new methodological framework which explores the shared worlds created by the chosen core texts. The majority of these texts deals in one way or another with both Ireland and its mythological counterspace, Tir na nÓg. These are shared worlds in the sense that they are culturally familiar to the intended audience for these texts. Le Guin writes that 'in the tale, in the telling, we are all one blood' (29); that the tale creates a community, the telling facilitates connectivity. If the listeners, the tellers and the readers are all one blood in the narration, the tale itself represents a shared experience. Through narrative, a community is created; 'we will all come to the end together, and even to the beginning' (29). Narrative is the thread that draws atemporal events together; in a larger sense, it is this notion of narrative connection that facilitates an examination of the chosen core texts in the context of cultural heritage. Through narrative, events are arranged in a 'directional temporal order analogous to a directional spatial order' (38); linear and spatial experiences are connected through narrative. Narrative is 'language used to connect events in time' (38). It carries meaning in towards its own centre and outwards to a listening community. Narrative is then a journey based on connections, on the links between the past, the present and the future which begins in memory, moves through experience and is projected into the imagination.

Hanne argues that every act of storytelling, even a story we tell to ourselves, is structured 'by the storytelling codes or conventions available to the teller' (14). These conventions find their origins in specific historical and cultural situations and 'operate in relation to a particular social formation' (14). The recurring narrative patterns associated with so much of Irish children's literature are in and of themselves founding 'codes [and] conventions' (14) and, as such, provide an imaginative framework for readers which encourages interaction, rather than limiting the meaning that can be produced and transmitted. Telling a 'previously "untold" story' (14) can disrupt the existing social and cultural order; reimagining a story, either told or untold, can be both disruptive and creative. If stories perform 'acculturating, mystifying or legitimating roles' (14), it can be argued that stories also function as creative texts, providing access points into traditional, cultural, historical and mythological systems and frameworks even as they originate within these systems.

Contemporary viewpoints

This critical methodology is also supported by extensive engagement with contemporary critical viewpoints on Irish children's literature. Pádraic Whyte's work on the representation of history in children's texts provides a specific focus on narratives of childhood in Ireland at the end of the twentieth and the beginning of the twenty-first centuries. He writes about the dramatic, and often drastic, economic, political and cultural, changes which transformed Irish society at this time and heavily influenced the evolving conception of Ireland as a nation. Whyte argues that these changes directly impacted 'children's culture and cultures of childhood in Ireland' (xi) during this period. I am concerned with these cultures of childhood and the ways in which they are represented through 'the centrality of narratives of childhood' (xi) in Irish children's literature.

Whyte brings a focus to bear on the 'relationship between representations of Irish history and constructions of childhood' (xi) in Irish fiction and in Irish texts for children, highlighting the lack of critical attention this relationship has received. My methodology operates in this gap, exploring the reimagination of Ireland's mythological, cultural and historical heritage through narrative representations of childhood in Irish children's literature. Whyte states that the link between past and present 'is a dominant concern' (xii) of Irish literary and social culture and that constructions of childhood in Irish children's fiction are used to explore aspects of that link. Le Guin's vision of narrative journeys connecting time and landscape can be used in conjunction with this statement to create a new critical paradigm within which the centrality of childhood experiences and the importance of cultural heritage in Irish children's literature is recognized for its meaning-making potential. This is achieved by engaging in a close textual analysis of my core texts. These texts offer evidence for a tendency in Irish children's literature to rehabilitate child figures out of a lack of connection with the past through their engagement with cultural heritage and their capacity for retelling and reimagination. If child development, perspective and trauma are 'utilised as modes of interrogation' with which to examine and deconstruct narratives of the past 'and relate them to contemporary Irish culture' (Whyte 145), then Irish fiction, and Irish children's literature in particular, is built and functions upon a cyclical pattern of retrieving, retelling, remembering and reimagining as the past is retold into narratives of the present.

Narratives of Ireland's mythical and historical past are also imbued with reimaginative potentiality. Valerie Coghlan and Keith O'Sullivan argue that Ireland's pasts offer a kind of refuge to contemporary writers of children's literature who may be reluctant to confront sensitive or even controversial issues in the lives of young people today (5). These 'intrusions of the past' (5) may be seen not only as escape routes from modern reality but also as access points into the mythic, cultural and historic pasts of the nation. The assertion that 'present-day Irish writing for young people remains heavily indebted to the past' (5) can be interpreted in a positive sense; the indebtedness they speak of can be seen in terms of exchange rather than as an unbalanced account. The significance of the existence of a literature for young people within a national literature cannot be denied, nor can its necessity be questioned (5).

Indeed, as children emerge as a 'discrete collective' and as a cohort of readers with 'a specific range of concerns' (Shine Thompson 15), they require a body of narratives that expresses their shared experiences. Literature, in this context, functions as a collection of imaginative narratives that 'assert the existence of shared identities, shared historical experiences, common values and concerns' (Cleary 76). Children require narratives of childhood, narratives which encompass all aspects of childhood experience, from the physical to the emotional. If Irish children's literature is part of what Appleyard calls 'a whole cultural tradition' (12) the assimilation of its content involves a familiarization with its 'specific ways of organizing [sic] and interpreting experience' (12); if learning to speak is synonymous with learning to tell a story (Le Guin 39), reading becomes synonymous with interaction, with precisely those processes of assimilation and accommodation. But the reading experience, like any other, is subject to and operates under broad ideological factors. Works of art 'are not received as single entities but within institutional frameworks and conditions that largely determine the function of [those] works' (Burger 12). Literary texts exist within a framework or community and the production of meaning must be understood as a communal enterprise. The framing conditions of 'purpose or function, production and reception' that ordinarily 'constitute the institution of art' (Zipes *Fairy Tale as Myth* 19) are, in the context of Irish children's literature, translated into retrieval, retelling, remembering and reimagination. Ideology itself 'may be conceived of as part of the content of a story' (Appleyard 13), transmitting or representing cultural, societal or authorial values. It may be 'more deeply embedded in the formal structures of setting, character and plot' (13), in the framework of the narrative itself. Or, ideology may be imposed on the text from the outside, 'in the learned expectations readers bring to the task of interpreting narrative conventions' (13). During the reading process, interaction occurs not only between the text and the reader but also between the text and wider society, through the reader.

Arguably then, interaction with texts is meditated through 'the cultural institutions, language codes, social rituals [and] customs' (14) within which the text is produced and within which the reader's identity and perception have developed. So, the reader's development is 'in part socially constructed' and is 'an artefact … of the particular cultural experiences that prepares the reader to read' (14). Reading can provide access to a cultural, social and mythological memory; access is gained through interaction with recurring archetypal narratives, stories, legends and histories which resonate through the collective consciousness of a nation or community. The communal aspect of the process is at least as significant as the individual. As an institution of cultural heritage then, Irish children's literature operates on a number of levels; though cultural and social systems of meaning 'are … prior to the reader in a historical and epistemological sense', the construction of 'any particular meaning' (14) requires an interaction between an individual reader and the culture, such as that which occurs between readers and the texts of Irish children's literature. The individual reader's construction of meaning leads to the 'incremental restructuring of the culture' (14); through interaction, and through the production of 'new' meaning, child readers reimagine, reshape and restructure the culture of Irish children's literature.

Iser characterizes reading as a 'framework' through which the virtuality of the text 'may be brought into being' (279). The interaction between the text and the imagination produces the 'virtual dimension' (279) of the text – the reality of the narrative. Any form of interaction with a text, its multiplicity of possibilities and its images of cultural heritage 'represents the fulfilment of the potential, unexpressed realit[ies]' (279) the text carries. It is a 'creative process' (279) which supports the cycles of retelling and reimagination that permeate Irish children's literature, and specifically the narratives examined here. Just as the reader activates the literary text, the literary text in turn activates the reader's creative faculties, enabling 'the world it presents' (279) to be imagined into being. This reciprocal creativity is especially significant in the context of Irish children's literature and the images of cultural heritage it presents to successive generations of child readers. If the imagination of the reader brings the text to life, into reality, then by interacting with the images of cultural heritage they encounter in Irish children's literature, child readers are actively retelling and reimagining the traditional, social, cultural, historical and mythological narratives of Ireland into new existences. This 'dynamic process of recreation' (288) is rarely a simple one. In looking back, in looking forward, in evoking memory and musing on the future, the reader creates interruptions, points at which the process of reimagination can occur. The potentiality for meaning-making inherent in this process of recreation facilitates the reader's imaginative engagement with the text. The young child reader's 'intermittent grasp of the boundary between fantasy and actuality' (Appleyard 16), both in everyday life and in terms of reading, echoes Iser's creative interruptions; these gaps and intersections between real and fantastical experiences stimulate the impulse to retell and reimagine. In the same way that 'narrative is incomplete until it is read' (Iser 28), the cycle of retelling and reimagining only reaches its meaning-making potential when child readers engage with it by reading texts that concern themselves with mythological narratives.

Imagination and memory

Bachelard argues that there is a fundamental connection between imagination and memory. In fact, the connection is so intimate that 'distinction is especially difficult' (20). This is particularly true in the realm of childhood memories, 'the realm of *beloved images* harboured in memory since childhood' (emphasis in original) (20). These are the images which contain, memorialize and symbolize childhood experiences. The memory is evoked by the image, and the image becomes the origin and the concern of a complex and meaningful reverie towards the past: 'the memory dreams and the reverie remembers' (20). Memory and imagination are connected in the process of evocation – in the retelling and reimagination of childhood narratives. If the 'imagination ceaselessly revives and illustrates the memory' (20) the imagination becomes the faculty through which we evoke the memories of our past experiences, our past selves, and narrative is the structure through which we can re-experience and reimagine them. If we can map the concept of reverie as an imaginative experience onto reading, the act of reverie-reading becomes a creative one where 'the imagining consciousness' (2), in opening out individual images, also opens out the world the reader is exploring. The flight out of the real and into an imagined narrative world expands our being in the real world of everyday experience; 'a world takes form in our reveries' and this dreamed or imagined world reveals to and teaches us the 'possibilities for expanding our being within the universe' (8). A reverie that is informed by images of cultural heritage must necessarily envision a world that is similarly informed by those images as the reader, or the dreamer, actively engages in the process of retelling, reimagining and re-experiencing those images. Through reverie, the 'imagination attempts to have a future' to create a 'dreamed universe' (8) through the process of reimagination.

Though they are flights out of the real and into the imagination, reveries 'help us inhabit the world' (20); reverie allows us to inhabit the world more securely, emplaces us in it more deeply by helping us to retell it, reimagine it and remember our relation to it, by involving us in its creation. The text itself becomes a manifestation of the connection between the real and the imagined world, the memory and imagination;

'it is at once a reality of the virtual and a virtuality of the real' (24). The physical text represents an access point into an imaginative community of narratives; the interaction between reader and text brings forth the potentialities of meaning the imaginary world contains. Reading leads seamlessly to dreaming and vice versa (65); because of the connection between memory and imagination, between memory and dreaming, when we read, when we imagine, we are simultaneously remembering and participating in the recurring and cyclical pattern of traditional narratives and stories upon which Irish children's literature is founded.

It is in the 'nucleus of childhood which remains at the centre of the human psyche' (108) that imagination and memory are most closely bound together; at the self's core, 'the being of childhood binds the real with the imaginary ... lives in the images of reality in total imagination' (108). Inventing or imagining is, in fact, a form of remembering, of drawing on past experience for inspiration, for creative interpretation; reveries which lead back to childhood bring to life lives which 'have [only] been imagined' (110). In the cyclic narrative patterns of Irish children's literature, child readers find this inspiration, this communal memory. Though this narrative cultural heritage originates in the past, it has a future – 'the future of its living images' (110) as they are reinterpreted and reimagined by generations of readers. Reverie, then, is a system of memory, a 'mnemonics of the imagination' (112); the child's imagination lives in their own fables, not in the 'fossils of fables' (117) they encounter. In reverie, especially reveries into narrative, child readers find their fables; 'the fable is in life itself' (118) and in the acts of retelling and reimagining that bring those fables out of the mythic past and into the present, into the imagined future.

Myths create different dimensions of experience within the world (Eliade *Myth and Reality* 135). As messages 'passed through the ages and over the generations' (Rennie Short 3), myths transcend the borders between the past and the present, as meaning is 'projected into a timeless future' (Eliade 52). When myths are reimagined, time is transformed into a series of experiences that are endlessly and continuously recapitulated. In the texts selected for study here, such experiences are emplaced in the landscapes of Ireland. This emplacement is framed by a narrative pattern of imagination and reimagination. Landscapes, real or imagined, 'are representational ... form[ing] part of the medium through which ... meaning is produced and exchanged' (Brace 121). Meaning here becomes synonymous with the stories produced and exchanged in these landscapes. If poesis is an 'invitation to discovery' (Buttimer iii–v), an imaginative call for new perspectives, then the representations of landscape, myth, time and selfhood in Irish children's literature constitute a poetics of imagination, an invitation to discover and to reimagine and to engage with the creative potentiality inherent in the liminal spaces presented by the narratives here. Myths, especially Irish myths, articulate experiences in landscape. The recurring mythological narratives in the chosen texts mediate a sustained imaginative engagement between the traditional and the contemporary that underpin experiences of childhood in Ireland.

This means that Irish children's literature is instinct with images and stories of cultural heritage. Any contemporary narrative is necessarily constructed with images and stories from the past and is influenced by a multitude of imagined futures. In the processes of retelling and reimagining, landscapes 'are created ... transformed, interpreted and reinterpreted across space and time' (Share and Corcoran 11). Meaning is generated in these landscapes when child figures engage in imaginative exploration. Myth, as an 'intellectual construction which embodies beliefs, values and information' (Rennie Short xvi), is also an imaginative construction, one that influences the representation of landscape, time and selfhood in Irish children's literature. In that context, mythic narratives, historical discourses and traditional stories are imbued with the significance of 'a complex cultural reality' (Eliade 5). In these texts, engagement with myth and with the cultural reality it influences is mediated through emplacement in landscape, experience in time and development of selfhood.

If place and time are the 'two pillars of identity' (Trigg xiii) and selfhood is constructed in the space between them, then for the child figures considered here, identity is constructed, at least in part, in the landscape, between experience and memory. The dialectic between landscape and identity is expressed in the movement of child figures through the environments they are emplaced in. Through movement, through exploration, these child figures, and by extension, child readers, experience 'the lived relation between identity, place and memory' (xiii). To overcome time, to access the temporal experience of repetitive mythic time, it is necessary 'to go back and find the beginning of the world' (Eliade 88). Recollection neutralizes the 'work of Time' (89) so that going back becomes a return, a return that is meaningful precisely because it has been undertaken before. Remembering disrupts the passage of time, if only for a moment, and retelling becomes a form of remembering. The landscapes in these texts support and sustain durable and lasting experiences of childhood (Bachelard *Reverie* 100–16). But it is 'not enough to know the origin' (Eliade 37). The stories that narrate and describe key moments in the cultural and mythological heritage of the nation must be retrieved, repurposed, remembered and reimagined into new narratives that transmit the significance of this heritage through accessible and arresting images. In order to move forward, we must go back; there must be a reciprocal return to the landscape through time, myth and selfhood.

This book synthesizes these critical approaches to myth, landscape, time and identity to provide the first full study of representative texts within the body of Irish children's literature that engage with these concerns. It fosters new relationships between these disciplines and establishes children's literature as a new arena for the application of these theories. It offers a new and relevant critical reading of key texts in the canon of Irish children's literature by offering a new poetics of childhood experiences, both domestic and mythic, and a poetics of cultural heritage and memory that demonstrates how the stories told by Irish children's literature are a form of cultural expression and transmission that link mythic pasts with imagined futures through the creative act of reading. I am concerned with the treatment of childhood, both as a concept and as a collection of diverse experiences in Irish children's literature, and how a pattern of recurring mythological narratives influences the genre. Focusing on texts that consciously engage with mythological narratives, I demonstrate that these texts constitute a vital and dynamic repository of images of cultural heritage.

Chapter 1

RETRIEVING: STANDISH O'GRADY, ELEANOR HULL, AUGUSTA GREGORY

The Celtic Revival: Cultural movement and cultural context

The Celtic Revival was a new departure in Irish cultural nationalism, a literary renaissance that began in earnest in Ireland in the late nineteenth century (Wilson Foster ix).[1] It can be described as a collection of diverse movements, each striving to engage with Ireland's cultural traditions and ancient pasts through myriad viewpoints and literary experiments. It is in no way surprising that tensions between these movements emerged regarding differing concepts of Irish selfhood, from notions of 'essence and origins' to a sense of identity 'based on lived and shared experience' (Watson *Politics and Poetics* 2) in a landscape negotiated on physical and metaphorical levels. As a series of cultural projects focusing on reconnecting the Irish nation with its ancient heritage and on re-envisioning its mythical past, the Revival and its cultural effects changed the Irish people's perception of themselves (McMahon 4), despite an endemic lack of unity among the Revivalists driving it.[2] It influenced representations of Ireland in contemporary literature, and in Irish literature for children produced in the English language in its wake.

The patterns of retelling that permeate Irish children's literature in English in the twentieth and twenty-first centuries have been largely inherited from the acts of narrative reimagination that characterized the Revival. In other words, the Revival movement provided a model of retelling that was taken up and further adapted by authors writing for children in its aftermath. The recurring mythological narratives that are retold and reimagined across this literature constitute a heritage of imagination. The texts examined in this chapter are 'products of their age' (Kiberd 4) to be viewed in relation to one another, and in relation to texts in English for children produced in Ireland in the decades that followed the Revival. If, as W. B. Yeats said, 'the arts lie dreaming of what is to come' (*Literary Ideals* 72), then the retelling of these mythological narratives simultaneously looked back to the pasts of Ireland out of which they emerged, and to the future, the shape of which they would influence.

This chapter brings a focus to bear on the patterns of mythological retrieval prevalent in the early part of the Celtic Revival, between 1892 and 1909, by analysing three retellings of the myth of Cuchulainn: Standish O'Grady's *The Coming of Cuculain* (1894), Augusta Gregory's *Cuchulain of Muirthemne* (1902) and Eleanor Hull's *Cuchulain the Hound of Ulster* (1909). These specific texts are chosen for consideration precisely because they can be considered to be representative of the aims of the Revival as expressed in literary texts that influenced narratives produced for children, with a particular focus on the use of childhood as a preparatory stage for citizenship. The cultural and imaginative effects of the Revival, and the aim of its central writers, to restore Ireland to a sense of its lost heritage and to retrieve mythological narratives out of that heritage, influence the production of literature in English for children in Ireland in its wake, a body of texts that is dominated by mythological narratives. O'Grady's and Gregory's texts, while not written specifically for a child audience, were part of the cultural discourse about citizenship and duty that influenced children's culture and literature at the time. Together with Hull's version of the myth of Cuchulainn, retold specifically for children, these texts are representative of the ways in which mythological narratives and heroic figures were used to engage child readers in the wider Revival movement.

The works of Revivalist authors such as Standish O'Grady, Eleanor Hull, Augusta Gregory, George William Russell, W. B. Yeats and others produced images of cultural and mythological heritage that permeated the contemporary literary and cultural spheres of Irish society, facilitating a dialogue about imaginative inheritance which in turn influenced literature produced in English for Irish children in the decades that followed.[3] The Revival, and the processes of retrieval and reimagination that gave the movement its dynamic momentum, becomes a starting point for the patterns of recurring mythological narratives that pervade Irish children's literature in the twentieth and twenty-first centuries. Authors such as O'Grady, Hull and Gregory retrieved mythological narratives out of the past in order to restore them back into cultural discourse so that the act of retrieving becomes one of the defining actions of the Revival movement, particularly in the context of literature produced for and consumed by children.

Towards the end of the nineteenth century in Ireland, one of the fundamental aims of that Revival movement, as propounded by organizations such as the Pan Celtic Society (1888), the Gaelic League (1893) and the Irish Literary Theatre Society (1893), was 'to preserve the cultural individuality of the … nation' (Hutchinson 1) by precipitating a return to the history and mythology that constituted the distinctive imaginative heritage of the Irish people. In essence, by presenting what was retrieved out of the nation's past to the nation's people, the cultural nationalist movement would achieve a revival of Ireland's national character. Defined or conceived of 'in terms of myths of common origins, distinctive cultural characteristics, and attachments to specific territorial homelands' the idea of the nation has existed 'from time immemorial' (3). The culture of a nation is thus constituted by these myths, characteristics and attachments, an imaginative heritage shaped and defined by experiences of time, myth, landscape and selfhood, articulated in literature and artistic expression. Cultural nationalism, then, in the context of the Revival, was a nation-building endeavour, where the foundations for that nation were to be found in the past, because nationalism, as Ernest Gellner writes, 'constructs and transforms a folk culture into a high culture' seeking an affirmation and validation of 'a state of its own' (xxviii).

The objectives of the Gaelic League at this time were Revivalist as opposed to political in nature, and the organization was seeking the spiritual and cultural regeneration and restoration of the nation, by promoting and facilitating 'a return to its creative source in the evolving Gaelic civilisation of its recent past' (Hutchinson 116). As early as the sixteenth century, Ireland was associated with the notion of a periphery, and with the older vestiges of a primordial '"Celtic" language' (Leerssen 7). The works of Celticists such as Ernest Renan and Matthew Arnold evoked journeys outwards 'in which one leaves the present and the quotidian pace of temporal progress' and 'moves out of time, into the past or into some mythical or primordial timelessness' (Hutchinson 116). Celtic mythology was and is associated with the past, just as the landscapes of Ireland were and are associated with the evocation of that past.

The Revivalists were arguing that this ancient culture had inspired the Irish people for countless generations. For them, looking forward was explicitly connected to the act of looking back, and to acts of recovery and retrieval. It is testimony to the diverse nature of the Revivalist movement, however, that we find 'rival versions of the national idea represented by separate linguistic and literary movements' (119). The former was concerned with a cultural and social revival based on the restoration of the Irish language itself. The latter was striving to create a singular and distinctive 'Anglo-Irish nation' (119) by producing a national literature in English, the foundations of which would be built on the legends and idioms of the disappearing Irish language. I want to focus on the latter stream of the Revival, and on the project of retrieval and retelling that was pursued in the name of such a national literature, where nothing less than a new departure in narrative technique would be demanded so that a 'new united nation synthesizing [sic] the Gaelic and English heritages' (120) might come into being. In the vision of leading Revivalist figures such as Yeats, Gregory and others, we find the template for the patterns of reimagination that influence Irish children's literature in English in the twentieth and twenty-first centuries.

The Celtic Revival was thus a revival in which genres were recreated, reclaimed and reimagined. The diverse streams within the movement of the Revival facilitated a communion between tradition and innovation that had hitherto seemed impossible (Schleifer 3). Within the larger Celtic Revival, the Anglo-Irish Literary Revival sought to create a new medium in the cultural life of Ireland, a hybrid language based on the emerging vernacular of the Irish people – 'an English rich with Irish idioms and rhythms' (Hutchinson 128) that could be used to articulate a new literature that would simultaneously recall a Celtic heritage and would look forward to an enlightened future. In order to 'preserve and thereby redeem an authentic Irish … culture' (Castle 41), the mythological narratives associated with Ireland's cultural heritage needed to be retrieved and retold.

Representation is one of the central practices through which culture is produced, and culture itself is concerned 'with the production and exchange of meanings' (Hall *Representation* 2). Culture is about shared meanings, and for meanings to be shared and exchanged, members of a culture must have access to a common language. This is because language is one of the media through which 'thoughts, ideas, and feelings are represented in a culture' (1). Representation through language is central, therefore, to the processes through which meaning is produced in a culture.[4] Language occupies a crucial role in the production and exchange of meaning because it functions as a representational system. If it is to allow members of a culture to perceive and understand the world in similar ways, those members must also 'share sets of concepts, images and ideas' (4). So, culture is concerned with the production and exchange of meanings, not just between individual members and groups in a society at a particular moment but across different time periods through cultural texts and artefacts. Meaning is produced when we 'weave narratives, stories – and fantasies' (4) around the cultural rituals and practices that structure our lives, and if those narratives remain accessible, they can continue to produce meaning for new generations of a particular culture.

Members of the same culture must share and understand the same symbolic language. Within their individual projects, the writers of the Celtic Revival were contemporaneously seeking to create a new set of symbols and images through which to retrieve the lost mythological and cultural heritage of the Irish people and restore it back into the contemporary present. They were seeking a narrative language that would allow them to simultaneously remember the past and imagine the future. They were trying to create, through retelling, what F. M. Barnard terms 'symbolic forms of life' (185). The movement towards the retelling and re-purposing of mythological narratives that developed during the Revival was, essentially, an 'invented tradition', a set of culturally reformative practices through which these writers sought to retrieve and restore a sense of Ireland's lost heritage by establishing a 'continuity with the past' (Hobsbawm 1). The Revivalist project, then, was a process of 'formalization and ritualization' [sic] (4) of Irish cultural and mythological heritage, through retelling and reimagination. In this context, Ireland's cultural heritage became a narrative, or a series of narratives, and a way of 'thinking and talking about communities … in space and time' (Gillman 21) connected by shared practices, rituals, experiences and memories.

Cultural memory: Images and rituals

Memory allows an individual to sustain a distinctive identity, not only through processing acts of recollection but also through interacting with and making meaning from memory images. It follows then that communities and societies also use memory to sustain and perpetuate distinctive, collective identities. Through memory and memory images, a society, or a nation, can maintain and transmit a sense of its collective identity to future generations (Boyer 9). Narratives that contain memory images can fulfil this function, especially narratives that are mythological in nature, and that encapsulate aspects of a nation's cultural heritage. These narratives not only facilitate what Boyer calls 'the collective construction of a common past' (9) but also the retrieval and reclamation of a common past previously deemed to be lost. Boyer also argues that memory is constructive. This implies that memory is a creative force, as well as a recreative or reconstructive one.

This is why any causal account of social identities (11), or any causal account of the prevalence of reimagined mythological narratives in Irish children's literature since the Revival, should include individual or narrative processes of representations of the past. The ideas of 'time present and time past' become, through narratives that retrieve and retell cultural and mythological heritage, 'time future' (Eliot 13).

The impulse to remember and to retell that informed so much of the imaginative fiction produced during the Revival was also an undertaking not to forget what had been recalled. A pattern was formed from the desire to remember and the perceived duty not to forget. While the Cultural Revival as a movement provided a creative space in Ireland within which engagement with mythological narratives and cultural heritage became connected to the rejuvenation of national identity, the notion of looking back in order to retell ancient stories was already a familiar one in Britain, especially in relation to the Arthurian cycle. Thomas Mallory's *Le Morte d'Arthur* was first published by William Caxton in 1485 and became the foundational text for many interpretations of the Arthurian myth, not least Tennyson's *The Idylls of the King* from 1859, which retold the entire myth for a Victorian audience, and Sidney Lanier's *The Boy's King Arthur* from 1880, a text specifically edited and retold for a child readership. The Irish Revival project was always infused with a sense of what had been lost out of the nation's cultural memory. The attempt to retrieve or at the least recreate that material necessarily involved a negotiation of Ireland's colonial past and present and its contemporary position in relation to British control. In contrast, the Matter of Britain, the narratives of Arthur's myth, was preserved through centuries and always available to be retold and reinterpreted. T. H. White's *The Once and Future King* from 1958 uses the Arthurian cycle to examine and satirize the contemporary political climate and the state of education in Britain. For Irish authors working within the Revival project, retelling was always connected to creating and recreating a national identity and a national mythological past. For British authors working with the Matter of Britain, this national past was always already established because the Matter of Britain had never been lost or forgotten.

But memory can also be understood within the context of the Platonic idea of anamnesis, the belief that 'when knowledge comes to be present ... it is recollection' (*Phaedo* 21). Knowledge and memory then are connected by the act of recollection, by the remembering of that which was and is already known.[5] If recollection involves the retrieval of memory-images from the past, then retrieval is also 'the repossession of truth' (Scanlan 11), be that truth cultural or mythic in nature. John Scanlan writes that the memory that seems to reappear from the past as recollection (and he deems this reappearance to be involuntary, and places it in opposition to the 'willed efforts of remembering') intervenes in the present 'as a kind of mythic temporality' (9–10) constituting a time outside of time. The creative projects of the Revival, and the acts of retelling and repurposing its writers engaged in, accessed this mythic temporality, precisely because the retelling and repurposing of mythological narratives brought the ancient pasts of Ireland into its present. The projects of the Revival were arguably concerned with cultural and mythological memories, or memory-narratives and memory-images, which are not only remembered but deliberately and consciously retrieved and reclaimed as well. The retrieval of such memories or images revealed a mythic connection between the pasts of Ireland and its contemporary present, as envisaged by the Revivalist writers. Memory also acts 'as an awareness of the distance between the past and the present' (116). The Revivalists, in attempting to retrieve and retell the narratives of Ireland's mythological past, wrote into this distance. So, the images of the past that were retrieved, especially in the specific context of the Revival, are 'remembered, narrated, and … woven into the fabric' (Assmann *Moses* 14) of the contemporary present of Ireland.

If the past is refracted through the present, then heritage, or the cultural and mythological inheritance of Ireland's people in this case, must involve an engagement with the past within the present. Objects, images and narratives from the past are brought back into view through recollection. Such objects and images must be engaged with imaginatively to 'reveal their hieroglyphic potential' (Scanlan 52). Hieroglyph is a Greek word meaning sacred writing,[6] yet hieroglyphic images are just that, images. So, with the phrase 'hieroglyphic potential', Scanlan is arguably referring to the capacity for objects, images and narratives to hold multiple meanings, and to generate multiple meanings. If we think of the past in terms of images that are at once distant, yet accessible to us through memory (56), then the past itself is accessible through memory, and through the meaning we can generate from memory-images.

So, these images are, by their very nature, dialectical, in that they promote and facilitate the discussion of ideas of the past, of identity and of culture. Scanlan further defines these dialectical images as thought-images, which '[fuse] time, experience and memory to suggest new possibilities' (101). In the dialectical image, as Walter Benjamin writes, 'what has been within a particular epoch is always, simultaneously what has been from time immemorial' (464). As such, what has been 'is manifest, on each occasion, only to a quite specific epoch' (464), the moment when this dream image is recognized as such. It is at this moment that the historian, or, in the context of the Revival, the author as well, takes up, with regard to that image, the task of 'dream interpretation' (464) or reimagination.

A mythological heritage comprising narratives such as those that were retold and reimagined during the Revival is both the predicate and the product of cultural memory. Within such a heritage resides the means to access the past, the means to imagine or construct an identity and the means to maintain a sense of cultural continuity (Assmann *Cultural Memory* 2). The existence of a mythological heritage facilitates 'the formation of tradition' (2). Every culture forms a connective structure that exerts a binding effect on its members on social and temporal levels. By creating images and archetypes, each culture provides a 'symbolic universe' of bodies of traditions that 'integrate different provinces of meaning' (Berger and Luckmann 120, 133) and allows members of these cultures to articulate realities that are outside of everyday experience. These are the imagined and remembered realities of a nation. These symbolic universes also create a link between the past and the present, precisely what the Revival writers strove for, by 'incorporating images and tales from another time into … the onward moving present' (Jan Assmann *Cultural Memory* 2). In the same way, heritage is produced in the present, through engagement with the past. Without the images, there would be no pattern to follow, because images are central to our ability to recall and to perceive the past.

A connection exists between memory and imagination, in that to evoke one, or to imagine it, is to evoke the other, to remember it (Ricoeur *Memory, History, Forgetting* 6). The image plays a central role in both the Aristotelian and Platonic categorizations of memory. The former focuses on 'the representation of a thing formerly perceived', the latter on 'the present representation of an absent thing' (5). Both of these representations are evoked through images. Such images can, in John Knox's terms, 'express … things as known in experience or as carried in memory' (22). The memory image is the product of remembering, and it is retrieved through the imagination. The relationship between heritage and culture, and between imagination and memory, is thus a complex and symbiotic one; they can both be classified as systems of symbols that produce meaning and preserve that meaning.

Cultural heritage can be most comprehensibly defined as 'the practices, representations, expressions, knowledge, skills that communities … recognise as part of their cultural heritage' (UNESCO Culture Sector). This definition endows the community, and indeed the individual, with the capacity to construct their cultural heritage from the 'instruments, objects, artefacts and cultural spaces' (UNESCO) available to them. This cultural heritage is transmitted from generation to generation, 'constantly recreated by communities and groups in response to their environment, their interaction with nature and their history' (UNESCO). Cultural heritage provides a sense of identity and continuity in time for these communities and groups. Traditional narratives are a vital aspect of this construction process, and in the ongoing recreation and reimagination of cultural heritage.

Cultural heritage is perpetuated through rituals because, as Constantine Sandis writes, 'they are the form through which cultural meaning is … handed down' (6). The recurring mythological narratives that permeate Irish children's literature are the textual rituals through which cultural heritage and memory are passed on and reimagined. The foundation of these connective structures is repetition. The repeated acts of retrieval and retelling engaged in during the Revival instituted 'recognisable patterns immediately identifiable as elements of a shared culture' (6) for the Irish people. These recognizable patterns have influenced the literature for children in English produced in the aftermath of the Revival, as new generations of authors sought to access the memories of a shared mythological and imagined past. It is through the written narratives of such traditions that repetition gradually gives way to re-presentation; 'ritual gives way to textual coherence' (3) in that contributors begin to interpret memory instead of merely preserving it. Through repeated patterns which operate within a broader tradition, 'memory of the past is brought to present life' (3).

Within traditional ancient Greek oral *epos*, the true thought is inherent in the remembered and ritualized patterns (Ong 5), rather than in the conscious intentions of the singer to organize the narrative in any specific remembered way (145). Meaning is created and recreated through the renewal of patterns, where the singer effects 'not a transfer of his own intentions, but a conventional realization [sic] of traditional thought' (Peabody 176) for his listeners, through re-enactment and reimagination. The singer is not transferring information. Rather, he is remembering in a public way, 'not a memorized [sic] text' (Ong 146) but the themes and images other singers have created before him. This is because the images and signs associated with rituals are not inherently meaningful. Rather, it is 'our response to our own perception of signs' that produces meaning, where meaning functions as 'a predicate of structure' (Peabody 6). The singer always remembers differently, recreating the pattern in his own way on this particular occasion for this particular audience. In the same way that 'song is the remembrance of songs sung' (Peabody 216), reimagination is the remembrance of stories told. If the oral song is produced through the interaction between the singer, the present audience and 'the singer's memories of songs sung' (Ong 146), then narratives can be said to be the result of the interaction between the author, the present readership and the author's memories of stories that have already been told. This tradition of remembering and transmitting also existed and thrived in medieval Ireland. Between 1400 and 1690, the corpus of bardic material consisted of 'ancient mythology, clan histories, saints' lives' (Meigs 12) and was shared among all ranks of society. This sharing across many centuries 'helps explain the persistence of an amazingly resilient cultural tradition' (12) in Ireland. Bards were employed as 'family retainers, tradition bearers, historians, poets, and skilled musicians' (Forde 122). In the days before literacy and print culture they were seen as the keepers and preservers of clan and family memories. As Maria Tymoczko and Colin Ireland note, the etymology of *fili*, the Gaelic word for 'poet' (from Indo-European *vel-*, 'see'), suggests that the poets of pre-Christian Ireland 'were regarded as seers, possessed of particular kinds of insight or mystical knowledge' (30), the articulation and expression of which required a specialized poetic language. This is why trainee bards studied Irish and Latin grammar, metrics, genealogy, law, *dindschenchas* (the lore of places), mythology and history. They operated within an ancient tradition of intensive memory training, 'inherited from a period when writing was regarded as an admission of … weakness' (31) in relation to memory. This corresponds to Yeats's Revivalist vision of a romantic poet figure, a modern-day bard remembering and retelling the country's past and heritage.[7] Individuals can experience 'the collective sense of belonging that is fixed to language and culture' (Scanlan 31) through oral traditions, and through engagement with the narratives preserved within them. These oral traditions, and the sense of belonging they promote, are largely swept aside in modern societies, persisting only 'against the tides of change … as echoes of a past that risks being overwhelmed' (31) by the passing of time. The figures at the centre of the Revival were writing against and beyond this tide, reaching back into oral traditions to retrieve narratives of cultural significance and heritage, even as they were in danger of being swept away.

The presence of the past in the present: Recovery and restoration

Much of the 'imaginative prose' coming out of Ireland from the 1890s onwards was part of the larger Irish Literary Revival movement, produced by writers who were seeking what would essentially be a 'native prose tradition' (Wilson Foster xvi), where the old and the new would meet to produce a new experience of Irish culture. These writers were connected through their involvement in various streams of cultural nationalism, an interest in mythology, a 'preoccupation with heroism ... [and] their promotion of an ancient Gaelic polity' (xi). Much of this imaginative fiction was the product of an attempt to articulate the heroic ideal in an Irish context that was simultaneously of the past and of the present, and of a search for the most appropriate narrative forms 'in which the old pagan romances might be recast for an awakening Ireland' (4). The myths of the past were retold in order to transform experiences of reality in the present. In the period of the Revival in Ireland, the past had a presence in the present, in the echoes of a lost heritage that waited to be reclaimed. In seeking to articulate that past-presence, the writers of the Revival engaged in a communion with the past, expressing their sense and experience of Ireland in 'renewed genres' (Schleifer 8). The language of the past became associated with the oral traditions of Ireland, which stood, and still stand, at 'an intersection of public and private life', where the boundaries between the past and the present were broken down through the act of narrating events that were depicted 'as simultaneous rather than chronological' (Thuente 96). Through retelling, the past was restored into the present, in a 'living oral discourse' (Schleifer 9) that remembered Ireland's heritage while imagining Ireland's future. So, the 'recovered past'[8] became a dominant concern in the writings of the Revival, writings which, by necessity, had to articulate issues of time, myth, landscape and selfhood.

At the opening of the Irish National Literary Society in Dublin in July 1892, George Sigerson delivered a lecture in which he connected Ireland's possible freedom from British rule to 'the monuments of the ancient Irish past' (Sigerson 110). Cultural and political freedom in the present remained in those ancient monuments, waiting to be accessed, and channelled into the future. The objective, then, was to bring the past into the present, and from this past-infused present to generate a future that simultaneously remembered the past and imagined a greater future. This new Ireland of the future would be made viable 'according to the degree that it repossessed the civilisation of its past' (Richards 122), in other words only to the degree that it recalled and reimagined its own heritage. If 'national liberation is necessarily an act of culture', then the Revivalists, in striving 'to return to the upward path of [Ireland's] own culture' (Cabral 43), were, in actuality, returning to the past to envision the future.

At a similar occasion hosted by the Irish Literary Society, London, in July of 1892, Sir Charles Gavan Duffy gave an address entitled 'What Irishmen May Do for Irish Literature', which would be developed in his second address a year later, 'Books for the Irish People'. During this speech, Duffy asserted specifically that the young people of Ireland must be given access to books that would 'carry them away from the commonplace world to regions of romance' (24); the youth of the nation needed access to the mythological and cultural heritage of the past. This access to 'the original creations of a civilisation' was explicitly connected to the 'healthy development of both individuals and nations' (Richards 123). Sigerson himself stated that there was 'a tone of sincerity in the ancient narratives which cannot exist in imported thought' (70). Here, a fundamental aim of the Revival movement was established: to reconnect the youth of Ireland with the ancient narratives of their national cultural heritage so that those narratives might be experienced in the contemporary present and inform the future that generation would create.

For the cultural nationalists an interest in the past was not enough. It was necessary not only to access the narratives of the past but also to bring them into active engagement with the narratives of the present. The oral traditions of folklore, legend and mythology were seen as a repository of culture, 'a store-house of memories unique in modern Europe' (Pearce 8) which could be used to restore a sense of the past into the contemporary present of the nation, and to recover a lost imaginative heritage. The ideas of recovery and restoration were therefore key to the aims of the Revival writers. Ernest Renan's concept of an undivided national inheritance resonated particularly within those aims. In 1882 Renan delivered a famous lecture at the Sorbonne in Paris entitled 'What Is a Nation?' in which he presented a definition of cultural nationalism that was to profoundly influence the Revivalist movement. In the lecture he stated that a nation was both a living soul and a spiritual principle, and that it existed both in terms of individual experience and collective thought. The spiritual principle of the nation was constituted by 'two things, which in truth are but one' (80–1), namely the past and the present. Renan defined the past in this context as 'the common possession of a rich heritage of memories', while the present was 'the will to preserve worthily the undivided inheritance which has been handed down' (81). The nation was experienced and perpetuated through the retrieval, possession, preservation and reimagination of heritage. It was a continuous enterprise, 'the outcome of a long past of efforts, and sacrifices, and devotion' (81) lived perpetually in the present.

George Russell, Yeats's contemporary and fellow cultural nationalist, wrote about the nation as both an imagined and an imaginative community, where communion through imagination was as binding as a national patriotism. Ideas of a country are formed from readings of history or contemporary politics, 'or from imaginative intuition' (5), and Russell argued that it was the Ireland of the mind, and not the Ireland of reality, that inspired the individual. The cultural nationalist writers of the Revival were creating and recreating Ireland through narrative. The ideal of Ireland 'grows from mind to mind' (5) echoing the stream of suggestion that Yeats reflected on in his own work. Culture and heritage were recovered, lived and reimagined through imaginative communion.

But collective memory is not merely a collection of individual memories, and not just a 'reservoir of ideas and images', but rather a 'reality of the past' (Irwin-Zareck 55) that is articulated by a body of narratives, cultural, social and mythological, and maintained by the society that remembers those stories. These remembered and reimagined narratives contribute to the ways in which communities imagine themselves as nations (Anderson *Imagined Communities* 6). We recount or narrate the past, both to ourselves and to others, in narrative form (Fivush and Bauer 268). We remember through language. It is only through narrative language that we can 'fully share the past with others' (271). It follows, then, that it is only through remembered narratives that the collective pasts of a nation can be reimagined. A connection can be established between an individual or personal past and a collective past, the 'origins, heritage and history' (Agnew 3) of any given community or society. The past thus defines the present, while highlighting the difference between 'memory as recollection' (3) and memory as imagination, where what is imagined is the past, present or future of a community. We dream and remember in narrative. It follows then that 'narrative meaning' is created and recreated, imagined and reimagined through the 'contextual links' (Hardy *Poetics of Fiction* 5) it makes with past experiences, in individual and communal contexts.

Yeats himself wrote on the nature of a communal or national imagination, wondering if a vision could 'divide itself in divers complimentary portions' and depending on the subjectivity of the visionary, might not the thought of an individual 'depend at every moment of its progress upon some complementary thought in minds perhaps at a great distance?' (*Collected Works* 216). He wrote of a community of imagination, where the thoughts of every member affect and were affected by the thoughts of every other. This was an image of an imaginative nation, and Yeats wondered whether there was a 'nation-wide multi-form reverie, every mind passing through a stream of suggestion' where there were multiple streams 'acting and reacting upon one another' (216). A nation was defined and connected, even 'bound together by this interchange among streams or shadows' where that connection was expressed through and experienced in his 'Unity of Image ... an originating symbol' (216). He wrote of objects or images acting as 'originating impulse[s] to revolution or philosophy' (211). This revolutionary potential resonated within the images of cultural and mythological heritage that dominated the narratives the Revivalists were concerned with retrieving. Running throughout this period of Yeats's work was the notion that the idea of a nation could not be kept alive 'where there are no national institutions to reverence, no national success to admire' and 'without a model of it in the mind of the people' (364). The model of which he spoke was arguably the idea of the nation, an idea that could be created and sustained through imagery, and specifically through mythological imagery, reclaimed from the past. Everyday life demanded 'a complex mass of images' (364) that were imbued with cultural heritage, against which contemporary audiences could react, and which they could reimagine.

The pasts to which Yeats and other Revivalist writers looked back were 'mythic rather than essentially historic' (Richards 123), pasts that could be reaccessed through the cycles of mythological narratives upon which so much of the imaginative fiction of the Revival was based. The recovery of these narratives out of the past facilitated an act of cultural reimagination where 'the material world and mythic worlds ... blend[ed] into an ideal whose purpose was ... to inspire identity' (123). Time and myth influenced the creation of cultural identity, inspiring a sense of selfhood in the new generation of Irish youth, precisely because myth, as an 'intellectual construction which embodies beliefs, values and information' (Rennie Short xxii), was also an imaginative construction, and one that influenced the representation of landscape and selfhood in Irish children's literature produced in the aftermath of the Revival. When myths are reimagined, time is transformed into a series of experiences that are endlessly and continuously re-presented. Myth does not set up an opposition between falsehood and reality; as an imaginative construction it contains within itself both 'fact and fancy' (Rennie Short xvi). Meaning is generated through the tension between what is real and what is imagined.

Malinowski wrote specifically on the nature of myths and how they generate meaning in primitive societies. There is a connection between the myths or stories and sacred tales of a tribe, and their rituals, their morality and their social organizations (Malinowski 9). Myth, in this context, is a validating rather than an explanatory force; it is a cultural structure. Malinowski argues that myth is not symbolic, but rather a direct expression or articulation of its subject matter, what he terms 'a narrative resurrection of a primal reality' (9). Myth, in its living form, 'is not merely a story told but a reality lived' (13). Though Malinowski's work emerges approximately two decades after the peak of the Revival movement, he, like Yeats, was influenced by Sir James Frazer's theories on the anthropological nature of myth, and on its cultural significance.[9] Building on Malinowski's 1926 text, Joseph Fontenrose writes that once myth and ritual become associated, one begins to affect the other. The rite suggests interpolations in the myth which suggest additions to the rite (Fontenrose 50). This theory of affect can be applied to the myths that were being retold during the Revival, in that the ritual of retelling mythological narratives added to the mean-making potential of those myths, and to their capacity to not only retell but also reimagine a lost history or cosmology of Ireland.

The myth of Cuchulainn

Three different versions of the myth of Cuchulainn produced during the Revival period place a specific emphasis on the hero's childhood with each author striving, in their own ways, to interrogate the ideas of citizenship, culture and heritage. These are Standish O'Grady's *The Coming of Cuculain* (1894), Eleanor Hull's *Cuchulain the Hound of Ulster* (1909) and Augusta Gregory's *Cuchulain of Muirthemne* (1902). Each of these writers had specific interpretation of the role of the author in such retellings, and of the value of the cultural heritage they were attempting to retrieve and retell. Hull and Gregory were concerned with presenting this mythological episode to a new and younger audience, with a view to reviving interest in such material, and to ensuring its preservation. Within the larger project of the Revival, these women were making a connection between the cultural significance of these myths and the capacity for Ireland's young people to restore their lost heritage into the present of the nation through imaginative engagement with new and authentic retellings. The fact that no fewer than three versions of the Ulster Cycle were available to be read by children during the Revival is evidence of the preoccupation that existed among writers at the time to not only recover lost material from Ireland's mythological past but also to ensure that this material was reintegrated and reimagined back into mainstream contemporary and literary culture. This could be achieved by introducing a new generation to the founding myths of Ireland's ancient civilization.

As Terry Eagleton writes, Standish O'Grady firmly believed that the history of one generation became the poetry of the next (13). Myth passes into present culture through the conduit of history, in what Eagleton sees as a kind of four-stage translation: the history of the people is encoded by myth, the myth is retrieved by the modern historian, then deployed by the artist and is ultimately restored to the people (13). The retelling of Irish history became, in O'Grady's vision of his own project, a series of imaginative processes, aimed at reconstructing the past. In his introduction to O'Grady's *The Coming of Cuculain* (1894), George Russell (Æ) stated that through O'Grady and his works 'Ireland has found again … what seemed lost forever', that being the governance of its own identity 'and its memories which go back to the beginning of the world' (xxiii). O'Grady's text, then, is nothing less than a project of retrieval, a narrative that recovered for a new generation, the memories of previous generations that were lost. Within the mythological episodes O'Grady retold are images of a cultural heritage that was being revitalized, even as it was being revived. Russell wrote again and again of these returning 'ancient memories' (x) accessed through narratives that had been retold for a new cultural context.

Russell also addressed the significance of reading, and how that act could be an act of exploration, and revival, if one read to recover a narrative that had previously gone untold or unheard. Many of O'Grady's contemporaries read as though they 'were bereaved of the history of their race' (x), reading so that they might recover what had been lost. Through 'the creation of great images' O'Grady's writings would go on 'recreating for generations yet unborn the ancestral life of their race in Ireland' (xi). Russell clearly envisaged a future for the narratives O'Grady had chosen to retell, and that his text would remain in circulation, having 'rescued from the past what was contemporary to the best in us today' (xvi).

The concept of Yeats's stream of unity resonated particularly in Russell's imagery, especially when he spoke about the 'submerged river of national culture' that would rise again within O'Grady's writings, and the harmony of a national consciousness and 'ancestral moods' (xv) that were evoked, recovered and remembered. Again, Russell, like Yeats, referred to the communal memory of a nation, stating that a society 'cannot carry with it through time the memory of all its deeds and imagination' (xv). Only what was valued most 'among the imaginations of the ancestors' was retained in that communal memory when 'a new era [began]' (xv). This provided a definition of the idea of culture and heritage that the Revival writers were operating within.

O'Grady's text begins with a statement that Cuchulain [sic] and his contemporaries 'are historical characters, seen … through mists of love and wonder' (v). Ireland itself, because of its Celtic culture, had been consistently associated with 'a mystical otherworldliness' (Leerssen 8), a 'mythical or primordial timelessness' (7) expressed for centuries by the symbolism of the Celtic mist that shrouds the country and its mythological history. O'Grady evokes that symbol here by having the figures whose narratives he was attempting to retrieve and retell be seen through it. These mists of love and wonder are associated then with perception, and with the ways in which Irish culture and identity can be seen. That mist might actually aid perception and bring clarity is an ironic concept, but the symbol is one that appears throughout the period examined here, especially in relation to mythological figures and landscapes. The figures O'Grady describes are figures 'whom men could not forget' but rather continue to celebrate 'in countless songs and stories' (v) generation after generation. By the time the Celtic Revival began these songs and stories may have passed out of cultural circulation, but they were available to be retrieved so they were also available to be remembered. When O'Grady speaks about the actual existences of these figures, he connects their authenticity and reality to the fact that 'mere creations of idle fancy do not live and flourish so well in the world's memory' (v). Walter Ong connects the heroic tradition of primary oral culture to 'the needs of oral noetic processes' (70). Taking the concept of *noesis* or intellectual thought and perception, Ong argues that oral memory works most effectively with 'heavy' or striking characters, figures whose deeds and exploits are extraordinary, public and, most importantly, memorable. So oral culture generates outsize or heroic figures, not necessarily for romantic or even moral reasons but simply to 'organize [sic] experience in … permanently memorable form' (70). Forgettable figures are not remembered. Ong posits that the same 'noetic economy' (70) can be perceived where oral settings still exist in literate cultures, citing the telling, and retelling, of fairy tales to children as an example. These, like myths, feature type figures that ensure memorability. Heroic figures like Cuchulainn and the men of the Red Branch Knights are retained within the narratives of oral culture, until those narratives are reimagined into texts. As Thomas Carlyle wrote in *On Heroes* (1840), the hero of one age becomes the god of the next.[10] The image Carlyle presents of the unity between past, present and future, the Life-Tree Igdrasil, spreads its bows over the project of the Revival, 'its roots down deep in the Death-kingdoms … its boughs reach always beyond the stars' so that the tree is 'in all times and places … one and the same' (*Collected Works* 38). This is the process of retrieving and retelling that O'Grady was engaged in. Indeed, O'Grady himself wrote on this process of heroes transitioning into gods – 'the formation of the Tuatha Dé Danann, who represent the gods of the historic ages' (*Cuculain and His Contemporaries* 38). So 'the history of one generation is mythologised in the next' (McAteer 37) with that mythologization being also an act of reimagination so that history becomes myth becomes imaginative narrative as each generation continuously brings the past into the present.

Indeed, O'Grady wrote that 'in history there must be sympathy, imagination, creation' (Marcus 19). There must be sympathy with the source material, imaginative engagement with the overall narrative and the capacity to create a new vision from these two. O'Grady, then, saw his project of retelling as a task of elimination and selection, to find within 'variant accounts ... the most genuine' (31). There was evidence in his work of 'a struggle between his sense of history as solid material fact and of the imagination as ... irreducible to material fact' (Foster *The Story of Ireland* 14–15). O'Grady's concept of history was a mythic one, and he struggled to articulate the relationship between history, myth and imagination that he felt Ireland's cultural heritage was founded upon. His were the first of 'the major imaginative works' (Eagleton 34) that began to emerge in the early moments of the Revival. As a Revivalist writer, he stood in the liminal space between the historical and the imaginative conceptions of Irish culture (McAteer 14), making deliberate decisions about the ways in which he retrieved the mythological material that formed, as he perceived, the bedrock of Irish identity.

This is reflected in the ways in which O'Grady articulated Cuculain's movement out of childhood and into adulthood in his text, and how this movement is emplaced in the mythical and historical landscape of Ulster. In O'Grady's retelling, Setanta, as the young hero is known until he is given the name Cuculain, is aware, even as a child, of the importance of his own lineage and heritage. The text relates how in the summer, the boy would often sit with the chief bard of his settlement, 'asking many questions concerning his forefathers back the ascending line up to Rury' (*The Coming of Cuculain* 21). It is implied that Setanta's compulsion to follow the road to the royal city of Emain Macha is connected to his awareness of his ancestry, and that his warrior's destiny is ultimately revealed to him because of this awareness. This resonated with O'Grady's larger project of retrieval, and of reimagination, in that a similar awareness of Ireland's history and mythology was necessary for a new generation of readers to access these narratives.

Setanta's awareness of his own personal heritage also directly influences his interaction with the landscape around him. As the end of his childhood approaches, he begins to dream of Emain Macha, even though his mother Dectera refuses to tell him about the road out of Murthemny [sic] that leads to the city. Setanta knows, however, that the road passes the mountain of Slieve Fuad, and he begins to focus his attention on the mountain, which he can see from the roof of the palace, as though he believes it will reveal something to him. He continues to dream of the city and begins to hear voices in those dreams. On the third night, one of the voices declares that their labour with him is in vain, that 'he is some changeling, and not of the blood of Rury' (24). Here, his stasis on the edge of childhood is cited as a reluctance to engage with his destiny. On the following night, when he climbs to the roof to gaze at the mountain, he is certain 'that Slieve Fuad nod[s] to him and beckon[s]' (24). In O'Grady's retelling, then, the landscape is the catalyst that sets the events of Cuculain's myth in motion. With this certainty in mind, Setanta travels swiftly 'for there [is] power upon him' (24). The landscape of Ulster supports his movement out of childhood and towards adulthood, so much so that when he emerges from the forest, he '[strikes] the great road which from Atha Clia [runs] through Murthemney to Emain Macha' (27) and sees the purple mountains of Slieve Fuad that have been beckoning him rising before him.

Ireland's ancient heritage manifests itself before Setanta on this journey, in the figure of a man with 'the port and countenance of some ancient hero' (28). His attire is strange, and it is clear that Setanta does not recognize him. O'Grady's narrator states that the figure is 'taller and nobler than any living man' (28) implying that this man does not belong to Setanta's present, to the Ulster of the boy's childhood, but to the mythological past. He leads a hound 'white like fire' (28)[11] by a bronze leash, and when he asks Setanta if he knows him, it seems that the young boy does not. The ancient figure, reminiscent of Lugh, the God of Light, in both appearance and standing, pledges to be with the boy always, and that he need fear nothing because of his friendship.[12] In this moment, the ancient past and the present are brought together in the midst of the mythological landscape of Ulster.

One of the seminal episodes in O'Grady's retelling of the Cuculain myth reveals how the young hero receives his name. Culain the smith hosts a feast for King Concobar [sic], Setanta's uncle, to which Setanta himself arrives late. In the context of O'Grady's larger narrative, and his efforts to synthesize history and mythology through imagination, the toast Concobar gives at the feast table becomes especially meaningful. The king speaks of the many heroes that the gathering has toasted, 'many heroes who are gone' and he proposes that they drink now 'to the heroes that are coming, both those unborn' (53) and those who are young, and still in their childhoods. He raises this toast specifically to his own nephew, Setanta, connecting the young boy to the future of the country, and to the future of Ulster itself.

Meanwhile, however, Setanta has encountered Culain's guard hound in the courtyard of the house. After a fierce skirmish, the hound is dead, and the young boy is shaken. Culain and the other men attending the feast stand and stare at the boy, him 'being so young and fair' (60). At first, they gaze at him with pity, because of his youth, but 'then with admiration for his bravery' (60). His white limbs are covered with his own blood, 'so cruelly had the beast torn him with his long and strong and sharp claws' (60). Setanta becomes a powerful image of the boy hero, poised on the brink of adulthood, having been blooded in his first battle.

Setanta pledges himself to Culain saying that he will himself 'take thy dog's place, and nightly guard thy property' and that he will continue to do this until a hound is located to take the place of the one he killed, and 'relieve [him] of that duty' (60). This focus on duty resonates throughout O'Grady's treatment of the narrative of Cuculain; the name Setanta takes on himself after this encounter means 'the hound of Culain' (60). As a young boy, Cuculain pledges himself to the smith he has inadvertently wronged, and as he grows older and matures into a warrior hero, he pledges himself to Ulster, to his homeland.

In O'Grady's own words, narratives such as this 'sum up … in a dramatic and picturesque form the essential qualities of historical characters'.[13] He treated the heroic figures of Ireland's mythological heritage as just that, historical characters whose actions and endeavours have been framed and articulated by and within a mythological context. His retelling of the Cuculain saga is an historical reimagination of a series of mythological narratives, retold precisely to restore those narratives into the contemporary consciousness of the Irish people. This episode is particularly significant, not just for O'Grady's treatment of the child figure but also for what that treatment of Cuculain's childhood imparted to the implied reader about duty, fate and the Irish connection to the landscape of Ireland.

In contrast to both O'Grady's and Eleanor Hull's versions of the Cuchulain myth, Augusta Gregory's retelling *Cuchulain of Muirthemne* (1902) was commissioned by a publisher. Initially Alfred Nutt, the British publisher, folklorist and Celticist, asked W. B. Yeats to undertake a retelling of one of the principal Irish mythological sagas, Cuchulainn the Hound of Ulster. Yeats declined, citing his own increasing workload, and his reluctance to undertake such a project while he still lacked what he felt was the appropriate narrative and linguistic form to tackle it. Instead, he suggested Gregory as a possible candidate. Having accepted, she chose to adopt the 'Kiltartan' idiom, the particular language and dialect used by the working-class peasants near her home in Coole, solving, at least in theory, Yeats's dilemma of form and language. She chose this speech precisely because she was 'afraid of being influenced', in spite of herself, 'by the French, German and bad English translations' (Gregory 8) of the material that were already in circulation. Her choice, then, was an attempt to not only retell the Cuchulain saga but also to retell it in as authentic a way as possible. In doing so, she achieved something singular within the work of the Revival writers – a retelling of an ancient mythological narrative that celebrated the past, but which was articulated 'in a speech living and spoken today' (15) by elements of her contemporary audience. The extent to which this retelling was actually accessible to the peasant community of Kiltartan is questionable, but Gregory's vision for the text's dissemination was nevertheless a theoretically inclusive one. Indeed, she retold the saga in such a way that there would 'be nothing in them that would offend ... especially if they were to be read by children' (8). Interpreted literally, this statement indicates that Gregory was aware of a child readership for her work. But her text was not written explicitly for children. Rather, her version of Cuchulain's myth marked a very particular point in the pattern of retelling and reimagination so prevalent in literature produced during Revival that would in turn influence the production of literature for children in the movement's aftermath. This was her particular Revivalist project – not only to collect these stories together but also to present them to a knowledgeable audience in a new format that might be easily preserved. She sought to bring these myths back into the contemporary experience of the people of Kiltartan, and of Ireland in general. She stated that while 'stories of Finn and Goll and Oisin' are almost ubiquitous in the Irish cultural landscape, 'there is very little of the history of Cuchulain and his friends left in the memory of the people' (10). Though these narratives may have existed in archaic sources and documents, they seemed to have passed out of common oral circulation. Gregory's version of the myth aimed to rectify this. Though her project was one of translation as much as retelling, she stated herself that she tried 'to take the best of the stories' (10) and in that way, from various parts, to re-present an account of Cuchulain's life and death to a new audience. Like Eleanor Hull, Augusta Gregory attempted to connect her endeavour to the larger pattern of retelling and reimagination that had transmitted these narratives for centuries.

In his preface to Gregory's text, Yeats stated that its stories 'are a chief part of Ireland's gifts to the imagination of the world' (Yeats 'Preface' 11), told perfectly for the first time in this volume. He discussed the art of storytelling itself, stating that no story that had been passed down from a previous generation or era retained the form 'it had when the storyteller told it in the winter evenings' (11). Every retelling, then, is an act of reimagination. He created a picture of Gregory as a curator of these stories, rather than an author; in this endeavour she put a shape on 'a great mass of stories, in which the ancient heart of Ireland still lives' (11) and she had done this without writing more than a few linking or connecting sentences of her own. No more, indeed, 'than the story-teller must often have added to amend the hesitation of a moment' (12). Her authorship here is likened to an act of oral storytelling, and the authenticity of her version is validated again. It is in the combination of her particular chosen form of narrative speech and her treatment of her various source materials that Yeats believed had 'called up the past [and] stirred the imagination of a painter or a poet' (12). The essential characters of these sagas must remain the same, but the details of their exploits remain to be reimagined, in that 'the strength of Fergus' may change so greatly that he, who a moment before was merely 'a strong man among many', becomes, in an expansive and imaginative retelling, 'the master of Three Blows that would destroy an army' (15). In his conclusion, Yeats specifically and explicitly connected the spiritual and cultural revival of Ireland to the retelling of these narratives to a new generation; 'if we will but tell these stories to our children that Land will begin again to be a Holy Land' (16).

Gregory's narrative gives precedence to an account of the day Cuchulain takes his arms. This episode occurs after his encounter with Culain's hound at the feast, on a day when Cathbad the Druid 'is teaching the pupils in his house to the northeast of Emain' (28). Among the eight boys with him, one asks him if his 'signs tell of any special thing this day is good or bad for?' (28). In reply, Cathbad tells the small gathering that if 'any young man should take arms today ... his name will be greater than any other name in Ireland' (28). But there is a qualification to his prediction; the span of this young man's life 'will be short' (28).

Cuchulain is 'outside at play' (28) when the prediction is made, so he is not a part of Cathbad's intended audience, but crucially, he hears what the Druid says, and is thus made aware of the significance of the day. Gregory places significance on the idea that he is playing when he hears the prophecy, emphasizing his status as a child, albeit a child with the mentality of a warrior hero. Cuchulain begins to structure his actions accordingly, already under the influence of the prophecy that will shape the rest of his life, and his development into a heroic figure.

He goes to his uncle, King Conchubar [sic], and declares his intention to take arms, thereby initiating the fate that the Druid has foretold. The king questions the young boy, asking who put this idea into his head. When Cuchulain replies that it was Cathbad, the king declares that he 'will not deny' (28) him, as though the authority of the Druid validates the actions Cuchulain will now take. The king, however, is under the impression that the Druid spoke directly to Cuchulain, while the boy himself is aware that he overheard the words of the prophecy and is choosing to take it and its implications on himself. Conchubar gives the boy his choice of weapons, and though Cuchulain tries them all, none are strong enough for him except the king's own. It becomes more and more apparent as Gregory's retelling of this particular episode unfolds, that Cuchulain is actively pursuing the end of his own childhood and is moving into a heroic adulthood as a warrior capable of wielding a king's weapons. Given the social and political climate informing the contemporary childhoods of Gregory's implied readers, this image of a warrior child actively seeking the point at which he can devote himself to his fate and his duties to his province becomes particularly significant, offering, as it does, a model of child citizenship.

Cathbad now enters Conchubar's room, and 'there [is] wonder on him' (28) and he asks if the boy is taking arms, as though he cannot believe his own eyes. When the king replies in the affirmative, the Druid declares that 'it is sorry I would be to see his mother's son take arms on this day' (28) again focusing attention on the tragic aspect of the prophecy he made to the gathered boys earlier. Confused, the king asks if it was not Cathbad who instructed the boy to do it, and when the Druid replies that he did not, Conchubar accuses Cuchulain of lying to him. Gregory's Cuchulain defends himself and expands on the prophecy, prioritizing his own interpretation. Cathbad again emphasizes the truth of his pronouncement, but now he does speak directly to Cuchulain, applying the prophecy to him, stating that 'there will be fame on you and a great name, but your lifetime will not be long' (28). It seems now that the boy is bound to the future the prophecy has outlined for him. He declares that he would care little if his life lasted only one day and one night, 'so long as [his] name and the story of what [he] had done would live after [him]' (28). The idea of Cuchulain's legacy and the ways in which he is remembered will become a trope in the literature produced for children in Ireland that engages with his myth. In Una Kelly's *Cuchulain and the Leprechaun* (1945), a comment is made on the presence of Cuchulain's story in oral tradition (see Chapter 3). In Pat O'Shea's *The Hounds of the Morrigan* (1985), Cuchulainn himself, disguised as an old man, asks the central protagonists, Pidge and Brigit, if they know of his heroic exploits (see Chapter 4). This is arguably the moment in Gregory's retelling when Cuchulain's heroic adulthood begins, as he crosses the threshold that separates his childhood from his fated future. When Cathbad declares that the young boy should step into a chariot so that they may 'see if it was the truth [he] spoke' (28) it is a step into that prophesized future, and into his destiny as the Hound of Ulster.

Eleanor Hull's *Cuchulain the Hound of Ulster* from 1909 shares a similar emphasis on historical context and authenticity with O'Grady's and Gregory's retellings.[14] Hull (1860–1935) was a writer and scholar of Old Irish and co-founded the Irish Texts Society in 1898 to promote the study of Irish literature and the publication of early manuscripts. She also served as president of the Irish Literary Society. In her introduction to *The Hound of Ulster*, Hull was at pains to situate the events she related in a specific, almost explicitly historical context. The narratives of King Conor Mac Ness and Cuchulain [sic] 'are supposed to have occurred, as we gather from the legends themselves, about the first century of our era' (Hull 9). The period referred to here is 'known to archaeologists as "late Celtic" […] i.e.

the period extending from about 400 B.C. to the first century of the Christian era' (10). Hull also wrote about the remains of weapons, ornaments and dress found in Ireland which support this supposition. The legends themselves were not the only evidence of such a culture, though the earliest written versions that exist 'are not earlier than the eleventh or twelfth century' (10). Until they were written down, these tales formed part of the oral culture of Ireland, 'handed down by word of mouth' (10) in an acquisition of knowledge that melded the body with the memory, with every bard and professional storyteller under obligation to know large numbers of romances by heart. Hull was clearly attempting to articulate the authenticity of the narratives she was retelling, relating a history of such retelling, reinterpretation and reimagination, to which hers was only the latest addition in a complex pattern. Hull was placing herself in a context and drawing attention to a dialogue of adaptation that she was contributing to, a dialogue that could be traced through the copies and versions of such tales that still existed. In the course of 'centuries of recitation certain changes crept in' to these stories, but the majority came to her contemporary audience 'much as they were originally recited' (10).

The storytellers who handed down the heroic tales of Ireland 'handled their material in a very free manner', according to Hull, 'expanding and altering as suited their own poetic feeling and the audience they addressed' (11), a method Gregory also outlined in the preface to her version of the Cuchulainn myth, *Cuchulain of Muirthemne*. In Hull's opinion, the later versions of the myth 'lack the brief dignity of the older versions' (11) but for her part she largely validated the work of former storytellers, scribes and bards, stating that her predecessors 'acted in a perfectly legitimate manner' and she had, by her own admission, not hesitated to follow in their example, adapting this material into 'a book written for the pleasure of the young' (12). Hull noted that the older form of the main story was often more restrained, and that there was a tendency, as centuries passed and the narrative was taken up by new generations of bards, and eventually, writers, to not only 'soften down the more barbarous and rougher portions, but to emphasise the pathetic and moving scenes' and augment these 'with touches of symbolism and imagination' (11). As the story was retold, layers of meaning were added to the foundation narrative. Hull reimagined her re-telling of the Cuchulainn myth into a narrative accessible for children, in order to restore them to a sense of the significance of Ireland's cultural and mythological heritage. Occasionally, she 'expand[ed] an imaginative suggestion indicated, but not worked out by the scribe' (11) in a continuation of a process of narration that had been ongoing for centuries.

In retelling the Cuchulain narrative for a child audience, Hull made specific editorial and aesthetic choices, in an attempt to retain the authenticity and wholeness of the source material. She drew specific attention to one specific act of artistic alteration she made, concerning the episode of Cuchulain's visit to Fairy-Land, commonly known as the 'Sickbed of Cuchulain', which, in her own words, required 'a slight modification of the central situation to make it suitable reading for any children' (11) who might encounter the book. She stated simply that this episode was 'too poetic and touching an episode to be altogether omitted without loss to the conception of the cycle as a whole' (11). Hull's project of retelling did not only involve repurposing the myth of Cuchulain for children but also preserving the essential components of that myth for a new generation.

The Hound of Ulster features a framing structure that differs from O'Grady's and Gregory's versions. In Hull's retelling, Meave [*sic*], the warrior Queen who will prove to be Cuchulain's greatest adversary, is privy to a Faery prophecy, foretelling the rise of a figure known as the Hound of Ulster. Setting out with Ailill, her husband, she seeks the truth of the prophecy, and the nature of the famed boy bearing this name. She summons Fergus Mac Roy and Cormac, King Conor's son, to the hosting of her army, and bids them speak of the boy Cuchulain. The two men relate their knowledge of the young warrior previously known as Setanta, telling of his remarkable boyhood in Emain Macha, the king's royal city.

Ailill asks the gathered men what they can tell Meave 'about this famous lad. What ages hath he? And wherefore hath he gained this name? and have his deeds become known to you?' (25). Hull has Fergus reply that his deeds are well known to them, 'for all the land of Ulster rings with this young hero's renown' (26). Here again, Cuchulain is specifically connected to the landscape of Ulster, and to his duty to that land by virtue of his birth. Fergus tells of Cuchulain's extraordinary childhood, how he surpassed all the chieftains' sons of Emain Macha when he was 5, of how he took arms when he was just 7 and of his journey to learn from Scatha the warrior woman of Alba. In his own time, Cuchulain has become a living legend in Ulster, as tales of his deeds travel across the province. He is, as Hull's Meave terms him, 'Ulster's Hound' (26).

Fergus identifies himself as Cuchulain's foster father, but he also alludes to Cuchulain's divine heritage, stating that he and others believe that 'he is of the offspring of the gods and that Lugh of the Long Arms, God of Light, is guardian to the boy' (26). This speaks to a detail in O'Grady's version of the myth, and to the moment when a mysterious figure leading a white hound appears to Cuchulain and offers his guidance and protection. Each of these retellings, though independent in their own right, were facets of the larger collection of mythological narratives that related the exploits of the Ulster hero. In Hull's version, Fergus is attempting to validate Cuchulain's reputation and presence in the consciousness of Ulster by presenting his lineage and history to Meave and Ailill. Though his father is Sualtach, 'a warrior of Ulster' (27), he was reared on Murthemne's plain, at Fergus's knees. Amergin the poet was his tutor, and King Conor's sister nursed him with Conall the Victorious in her home. Fergus also speaks of the judge Morann's prophecy concerning the infant Setanta. The judge foretold that 'his praise ... will be in all men's mouths, his deeds will be recounted by kings and great men, warriors and charioteers, poets and sages' (27). From the moment he is born, he is bound to Ulster, to 'give combat ... against her enemies' (27).

The conversation staged among Meave, Ailill, Fergus and Cormac becomes a narrative of Cuchulain's childhood, of his 'feats ... as a little boy' (28). Fergus relates how, as a tiny child, 'not much past four years old', Setanta was told a long tale of the boy-corps of King Conor in Emain Macha, the troop that the king had established 'for all the sons of nobles and of chiefs, to train them up in strength and bravery' (28). He was told that the king had set aside a playground for the boys, close to his own fort, and that 'there every day they practised games of skill, and feats of arms' (28). The moment the boy Setanta sets off for Emain Macha, with his hurl, his ball, his throwing javelin and his toy spear, marks the first of his childhood exploits as a child warrior. He travels through the landscape in an extended series of playful movements, striking his ball and driving it before him, then throwing his hurl, then his javelin, then his spear, 'always running on' (29). He is never still, 'scarce feeling tired' (29) so engrossed is he in his game.

When Cuchulain reaches Emain Macha, he finds the boy-corps engaged in a game of hurling, under the charge of one of Conor's sons, while the king himself watches the game. Ignorant of the etiquette the situation demands, Cuchulain joins the game, only to be received with hostility by the boys of the corps. Soon, Cuchulain is seized by 'his hero-fury' (30). His hair rises up on his head 'and in his wrath and fierceness it seem[s] as though a light pour[s] forth from each single hair, crowning him with a crown of fire' (30). He grows larger and taller, and the boys of the corps are suddenly terrified by him. Setanta attacks and quickly overwhelms them, though they outnumber him by almost 150 to 1.

The king himself intervenes, articulating the fact that 'this is no gentle game' (31) Setanta is playing with the boy-corps. The young warrior defends himself, stating that he did not receive the reception due to a welcome guest. Conor explains the rules of the boy-corps to Setanta, 'that a new-comer must go under their protection, so that they will respect his life' (31). In response, Setanta asks openly for the king's protection, and Conor is taken by the boy's spirit and bravery. So, the boy-corps accept the little boy into their ranks, but he continues to play roughly with them until the king is forced to question him again. He declares that 'until they place themselves under [his] protection as [he is] placed under theirs' (32) he will not ease his treatment of them.

Fergus uses this episode to illustrate to Meave and Ailill the truth of the rumours and stories they have heard, and how a young boy who was capable of such feats at the age of 4 or 5, 'now being turned seventeen [proves] a formidable foe to Connaught in time of war' (32). Meave is forced to agree. This narrative of Cuchulain's childhood becomes a validation and authentication of his status as a heroic warrior figure, bound to Ulster and its people, which resonated within Hull's larger concern for her project of retelling. If O'Grady was concerned with imaginative history, and Gregory with appropriate language, then Hull was striving for narrative authenticity in her version of the Cuchulain myth. This episode with the boy-corps at Emain Macha features in both O'Grady's versions of the Cuchulain myth and in Gregory's. Hull's is the not only retelling to mention the incidence of the hero-fury which comes over Setanta. In O'Grady's version, Setanta seems to lose control over or connection with his body as the battle rage takes over.[15] In other versions, however, this hero-fury does not occur until Setanta is full grown, and has taken the name of Cuchulain, the Hound of Ulster.

Each of these episodes, O'Grady's narration of Culain's feast, Hull's presentation of Cuchulainn's childhood deeds and Gregory's relation of Cathbad's prophecy, though retold by different authors with different intents, share a certain commonality. They all place emphasis on the significance of Cuchulainn's childhood in Ulster, of the importance of the landscape in the development of his character and physicality and of the nature of the doom or prophecy he took on himself while still a young boy. They are differing yet similar accounts of the heroic childhood of a mythic figure, preserved through acts of translation, narration, preservation and retrieval, chosen specifically by three leading Revivalist writers to be retold for an audience that included potential child readers. The previous versions of the Cuchulainn myth that these retellings speak to are part of a pattern of cycles of reimagination and reinterpretation spanning centuries. If cultural heritage is a kind of communal or transcendental remembering, then in the context of these repeating cycles of retelling, the Revival project itself is illuminated as part of the continual process of remembrance and retrieval.

The return to the past

Cultural memory can focus on fixed points in the past, but it is unable to preserve the past as it was. Instead, it can only prompt recollection. The preservation of the past tends to be condensed into symbolic figures to which memory attaches itself until even myths themselves become what Assmann calls a 'foundational history … narrated in order to illuminate the present from the standpoint of its origins' (*Cultural Memory* 60). The writers of the Revival were engaged in the retelling and reimagination of the myths of Ireland's cultural heritage in order to contextualize the present in terms of that lost past. This past or, rather, these pasts were and are made present by 'cyclical repetition' (74), by the retelling of tales that have always been retold. As oral cultures move further into contact with print culture, the element of repetition and representation recedes, and the tendency to reimagine comes to the fore. Knowledge of a mythological heritage facilitates a textual continuity that 'entails a framework of references … within which … texts may remain present, effective and accessible' (86) even over a period of centuries. This continuity would manifest itself in literature produced for children in Ireland in the decades following the Revival precisely because that framework of references, once established, was returned to and reused again and again. The Cuculain of Standish O'Grady's 1894 would journey out of the nineteenth century and appear as Cuchulainn in the twentieth century in a text such as Pat O'Shea's *The Hounds of the Morrigan* (to be discussed in Chapter 4), utterly reimagined yet fundamentally recognizable.

There was a resonance between the myths that are retrieved and retold by these authors during the Revival and the reimagined mythological narratives so prevalent in Irish children's literature in the twentieth and twenty-first centuries. In 'Nationality and Imperialism', an essay by Æ, the spirit of the nation and the national being were described as being 'older than any name we know … not earth born, but the synthesis of many heroic and beautiful moments' (Russell 'Nationality and Imperialism' 15). These were moments that occurred outside of time, in a kind of sacred temporality that accounted for what Æ called the divinity of their origin. This sacred, mythic past became an essential part of the cultural expression of the nation. Together, Yeats and Æ asserted the centrality of the historic and mythic pasts of Ireland to any conception and articulation of Irish culture and identity (Richard 129), explicitly connecting the retelling of these narratives to the future of the nation. Yeats wrote that 'the legends will have a predominant influence in the coming century' (Yeats 'John Eglinton' 19) positing the conviction that the past would become again a presence in the present. This revelation of the cultural heritage of the past within the present informed the poet's work during this Revival period. He stated that 'the renewal of belief which is the great movement of our time, will more and more liberate the arts from "their age," and from life' (19). The Revival, then, was not a matter of creating something new, but retrieving something that had been lost, and renewing it. This act of renewal, or reimagination, was the liberation Yeats spoke of; through retelling and reimagination the mythological narratives of Ireland's heritage became timeless, and accessible to all, whenever they were retold. Within the Revival, Yeats sought 'the revelation of a hidden life' (36), a life that had all but been lost, but which remained to be retrieved. The purpose of art is to precipitate a return to the past, for the individual 'can only return the way he came and so escape from weariness' (Yeats 'The Autumn of the Flesh' 74). Art, then, is 'to lead us back on our journey' (74), a journey that must, by its very nature, be cyclical – a return to the past that would lead to a rejuvenation of the present.

In this context, Æ believed that the individual forms an ideal of his country from his reading of history, and this ideal was to be realized in a national literature, the central concern of which would be 'the creation of heroic figures, types, whether legendary or taken from history, and enlarged to epic proportions by our writers' (Russell *Imaginations and Reveries* 19). The aim of the Revival, then, was literally to revive the pasts of Ireland through narrative, 'to let that spirit incarnate fully which began among the ancient peoples' (17). This particular aspect of the project could only reach its full potential with a new generation of readers, which included child readers, prepared to engage imaginatively with the images of cultural heritage presented to them in this new national literature. Traditions were preserved and renewed for newer generations as these narratives were continuously retrieved and retold. The future, for the Revivalists, was always yet to be achieved. The project of the Revival was a future-oriented one, to reclaim and recover a lost mythological heritage, to infuse the present with a sense of that heritage and to transmit it into the future. Children, and child readers, in their role as citizens-in-waiting of a new and more enlightened Irish nation, were necessary for that future to materialize. In attempting to restore a lost cultural and mythological heritage, writers such as Yeats, O'Grady, Gregory and others were, in essence, attempting to reconnect the present to the past. The Revivalist writers were seeking to use what Knowles and Malmkjaer call 'the reality-creating potential of language' (ix) so that they might retrieve and retell a lost mythological past for Ireland. The impulse towards recovery and reimagination within the movement strove for a reciprocity between narrative forms and what Barbara Hardy calls narrative acts of mind, 'transferred from art to life' ('Towards a Poetics of Fiction' 19).

The texts chosen and analysed here constitute a heritage of stories, mediated through and experienced within the landscapes of Ireland. These stories and the cultural images they contain are components in the larger cultural system of Irish children's literature and can be fully understood only within the context of that system, in the world in which they 'come to life' (Brown ix). Images which encapsulate cultural heritage are accessible through this system, and through reimagined narratives. We look to 'ideas, images, and symbols' (ix) to create a sense of individual and communal identity, and these must be created and recreated as those identities change over time.

In this context, the interconnectedness that exists between images and memories allows for a transfer of meaning between them. Images of cultural heritage can evoke memories of a national past. This is precisely because a sense of subjective orientation in time, as it passes, is linked to memory, not only from the past to the future but also from the future back towards the past, across the living present. If an exchange or series of exchanges can take place between the living memory of individual persons and the public memory of the communities, societies and nations to which those individuals belong, can these exchanges not take place through different media? The mythological narratives which were retold during the Revival, and which went on to influence so much of the literature produced for children in Ireland in its aftermath, operated as one of those media, as sites of cultural and imaginative interaction. And while it can be argued that the writings of Revivalist authors such as Yeats, Hyde and others sought to direct the people towards the past, not to open the future but rather 'to encourage an endless reprise of the moment in which the Irish most fully realised their national destiny' (Richards 10), this return to the past was not and is not an endlessly circular reprise, but the expansion of a pattern of reimagination that facilitated the preservation and the revitalization of Ireland's cultural heritage. As the next chapter demonstrates, that approach to retelling and reimagining Ireland's cultural heritage fundamentally influenced the literature for children produced in the decades following the Revival.

Chapter 2

RETELLING: ALICE DEASE, ELLA YOUNG, VIOLET RUSSELL, PADRAIC COLUM, JAMES STEPHENS

Citizenship and national identity: Independence and heritage

The repository of myths, images and literary modes that so concerned the writers of the Celtic Revival was 'the inheritance that the nineteenth and early twentieth centuries had bequeathed to the citizens of a new state' (Brown 68). These myths and the ways in which they were retrieved by the Revival movement had done 'more than anything else to draw the attention of the outside world to the separate national existence of Ireland' (Boyd 7). The texts to be considered in this chapter were published between 1907 and 1920 and contributed to that sense of Ireland's separate national existence, especially considering that they were published for children, for the future citizens of that separate Ireland. This thirteen-year period saw dramatic events and changes occurring on the island of Ireland.

In 1908 Pádraic Pearse, a leading figure in the Irish revolutionary scene, founded his boys' school at St Enda's in the Dublin suburb of Ranelagh. The majority of the pupils would eventually join the IRB and the Irish Volunteers. Pearse's vision for the school would, ironically, be later reflected in the educational policies of the emerging Irish state – using Irish mythology and cultural heritage to engender a sense of national identity and citizenship. Pearse focused particularly on the figure of Cuchulainn and his association with the notion of blood sacrifice which would so fundamentally influence his conception of the 1916 Rising. While the authors considered here were retelling and repurposing narratives of the Fianna Éireann and introducing new generations to the cyclic notion that the soldiers of Ireland would return to fight for the nation again, the social and political climate of contemporary Ireland was reaching a crisis point. In 1912, when H. H. Asquith introduced the Government of Ireland Bill into the Westminster Parliament, nearly half a million Protestants signed the Ulster Covenant, pledging to oppose Home Rule in all forms. Meanwhile, the social conditions in Dublin were spiralling out of control with the urban slums cited as the worst in Europe. A six-month strike staged in 1913 by the Irish Transport and General Workers Union failed to make gains for the workers, meaning no improvement in living conditions. By the outbreak of the First World War in August 1914, the majority of the Irish population were largely supportive of Britain's cause with the promise of the implementation of Home Rule in the offing, prompting many Irish men to join the British Army. However, as the War dragged on, Irish Republicans saw an opportunity to present the case for Irish independence to the world. The 24th of April 1916 marked the beginning of a week of rebellion against British rule in Ireland, largely against the wishes of the general population. But in executing the leaders of that rebellion, the British government managed to turn the tide of public sympathy towards the rebels, and towards the struggle for independence. The 20th of January 1919 marked the first sitting of Dáil Éireann, a powerful political gesture of defiance against British rule. Between 1919 and the signing of the Anglo-Irish Treaty in 1921, Ireland was engaged in a guerrilla war with the British government which would eventually lead to the Irish Civil War.

In this period alone then, the conception of Irish independence, heritage and citizenhood changed dramatically, not only because of the larger global experience of the First World War but also because of the national and local experiences of rebellion and social deprivation. The literature produced for children in this period was written out of a time of social and political turbulence while looking back to the ancient traditions of the country's mythological heritage to not only provide context for the contemporary moment but also to connect a new generation to those traditions. There was a continuing need to connect the contemporary public with the pasts of their country in an attempt to articulate a national identity that was continuously changing. Responding to this, authors such as Ella Young (1867–1956), Alice Dease (1874–1949), Violet Russell (1868–1932), Padraic Colum (1881–1972) and James Stephens (1880–1950)[1] began to retell the myths and folkloric tales the Revival movement was so intent on retrieving, and in doing so, repurposed them for a new child audience. These authors began to adapt mythological material to achieve a new objective – to engage child readers in a cultural discourse about national identity and mythological heritage.

Mythology in culture

Mythology refers to 'the body of inherited myths in any culture' (Coupe 4). It is an important element of any national literature because literature can be seen as 'a means of extending mythology', in that literary works can 'create or recreate certain narratives' (4) which are taken to be fundamental to a particular culture or society's understanding of the world. The Revival writers not only sought to engage with that understanding but also to augment it. In order to retrieve lost pasts and lost selfhoods for Ireland, some employed mythic paradigms in their writing, setting their narratives outside or beyond historical time, in sacred or even primal time – time that does not pass. The concept of an ever-present otherworld where temporality is suspended is one 'that pervades Irish tradition' (Minahan McGinn 68). Many of the mythological narratives retrieved and repurposed by the Revivalist writers were concerned with the 'relativities of time and space that characterised the interaction of the two worlds' (68), the second of these being ancient Ireland or Tir na nÓg.

This focus allowed the Revival writers and those working in its aftermath to bring the pasts of Ireland into dialogue with their contemporary present, precisely because the essential action of these myths takes place 'in another realm or at another level entirely' (Knox 65) and because myth enlarges ordinary or profane time. On the other hand, Paul Ricoeur has noted that ritual brings mythic time 'and the profane sphere of life and action together' (105). Myth is enacted and re-enacted through ritual, and through participation in ritual, mythic time becomes accessible. For the Revivalist writers, then, participation in the ritual of retelling provided access to mythic time, and to a lost heritage. If 'the true myth is never consciously invented' but rather is a 'cultural inheritance' (Knox 24) then the work of the Revival writers who engaged with and repurposed the mythological narratives of Ireland's ancient pasts was fundamentally a project of reimagination. The cultural inheritance constituted by these mythological narratives also includes the meanings attached to artefacts and traditions inherited from the past (Duffy 194). In this context, the repurposing and reimagination of mythological narratives from Ireland's ancient pasts is in itself an act of preservation, even as it is an act of renewal. In much of the imaginative work produced during the Revival and after it, especially the texts that retell and reimagine mythological narratives, events are related by and articulated through what Wesley Kort calls patterns of repetition (16). Expressed through circadian or seasonal cycles of nature, and often personified in figures such as An Dagda, the father of Aengus Óg, time and its passage is intimately associated with the landscape. These narratives are rhythmic plots, and they are suggestive of aesthetic and spiritual life, in the manner of rituals and festivals (17). The idea of reimagination resonates particularly within rhythmic plots because these tend to favour the past, and 'the repetitions of rhythmic time carry the strongest suggestion of return' (17).

Much of the children's literature from this period, 1907–20, was based on mythological narratives and formed part of the larger scope and purpose of the Revival – to reconnect the Irish population with a lost mythological heritage. This facilitated an engagement with ideas of national and cultural independence. Time, landscape, myth and selfhood are the themes that dominate the mythological narratives prevalent in Irish children's literature, from the time of the Revival to the modern day. The writers of the Revival turned particularly to myth in their attempts to express a changing nation's concerns with issues of authenticity, identity and place. The focus here is on the retelling and repurposing of mythological narratives in literature for children in the early twentieth century in Ireland because myths especially seem to express or articulate the emerging nation's preoccupation with issues of cultural legitimacy, community, and shared experience. This reimaginative tradition, which, as we have seen, was precipitated by Standish O'Grady, Eleanor Hull and Augusta Gregory, and developed by the writers examined here, has influenced Irish children's literature for generations. Through an analysis of selected episodes from Alice Dease's *Old Time Stories of Erin* (1907), Ella Young's *Celtic Wonder Tales* (1910), Violet Russell's *Heroes of the Dawn* (1913), Padraic Colum's *The King of Ireland's Son* (1916) and James Stephens's *Irish Fairy Tales* (1920), this chapter will examine how literature for children in Ireland developed within and immediately after the Celtic Revival, and in the early part of the twentieth century. These texts are representative of a body of literature that was being created for children in this period, based on mythological narratives.

Terry Eagleton writes that in the modern epoch, culture becomes one means by which a fragmented or divided society can be held together (35). With this in mind, he argues that intellectuals, as cultural organizers, should assume higher profiles in such societies. As societies mature and modernize, and as 'tribal bonds, feudal fealties or an absolutist state can no longer hold a people together' (35), shared language, education and belief systems come to the fore instead. If, as Eagleton states, 'culture is the very medium of nationalist struggle' (35), it corresponds that intellectuals should play a more active role in colonial societies than in metropolitan ones. The texts discussed here, and the authors who produced them, use the medium of culture to address issues of national identity, tradition and mythological heritage, each seeing their work as 'an integral part of nationalist consciousness raising' (Foster *Vivid Faces* 81).

The writers of the Revival, and especially those associated with the literary movement, were concerned with the articulation of a shared past and with the narrative reconstruction or reimagination of Ireland's lost mythological past. Any act of remembering involves retrieving a narrative, an image, an object out of the past, and bringing it into the present. Memory, then, corresponds to imagining or reimagining the past. Because memory, like narrative, is constructive, the retold and repurposed narratives produced during the Revival were attempting to give precedence to collective representations of the past. As Thomas Hobbes states, 'Imagination and memory are but one thing' (16). He holds that we only refer to imagination as memory when we wish 'to concentrate on imagination as a form of perception relating to the past' (Leijenhorst 96). When the object of which we are thinking is removed from us, our sense of it diminishes. As the distance between it and us grows, that sense only diminishes further. Our imagining of the object then moves into the realm of remembering, where remembering becomes an imagination of the past. When we wish to express the object itself, this is imagination. But when we wish to acknowledge the sense that the object is far away from us in both place and time, this is memory. The act of retelling, especially as employed by the authors discussed here, is simultaneously an act of imagination and memory, in that the original myth is expressed, but the antiquity of that myth is also acknowledged. Distance from the past is an indication of a need to return to the beginning, for renewal, so that the pattern can begin again (Kort 17).

Alice Dease: The compromised hero

Alice Dease's *Old Time Stories of Erin*, an anthology of folk tales and mythological tales, was first published in 1907. The stories chronicle seminal moments in the history of ancient Ireland, from the arrival of Christianity to the reign of Cormac Mac Art, and key episodes from the Ulster Cycle of Mythology, including the saga of the Brown Bull of Cooley, and the appearance of the Morrigan, the queen of war and destruction.[2]

Dease propounded a particular view of the narratives retold in this collection. She stated in her own foreword that they 'cannot be relied upon as records of cultural events' (Dease *Old Time Stories of Erin* i). These stories operate outside of ordinary, quotidian time, in something closer to Eliade's continuous sacred time. It was their poetical or even metaphysical value that Dease was concerned with, and the ways in which these folk and mythological narratives helped 'to mould the destiny of a people in its early civilisation' (i). She was retelling these stories primarily because the heroic tales of ancient Ireland 'are unsurpassed in interest by those of any other nation' (i) but also because the cultural values contained within them were relevant, even essential, to the contemporary Ireland in which she was writing, and in particular, to the then burgeoning cultural scene in Dublin, a city 'defined by political subcultures' (Foster *Vivid Faces* xxii). These are heroic tales characterized 'by vividness of imagination and wealth of incident' (Dease i) and they are tales which lend themselves to reimagination. It corresponds that a writer associated with the Revival, with a movement intent on rejuvenating a stagnating Irish culture and society, should turn to such myths for inspiration, 'especially those which are of exclusively Irish growth' (i).

The tale of Cuchulin [*sic*] that Dease chose to retell is hardly typical of the archetypal hero story preferred by other Revival writers and is perhaps less well known than other narratives of his exploits.[3] The tale of 'The Grey Clown' is significant within Dease's collection for its exploration of heroic action, valour and the nature of morality and ethics. Though the majority of the Revival writers were interested in representing the figure of the hero, and in articulating the essence of heroism itself as embodied by Cuchulainn, Dease's retelling is a rather less flattering version of Cuchulin than those of her contemporaries, exploring his flaws and frailties as well as his mythical abilities and heritage, and using a traditional mythological template to produce a retelling that is provocative as well as imaginative.[4] This particular episode is also evidence of a continuing contemporary interest in the myths of Cuchulin and his men, following on from Standish O'Grady, Eleanor Hull and Gregory's retellings from 1892, 1902 and 1909, respectively.

The narrative opens with a description of the Red Branch Knights, resident at Emania, (Emain Macha) at a time when Midir, father of the beautiful and renowned Blanaid, is king of the island of Fir Falgia. The Knights have 'such a great love of fighting' (Dease 1) that they are not content with disputes and adventures at home, so they take to the sea, challenging Alban and Pictish champions to fight. There is a subtle note of judgement in these opening paragraphs, with Dease's narrator being at pains to illustrate the fact that the Red Branch Knights set out from Emania to cause violence for sport. Indeed, instead of disembarking in peace at their destination, 'and taking what they required without opposition', they are confronted by armed men and are forced to fight 'with all their skill and all their valour' (2) in order to win a battle that they themselves have precipitated. Dease is specifically addressing the issue of violence in the Ulster Cycle, and the problematic connection between this issue and the ideology of heroism propounded by the writers of the Revival (Wilson Foster xi). In this period, Cuchulainn is reclaimed out of the lost past of Ireland and is established as a cultural and mythological hero. In other Revival retellings, Cuchulainn and the Red Branch Knights are associated with integrity, valour and moral fortitude; in this retelling Dease is explicitly encouraging her child readers to question the nature of heroism and its susceptibility to corruption.

King Midir's palace on the cliffs of the island is so strongly fortified that 'even the great Cuchulin, the youthful leader of the band' (2), cannot devise a plan to penetrate it. Never before has the young hero 'seemed so near defeat' because 'in all the combats of his youth his invariable successes [have] been amazing' (2). Cuchulin is a youth not accustomed to defeat. Dease portrays the ostensible hero of the narrative as a somewhat arrogant figure, assured of his own success, yet confronted with the possibility of humiliation in battle. The figure of the youth was to become a central one in the discourse of Irish nationalism throughout the course of this decade, and in the lead up to the 1916 Rising. Dease was consciously writing into this discourse, problematizing the archetypal imagery and symbolism of Ireland's heroic and mythic pasts. As early as 1903, the political activist Arthur Griffith (who would go on to found the Sinn Féin organization in 1905) recognized that structured boys' brigades could be turned into 'a great national force' (Griffith 1). Na Fianna Éireann, founded in 1902 and reconstituted in 1909, was an Irish nationalist uniformed group designed to further the cause of independence through youth involvement. Its members were not only given military and physical training; they were also, as Marnie Hay has pointed out, educated about Irish culture and heritage, in a promotion of 'an idealised image of Irish nationalist youth that emphasised the importance of patriotism and morality' ('Moulding the Future' 447). Fundamental to the organization was the acknowledgement that the youth 'were the future of the Irish nationalist movement' (446). The figure of the youthful warrior or hero was central to the philosophies surrounding Irish independence at this time, and young boys and girls were exposed to this through a variety of different media, including cultural activities organized by women's groups such as Inghinidhe na hÉireann and columns for children in national newspapers.[5] As a mythological hero, Cuchulainn and the retellings of the myths featuring his exploits were employed in this cultural education.

Among the men who have followed the Red Branch Knights from Ireland is a stranger known as Curoi, the Grey Clown. He is older than Cuchulin, and this will prove significant as the young champion endorses Curoi's plan only because a quality in his voice and the authority he assumes shows that he is 'a man more used to command than to obey' (3). His age serves to legitimize his experience and skill. Curoi demands payment in the form of a jewel from the castle if his plan comes to fruition. Cuchulin, finally overcome with curiosity, demands to know the man's true identity, and how he might 'have come to learn the hidden secret of a foreign kingdom' (5). The Grey Clown reveals himself to be Curoi Mac Dare of Slieve Mish, and just as Cuchulin is the leader of the Red Branch Knights, so Curoi is the leader of the Munster Order of Chivalry. Cuchulin immediately declares that Curoi should assume a position 'as a brother knight' (6) as the attack unfolds, but the older man will not agree. Unlike Cuchulin, Curoi goes into battle as an ordinary soldier. Cuchulin and Curoi are set up in opposition against each other here – youth against experience, arrogance against pragmatism. As men of similar social and military status, it is easy to draw comparisons between their actions and conduct, and Dease's readers are encouraged to question the heroic qualities of these two men.

The plan is successful, and Midir's castle is captured. As the Champion of Erin is 'not one lightly to break his word' (7), as soon as the castle is in his possession, Cuchulin sends for Curoi the Clown. Cuchulin is ready to 'redeem his promise' (7) but it quickly emerges that the jewel Curoi has set as his payment is in fact Blanaid, the king's daughter. Cuchulin is caught in a conflict between his sense of personal outrage and the strictures of his duty as a Red Branch Knight and the traditions that bind him. His outrage is undermined by the fact that he, as a direct consequence of his decision to set out from Emaina with violence, has precipitated this situation. But he states that by his vows, he is 'bound to protect a maiden in distress' and so, if Blanaid chooses him for her champion, 'this last vow shall free [him] from the first' (9). The action of the rest of the sequence thus comes, in this moment, to rest on Blanaid's choice between two male aggressors; it is she who will ultimately suffer as the warrior vows that bind Cuchulin and Curoi are played out to their final effect.

Cuchulin approaches her 'with a confident air' (9) and drops on one knee before her. Without glancing at Curoi, Blanaid places her hands in Cuchulin's. The gesture is unmistakable, yet the girl speaks 'no word in answer to his question' (9): her silence becomes a signifier within the episode of her lack of power and agency. Cuchulin, for his part, is 'anxious to pretend to keep his word to his defeated rival' (10) and it is this idea of the contradictions between appearances and duty that makes Dease's portrayal of Cuchulin in this episode so compelling, and so challenging, to her contemporary child reader. The hero is concerned with appearing to keep his word, and this implies that he worries more about his reputation than his actions. So, when Curoi spirits Blanaid away, contrary to both hers and Cuchulin's wishes, the latter perceives it as a slight, and vows to retrieve the woman he has already claimed as his prize. Again, Blanaid's lack of agency is evident; she must wait to be rescued, since there is clearly no way for her to alter her situation herself.

Cuchulin catches up with Curoi and his party before they reach the sanctuary of Slieve Mish, and significantly, Curoi turns to face the oncoming hero, waiting 'with drawn sword the coming of Cuchulin' (13). There is a sense of honour inherent in his actions as rather than continuing to run, he turns to face Cuchulin and his challenge, as though certain of his own righteousness. An epic fight erupts between the two, with the older man gaining the upper hand. Dease's narrator explicitly states that although Cuchulin 'had treated him so badly', the Grey Clown admires his courage, and his skill, and does not wish 'to deprive the kingdom of Erin of the services of so great a champion' (14). Again, Cuchulin's fate is affected by his status as a warrior hero. Curoi chooses instead to humiliate Cuchulin by cutting his hair, knowing that this will force the hero into hiding for a year, until his hair grows long enough to fall to his shoulders again; shorn hair is a mark of shame within this warrior culture. Cuchulin must live the physical as well as the psychological effects of his punishment. He is also aware of the gravity of this punishment because it is a direct consequence of his poor conduct. It is rare that Cuchulin is bested in battle in the stories surrounding his exploits, and that the consequences for this defeat should be so humiliating, and so far-reaching, speaks to the image of Cuchulin Dease is trying to present: a flawed hero subject to misjudgements and poor conduct.

Dease takes up this narrative again in another episode entitled 'When the Stream Ran White'. During his enforced retreat from the world following his humiliation at the hands of Curoi, both Leary and Conal Kernach, 'friends and brother knights' (15) of Cuchulin, have adventures of their own and dispute his right to the Champion's share at feasts.[6] Neither the Druids nor the Brehon judges can solve the matter, stating that 'no man who was not himself a warrior could fairly decide so difficult a question' (15). So, the champions must look to Munster for judgement, and the Grey Clown, Curoi. The three Ulster champions set out to reach Cahir Conree in Kerry, the stronghold and meeting place of the Clan Degaid. The *cahir* is a great house 'built in the same fashion as their own Emania' (18) and overlooks the waters of Tralee Bay, following the course of the river Fin Glas, from its mouth towards its source. Not only is Dease's narrator at great pains to emplace the *cahir* in the landscape of Munster, but there is also a sense here that Cahir Conree is being set up as a mirror image of Emania, the stronghold of the Red Branch Knights, even though the Knights themselves are far from their native province. In the courtyard of the *cahir* they find a 'clear deep spring from which the river flow[s]' (18), and beside it is a lady Cuchulin recognizes as Blanaid, now the wife of Curoi mac Dare. This image of Blanaid beside the spring foreshadows the later events of the narrative, connecting her to the water that will initially provide the means for her escape but will ultimately result in her demise. Dease's portrayal of Blanaid here is perhaps related to or inspired by the figure of Boann, the river goddess who created the Boyne, losing her life in the water in the process, having striven to gain wisdom from a forbidden well. Blanaid's troubled life and tragic fate echo within Boann's narrative; it is only when both women are lost in violent flowing water that they attain a certain kind of freedom from the fates they have been committed to by the powerful male figures in their lives.

The episode progresses as Blanaid's ladies in waiting ask the champions to defend their mistress from creatures that have been attacking the *cahir* under cover of darkness. On the first night, Leary prevents the creatures from entering but does not kill any of them. Conal performs in a similar fashion on the second night. On the third night, Cuchulin is 'so skilful and so brave' that when morning comes, the heads of nine of the attacking men are lying on the castle floor 'as trophies of the young man's victories' (21). Consequently, and despite what has previously occurred between them, Curoi awards Cuchulin the Champion's share when he returns home.

Having been accepted into the *cahir* 'as a youth most qualified to keep perpetual watch over a king's palace' (22), Cuchulin learns from Blanaid that she did not want to flee Midir's castle with Curoi, and views him not as her husband, but as her captor. The Ulster Champion decides to rescue her, and Blanaid suggests that he should hide himself in the neighbouring woods, near the mouth of the river that follows from the castle well, until a day might come when Curoi would be alone and unguarded. Then she will send a message by the stream to tell Cuchulin to come to her. Her plan, while initially seeming duplicitous at best and treacherous at worst, is more complex than it first appears; it is only through deception and betrayal that she can regain whatever freedom might be available to her in this society. She cannot take arms against her husband herself, so she must employ or entreat Cuchulin to do so for her. Her plan is not then treacherous but merely necessary, even inevitable. She tells Cuchulin that 'when the stream runs white' (23) he will know the time has come. The stream and the surrounding landscape become integral parts of the plan; the river itself rises from within Curoi's own grounds, just as the plan against him rises from the heart of his castle.

When Curoi is gone, Blanaid empties milk into the stream until it runs white and, according to Dease's narrator, 'to this day the river is known by the name of the Fin Glas, or the White Water' (24).[7] Cuchulin receives the message, meets Blanaid at the *cahir* and later, when Curoi is asleep, the hero wakens him, and cuts his head off, killing him without giving him the chance to defend himself. His widow, described by Dease's narrator as 'the heartless Blanaid', then leaves the mutilated body lying on its couch, and gathers together 'all the jewels and the things of value Curoi had brought to her from foreign countries' (26). On one level this might be seen as Blanaid reclaiming her identity and her agency, in that she was once referred to by both Curoi and Cuchulin as a jewel but Dease's narrator instead emphasizes the 'faithless' aspect of her actions. Curoi's poet Ferketne, described as a 'faithful friend' (26), in direct contrast to Blanaid, follows the fleeing couple until they reach the kingdom of Ulster and then succeeds in overtaking them, just as Cuchulin once followed Curoi as he fled with Blanaid. Cuchulin has taken Blanaid to a dwelling by the eastern sea, and one evening, as they are walking on the high cliffs of the promontory of Kenbarr, Ferketne attacks them, pulling Blanaid over the edge of the cliff so that they both fall to their deaths in the water below. Again, the girl's fate is literally pulled out of her hands by a man concerned with issues of fealty and honour. Dease never reveals whether she was happy with Cuchulin or whether the choice to leave him is available to her.

The episode concludes with Dease's narrator's judgement of Cuchulin, who, though fated 'to live for many a day, to fight and win in frequent conflicts until his time also came to die' (28), would always carry the weight of his part in Curoi's death. But it is stated specifically that though the champion's heart was heavy with remorse for the fate of the Grey Clown, he was not concerned for the death of Blanaid, 'who had only earned for herself the merited reward of her own perfidy' (28). This stands even though her actions were forced upon her by the actions of both Cuchulin and Curoi, neither of whom were content until they were in possession of her. Thus, whatever agency Blanaid may have claimed for herself in escaping from Curoi is compromised by the narrative's conclusion, which, while redeeming Cuchulin to a certain extent, condemns her actions. Cuchulin's redemption is mediated through his status as a hero while Blanaid's ruin is a direct result of her compromised position as a woman in a warrior society. Male action, however destructive, is prioritized over female action. Even though Cuchulin experiences that redemption, and Dease does succeed in introducing an alternative narrative of the heroic figure in Irish mythology into the contemporary cultural discourse in which she was engaged, there is still little emphasis placed on the heroic female figures in Irish mythology.[8] The model of the hero presented here is a gendered one. In her reimagining, Dease tells a new story which complicates the idea of the male hero figure in cultural and nationalist discourses but further subjugates the female figure. She uses Blanaid's death and Cuchulin's shame and the ways in which their fates are connected to the landscapes they move through to interrogate the narratives surrounding the struggle for Irish independence. The landscapes depicted in Dease's narrative and in the other texts considered here are what Frances Yates calls 'memory places' (xi), existing as they do in both the ancient pasts of mythic Ireland and the contemporary cultural present of the Revival. In fact, the role of landscape and the significance of place in the ethos of the movement cannot be overestimated (Wilson Foster xvi). The primacy of landscape in the mythological narratives of Ireland's cultural heritage, and especially in the retellings of the myths discussed here, provided an imaginative stimulus for the writers of the Revival, in the form of an opportunity to bring the past into the present through place.

The primacy of landscape: A creation myth for Ireland

As John Wilson Foster has noted, cultural landscapes function as 'allegories of meaning' (xvi) and these allegories operate in multiple paradigms, be they imaginative, mythological or temporal. The images of landscape presented within these narratives are carriers of heritage, rich in Wilson Foster's 'signs of identity and social codes' (4) that work towards the creation of a collective cultural memory, supporting meanings and associations that evolve through time, endlessly changing. The landscape of Ireland becomes what James Anderson calls 'the receptacle of the past in the present' ('Nationalist Ideology and Territory' 24), articulated through these repurposed mythological narratives. Within the Revival period then, every act of retelling was a renegotiation of those landscapes. These mythological narratives 'are embodied in [those] emblematic landscapes' (Duffy 196). Thus, the Irish landscape is an 'archetypal national landscape' (Gruffud 219) shaped by imagery, myth and memory.

Ireland's landscapes provided many Revival and post-Revival writers with inspiration, and Ella Young was no different. She saw the west of Ireland in particular as what Rose Murphy calls 'the sacred source of pure Celtic culture' (1), a culture that could still be accessed and revitalized through the retelling of myths and folk tales. Her project then, with *Celtic Wonder Tales* (1910), was one of adaptation – the retelling and repurposing of 'Ireland's native oral literature' (2) for a new generation. She sought, like many of the Revival writers, to recover 'a lost inheritance' (142) through the act of retelling the stories of Ireland's ancient past. Padraic Colum wrote of Young's storytelling project that when she retold something from myth or folklore, she was 'not merely relating an interesting legend [but] telling a part of a sacred history' ('Ella Young: A Druidess' 6) and contributing to a wider cultural dialogue promoted by the values of the Revival. The retold stories in her collection illustrate what Colum called 'the traditional Celtic impulse toward journey [and] movement' (6) and towards an engagement with landscape and time through these tropes.

A key episode in Young's *Celtic Wonder Tales* collection is a story entitled 'The Earth Shapers'. With it, Young produced a creation myth for Ireland, including prominent figures from the Mythological Cycle of Irish mythology. The episode is dedicated to the Sacred Land, an allusion to Ireland that establishes a connection between the landscapes depicted in Young's collection and the landscapes of contemporary Ireland. Young sets the story in Tir na Moe, the Land of the Living Heart, where Angus the Ever-Young (an alias for Angus Óg and a figure who returns time and again in the literature for children produced in the aftermath of the Revival[9]), Midir the Red-Maned, Ogma the Splendour of the Sun and the Dagda are listening to Brigit singing. These are central figures in the cycles of Irish mythology – members of the Tuatha Dé Danann, the people of the tribe of the Goddess Danu and the supernatural rulers of mythic Ireland. Brigit's song tells of a gift from the gods, a 'wonder-sight' (3). It is at once a wave, a star, a flame and a sacred bird, 'ours, if our hearts are wise, to take and keep' (4). The silence that follows the cessation of Brigit's singing is an interpretive space – a meaningful silence at the heart of Young's narrative wherein the other Dé Danann gods, and especially Angus, are trying to quantify the imagery in the song they have just heard. The song and its music are both strange to Angus, and he says that they swept him 'down steeps of air – down – down – always further down' (4). Bachelard writes that the path of reverie is 'a constantly downhill path' where the consciousness relaxes and 'wanders and consequently becomes clouded' (Bachelard *Reverie* 5). Angus has experienced a reverie; he says that Tir na Moe became like a half-remembered dream to him, like the clouding Bachelard associates with the movement into reverie. If we see Angus's experience of being swept downwards by Brigit's song as a reverie, then the song itself becomes an imaginative evocation of the space that will be reshaped as Ireland. To evoke something is to summon it, or to imaginatively recreate it, as in an evocation of the past.[10] The act of evocation comes from the Latin *evocare*, from *e-* meaning out of and *vocare* meaning to call. To evoke something, then, is to call it out, 'to recall (a feeling, memory, or image) to the conscious mind' (OED). It is, in a sense, a reverie in reverse, when the conscious mind calls something to it, instead of moving towards it through dream. To evoke something can also mean to elicit a response from it; it is a gesture or an action that invites interaction. It can involve invoking a spirit or a deity or imbuing a present action with the essence of a past endeavour. And to call something, one must have a sense that it is there. In the context of the Revival, this means an awareness of heritage. Evocation was at the heart of Young's project, and at the centre of 'The Earth Shapers'; it is an act of recall and an 'activation of past moments into the present'.[11] By evoking Ireland's mythological past, and simultaneously reimagining it, Young was imbuing her writing with a sense of heritage. It is the future that Young is evoking and imaginatively creating through the focal point of Angus's strange experience, as the Earth is transformed from a space where there 'is neither silence nor song' (Young *Celtic Wonder Tales* 4), where there is neither meaning nor thought, into a space that supports imaginative and creative engagement. The gathered lords are troubled by the mention of the pit, and they urge Brigit to 'let the thought of it slip from yourself as a dream slips from the memory' (4). She is being told to forget the idea of the Earth, before it is even properly formed. Young is establishing a connection between the sacred thoughts of the gods, the Dé Danann lords and an Ireland as yet to be created, associating both the idea or dream of Ireland and the landscape itself with the mythical race.

So, when Brigit tells the gathered lords that the Earth 'wails all night because it has dreamed of beauty' (5), she is trying to convey the idea that there is already a connection between the Earth and Tir na Moe. The Earth has dreamed of the beauty of Tir na Moe, 'of the star that goes before the sunrise' (5) and of music like the music of her song. And here too Young imbues the Earth with a kind of consciousness, a sentience that is waiting to be awakened, and to be imagined. Music is associated with divinity, and with the sacred landscape of the Dé Danann lords' domain; this space embodies the idea of Celtic culture that Young sought to engage with in her work. Brigit's song is connected with the Earth in the chaos before its creation. Angus now 'cannot shake the thought of the Earth from [him]' (5) because of the song, its words and its music. In Brigit's eyes, it falls to the lords to 'look into the darkness and listen to the thunder of the abysmal waves … to make gladness in the abyss' (5). The landscape of the Earth must be interpreted before it can be recreated, and before it can be reimagined by the gods. All places are to a certain extent imaginary, 'because they cannot exist far beyond the socially constructed images which we form of them' (Graham 3).[12] If place is already an imaginative construct, Young seems to suggest that the narratives that unfold within it are symbiotically charged with an imaginative potential.

Brigit then declares that together the lords of the Dé Danann, Midyir, the Dagda, Ogma the Wise, Nuada Wielder of the White Light and Gobniu the Wonder-Smith 'will remake the Earth' (6). Brigit throws down her mantle, and where it touches the Earth it spreads itself 'unrolling like a silver flame' (6) taking possession of the place Midyir has cleared for it and evoking once again the imagery from her song. Only Angus, the youngest of the gods, does not have the patience to wait until the mantle can cover the whole Earth. He leaps down and stands with his two feet on it. Instantly it ceases to be fire and becomes 'a silver mist about him' (8). The others follow him and the 'drifting silver mist close[s] over them and around them' and through it they see 'each other like images in a dream – changed and fantastic' (8). The silver mist is associated with perception, with a new way of seeing, just as Standish O'Grady cloaked his mythological figures in a mist so that they might be seen again.[13] At this moment in Young's retelling, the gods themselves are reimagined through their contact with the Earth. They have become part of the reverie inspired by Brigit's song. The landscape is changed still further by the Dagda, who scatters green fire from the Cauldron of Plenty. It is Angus who lifts 'the greenness of the Earth' and shapes it, playing with it 'as a child plays with sand' (8). This image of Angus playing with the sand, a natural element of the Earth, speaks to Young's particular project of reimagination; the child readers this narrative is intended for must engage with it imaginatively, as Angus does with the Earth, reshaping it, and re-envisioning it with their own experiences. In this moment within the narrative, Young connects the metaphysical myths of the gods with the physical landscape that will become Ireland.

When Brigit lifts her mantle again, the Dé Danann see 'everything clearly' (9); they are no longer in a dream. The reverie that has led them here has left them emplaced in this landscape, an island 'covered with green grass and full of heights … and winding ways' (9). Brigit lays the Stone of Destiny into the green grass so that the lords 'may have empire' (9). The land they have created is thus consecrated. As the Stone sinks into the earth 'a music [rises] about it' (9) and rivers of water begin to flow through the land. Music becomes associated with life and movement in the landscape. The Stone of Destiny, or Lia Fáil in Irish, is central to the creation myth Young is reimagining. It is situated at the Inauguration Mound on the Hill of Tara in County Meath, which served as the coronation stone for the High Kings of Ireland until *c.* 500 CE.[14] The Stone of Destiny plays an integral role in both the mythology and the history of Ireland, and Young's decision to use it here as the means by which the Dé Danaans takes possession or empire of the land that will become Ireland established it as the point from which their authority emanates. Young was writing into a mythological tradition concerning the origins of the Stone, multiple versions of which exist; the *Lebor Gabála Érenn* (*The Book of the Taking of Ireland*) states that it was brought to Ireland by the Tuatha Dé Danann.[15] The *Lebor* is a collection of poems and prose narratives that chronicle the history of Ireland from the creation of the world to the Middle Ages. It tells of Ireland being settled six times by six different groups or tribes – the people of Cessair, the people of Partholón, the people of Nemed, the Fir Bolg, the Tuatha Dé Danann and the Milesians. The fifth group represents Ireland's pagan gods, and the final group the Irish people or the Gaels (Koch 1693–5). According to the *Lebor*, the Dé Danann had travelled to the Northern Isle where they learned skills and magic in its four cities: Falias, Gorias, Murias and Findias. They then travel to Ireland bringing a treasure with them from each city, the Stone of Destiny from Falias, the Sword of Light from Gorias, the Spear of Lugh from Murias and the Cauldron of Plenty from Findias, all of which Young references. Her narrative was clearly inspired by the *Lebor Gabála* but in her retelling the Dé Danann create Ireland, rather than discovering it. The empire Brigit speaks of when she lays the Stone of Destiny down on the grass will be realized in the Dé Danann's engagement with this new island, as they make themselves 'the smiths and artificers of the world' to 'fashion and refashion' (9) the things they find until everything is as beautiful as its image in the Land of the Living Heart; the Dé Danann's project begins to reflect Young's project of narrative reimagination. It is Brigit who ultimately names the island, calling it the White Island, the Island of Destiny, connecting it once again to the Stone of Destiny and, finally, Ireland.

Young has been described as an artist with an abiding interest in fairy tales, lore and romance and a high-profile female figure in the nationalist movement, but also as something of a dilettante whose work was intended primarily to be fashionable rather than culturally significant (Foster *Vivid Faces* 133). But her *Celtic Wonder Tales* represents a new departure in the literature available to children during this period in that they constituted a comprehensive mythology of Ireland mediated through the Revivalist ideas of recovery, retrieval and reimagination, from foundation and creation myths to narratives dealing with issues of national sovereignty and identity. This particular tale established the cultural essentiality of Irish mythology in the context of the Revival period; Young retold a creation myth for Ireland, fundamentally connecting the evolution of the Irish landscape to the enlightenment of the Tuatha Dé Danann figures. So begins Irish civilization, infused from that beginning with the energy of this mythic race. If the Revival project was an attempt by various writers to recover Ireland's lost cultural heritage and to re-engage a new generation with that heritage, then Young was arguably attempting to claim a mythological authenticity for that project with 'The Earth Shapers'. In reimagining the beginning through mythology, and in presenting that reimagination in a collection written specifically for children, Young was endorsing the capacity for Irish mythology to express and articulate contemporary experiences of culture and heritage.

Authenticity and oral memory: The return of the Fianna

Violet Russell presented a similar project of retelling in her *Heroes of the Dawn* (1913), an anthology of tales from the Fenian Cycle of Irish mythology. In reimagining the narratives of Fionn and the Fianna for a new child audience, Russell was aligning herself with the aims of the Revival.[16] Her introduction to her collection addresses two named figures, her sons Brian and Diarmuid, and urges them to remember the stories they were told as children, the 'stories of ancient days' when 'the folk of the other world were part of everyone's life and everyone's belief' (*Heroes of the Dawn*, ix). Here, these stories are intimately associated with childhood. Russell was advocating a revival – a reconnection to and a restoration of a culture where mythology was resonant and embedded in everyday life.

So, even within her introduction, Russell addresses the idea of a retelling, and of stories that have already been told. She exhorts her two addressees to remember and to recall the stories they heard when they were children and could not read for themselves. Russell states that she has 're-written some of those [stories] about Fionn and his warriors' so that other children, wishing as Brian and Diarmuid did 'to know something about the old gods so often mentioned in the legends' (ix), might be facilitated in their desire for knowledge. These stories are not those legends. They are conduits to the heritage the old legends contain. In rewriting these stories, then, Russell clearly meant for them to be read anew by a new generation. For Russell, this particular project of retelling was geared towards renewing and restoring the value of these stories, which was 'something more than mere adventure or enchantment' (ix). She would have her children, and the child audience for whom this collection was produced, see in them 'a record of some qualities' (ix) valued by the heroes of ancient times. This notion of providing information and background to the mythological narratives of Ireland was crucial to Russell's authorial project. The preservation of these narratives was not enough unless the children who would read them were knowledgeable enough to understand and respond to them. The stories were retold specifically for children so that children might be engaged with the narratives of Ireland's ancient past. In this context, reimagination became the means through which contemporary culture, and specifically contemporary children's culture, might be reinvigorated by these myths. Russell envisaged a social and a cultural impact from the tales of Fionn and the Fianna where the 'thought and speech and action' of her readers might be imbued with the 'absolute truthfulness and courtesy' (ix), so valued by these mythic heroes. In this way, the stories became a living inheritance for their readers, where reading them offered the possibility of gaining and assimilating these specifically Irish heroic qualities. Russell attempted to restore the cultural values of the Fianna to the contemporary Ireland of her audience by positing the idea that her narratives offered more to a new readership than generic adventure and enchantment. They provided a connection to the ancient mythological pasts of the country.

'The Slumber of Fionn' is one of the key sequences in Russell's collection, illustrating the core aims of the Revival itself, retrieval and reimagination, and the concept of cycles and patterns in Irish mythology. As was observed earlier, many of the mythological retellings produced in this period are structured by what Wesley Kort calls a 'rhythmic plot' (16) and 'The Slumber of Fionn' is no exception. In a rhythmic plot, events are related or connected by patterns of repetition, and rhythmic time is expressed through recurring cycles, often circadian or seasonal (16). The retold myths of the Revival period conform particularly and fundamentally to this rhythmic structure, not only because time is often expressed in circular patterns within them but also because the patterns in such plots tend to favour the past; repetitions of rhythmic time are evocative of return (17). Returning to and evoking the past was one of the key focuses of the Revival movement. The further from the past the pattern extends, the stronger the tendency 'to return to the beginning for renewal' (17) so that the cycle can begin again. In the context of the Revival, and the literature for children produced in its aftermath, the cycle begins again through reimagination.

'The Slumber of Fionn' opens in Donegal, where a hill lifts itself over a bog, a place filled with 'the dead remains of a forest that was there thousands of years ago' (Russell *Heroes* 248). Ancient landscapes such as the one depicted here are a notable feature in Irish children's literature. Patricia Lynch's *The Turf-Cutter's Donkey* (1934) (discussed in Chapter 3) is set almost entirely on a bog in the west of Ireland, a landscape that supports a number of different temporal paradigms. Siobhan Dowd's *Bog Child* (2008) (discussed in Chapter 4) is also centred on a bog landscape that facilitates an exploration of and an engagement with the realities of the border culture of Northern Ireland and the Republic of Ireland. A sense of the ancient quality of this landscape pervades Russell's narrative. It is a landscape that has changed and changed again, endlessly, through the passing of time. Russell's narrator states that 'it is many, many years now' (248) since anyone walked through the valley at the foot of that hill, implying that this narrative is set in a rather more recent past than the ancient times of Fionn and the Fianna, within living memory. The man walking through the bog is a knowledgeable operator in this rural landscape, yet when he sits down to rest, he sees, near to the summit of the hillside, 'a small dark cleft in the mountain' which he 'never remembered to have seen before' (248). It is not that he has forgotten the existence of the cleft; rather, he had no knowledge or memory of it until this moment. This implies that the cleft has not always been accessible or indeed visible in the landscape, or at least has not been in his lifetime. Here then is evidence of a pattern of concealment and revelation in this ancient and enduring landscape, mediated through time and its rhythmic passing.

As the man looks at the cleft, he remembers 'the legends his mother had told him, when he was a child' (248) about this mountain, just as Russell in her introduction exhorts her addressees to remember the stories they have been told about the ancient pasts of Ireland. The landscape evokes his memories of these stories. According to the legends about the mountain, 'there were mysterious beings dwelling in vast caves inside it' but the entrance to the caves 'could never be found' (249) because it was hidden by enchantments. These stories chart the lie of this landscape; they are the lays that map it, yet they simultaneously retain its secrets. Russell starts to build a sense of anticipation into the narrative; if the entrance to the cave has been revealed, there must be a momentous or ominous reason for that revelation within the landscape. The man continues to stare at the cleft, 'half expecting to see it vanish and become green, like the rest of the hillside' (249) but it remains visible, and present in the landscape of Donegal.

The cleft is in fact 'a very wide and lofty entrance to an immense cave' (249) that seems to penetrate deeply into the interior of the hill, and into the very heart of the mountain itself. The man walks some distance into the cave and comes to a larger one, 'shaped like a vast circular chamber' (249) that is filled with a golden light. This moment in the text becomes an example of Northrop Frye's conception of symbolic meaning (*Anatomy of Criticism* 74). On the one hand, the man is trying to go beyond his knowledge of the mountain and the stories that surround it – outwards from his memories to what those memories might mean. On the other hand, as he moves further into the mountain, and into the circular chamber at its core, he begins to pursue the meaning of this revelation inwards, trying to find its place in the larger pattern of his knowledge (*Anatomy of Criticism* 73). If, as Frye states, the final direction of meaning in all literary verbal structures is inward (73), then the man's movement into the mountain is a movement into an engagement with the legends he has remembered, and the new meanings they might produce. He stands on the threshold, in the liminal space between the Ireland he knows and an ancient mythic past, for 'lying on the sandy ground [is] a multitude of armed and gigantic men' their hands gripping unsheathed swords, and beside each lies a wolfhound 'as though asleep' (249). He is gazing on an image from Ireland's lost mythological heritage, but it is an image made manifest in reality before him.

In the centre of the circular chamber lies 'a more stately warrior than the others' with flowing silver hair and a banner at his head 'with a golden sun rising above the horizon' (250). The man thinks 'they must be warriors who had died long ages ago' (250) but that they remain as vital as men who are alive, as men who only sleep. Discovering a 'horn of great antiquity' in the sand of the cave, the man places it to his lips and breathes into it so that 'a musical humming note' (250) fills the chamber.[17] At the sound of the horn, the sleeping hounds raise their heads, and the warriors sit upright, their weapons and shields clashing. They are woken by the sound of the horn. This wakening out of sleep is another element of the rhythmic pattern which structures Russell's episode; Kort states that the 'alternation of torpor and awakening' (17) is suggestive of aesthetic and spiritual life. The repetition of these acts, separated by lengths or spaces of time, contributes to a rhythmic pattern, of a returning to the end from the beginning, only to begin again. The warriors Russell depicts have moved from wakefulness to slumber numerous times across Ireland's history; they will return to sleep now so that they can be woken again in the future.

The silver-haired warrior is the only one who speaks, and he asks, 'Is the time come yet?' (Russell *Heroes* 250). But the warrior's question remains unanswered, as the man flees from the cave in fear and does not say a word. Because he has recalled the legends about the mountain, he knows that 'these ancient warriors [are] Fionn and his heroes' who have waited in sleep 'for the coming of the day when the war-music of the Dord-Fian, the great trumpet of the Fianna will echo through the cave' (251). Russell's narrator explicitly states here that this moment is not the moment the warriors are waiting for, even though the cave has been discovered, and the horn sounded. When the foretold day comes the warrior 'will ask again the question', and it 'will no longer remain unanswered' (251). Their waiting then, in Russell's retelling, becomes part of the cycle of rhythmic time passing. In this way, the myth of the Fianna's return becomes a perpetual one, because it has yet to be fulfilled, and because the cave remains to be found again in the landscape of Donegal. So long as the story is told and retold, the potential remains for the Fianna's return to be imagined and reimagined.

Russell, perhaps more than any of the other authors discussed here, produced stories specifically for a child audience, stories that were essentially retold myths. By using her introduction to address her sons, and to remind them of the child readers they once were, she created a very specific context for her collection. As Barbara Wall states, 'If a story is written *to* children, then it is *for* children' (Wall 2) (emphasis in original) even if it is also meant to be read by adults. By addressing her stories to children, Russell incorporates the ideals of the Revival into the production of literature for children in Ireland.

Oral culture: Heavy figures to ordinary life

In oral cultures, 'all cultural knowledge … is stored in the mind' (Goody 76) primarily because there is no alternative available, no textual archive to call on. Within such cultures, as previously noted, oral memory works effectively with what Walter Ong calls 'heavy characters' whose deeds are 'striking, singular, and archetypal' (Ong 70). In the heroic traditions of Irish mythology, figures like Cuchulainn, Fionn and Aengus Óg function as such 'heavy' figures who are remembered through renewing and recurring cycles because of the distinctive and momentous nature of their actions. Put simply, the stories told about them make them difficult to forget. The cultural memory that permeates Irish children's literature is thus connected to the oral culture that the writers of the Revival were keen to preserve and to reimagine. But such memory figures need, as Jan Assmann states, to be given substance 'through a particular setting and to be realised in a particular time' (*Cultural Memory* 24). Such figures, and the narratives that surround them, are remembered in place and through time. Far from precluding images, oral cultures actively produce images, through oral narratives. So, oral cultures use heavy heroic figure and the images that are generated by their actions to organize experience, individual and collective, into 'permanently memorable form' (Ong 69). This is the process that Ong has termed 'noetic economy' and as previously noted, it is still discernible where oral settings influence literate cultures, 'as in the telling of fairy stories to children' (69). A noetic process is one specifically related to the intellect and its operation.[18] It also refers to something that exists on a purely intellectual basis, corresponding with Ong's theories about oral literature and its transference between generations through storytelling and memory. If a noetic economy exists on an intellectual basis, its potential to transcend the limits of language and even culture is extremely powerful. The project of the Revival used the same noetic economy, not only to tell stories to children but also to retell myths to a nation. As these oral noetic structures, or frameworks of cultural perception and memory are altered by print culture, Ong argues that narrative relies less on these heavy figures, until it can comfortably articulate 'the ordinary human lifeworld typical of the novel' (Ong 69). In the space of a century, we can trace a journey from Yeats's mythical 'Wandering Aengus' (1899) to Kate Thompson's roguish Aengus Óg (2005), discussed in Chapter 4. These evolutions can be traced through the retellings of these myths that have occurred. The Angus Óg of Ella Young's 'A Good Action' looks forward to the irreverent Aengus Óg that walks through modern-day Kinvara and Tir na nÓg with equal ease in Thompson's text. Young's Dagda sits with his back to an oak tree in the story. His hands are 'as hard as the hands of a mason, but his hair [is] braided like the hair of a king' (*Celtic Wonder Tales* 21). Angus Óg himself is dressed in rags, his hair 'matted like the hair of a beggar' but 'his eyes [are] smiling' (21). Young's narrative articulates the incongruity between the divine nature inherent in the two figures and their ordinary appearances, an incongruity that also pervades Thompson's later work. The Dagda tells his son to 'remember that I am one of the gods: it is not necessary to talk sense to me' (22), a statement that Thompson's Dagda might make less than a hundred years later. So, the reimagination of mythological narratives in children's literature in the aftermath of the Revival and into the twenty-first century brings noetic heroic figures into the ordinary human lifeworld. Oral culture is thus retrieved and renewed through print culture.

The role of the Seanchaí in the Revival

James Stephens (1880–1950) was an Irish novelist and poet who produced numerous retellings of Irish myths throughout his career, including *Deirdre* (1923), *In the Land of Youth* (1924) and his *Irish Fairy Tales* (1920). He became, through these retellings, 'perhaps the nearest thing to a shanachie' [*sic*] the Revival produced (Wilson Foster 214). Stephens began his initial career as a poet, under the influence and tutelage of Æ (George William Russell), husband of author Violet Russell, and a leading figure in the Literary Revival. As a socialist and fluent Irish speaker, Stephens became a unique contributor to the literature of the period. In contrast to the other authors focused on in this chapter, Stephens did not consider himself a writer for children; yet, as this examination of his *Irish Fairy Tales* will demonstrate, his work resonated within and contributed to the body of literature that was being produced for children during this period.

Though Stephens chose episodes and elements from the Fenian Cycle for his fairy-tale collection, and chose to call his narratives fairy tales, he referred to *Irish Fairy Tales* as 'an original book' (*Letters* 253). Standish O'Grady had published *Finn and His Companions* in 1891 and Stephens was at pains to demonstrate that the sequence of his tales, especially those concerning Fionn, was his own and not O'Grady's. The similar yet differing projects of these two authors mark a certain tension between versions of mythological tales and models of heroism; O'Grady and Stephens were striving to achieve different aims with their retellings, with the fairy-tale form becoming the medium through which Stephens retold the lost stories of Finn's mythology. Fairy tales tend to be short narratives, episodic in nature. The fairy tale also tends to be secular. Using a form like this, relatively free of religious influence, suited Stephens's creative and nationalist project. The focus of fairy tales has always been 'on finding magical instruments, extraordinary technologies or powerful people or animals' that will allow the protagonists 'to transform themselves along with their environment' (Zipes *Irresistible Fairy Tale* 2). In Stephens's version of the fairy tale, which is his version of Fionn's childhood, the magical item is Fionn's own identity, his ability to grow into his heritage and assume his rightful place as an Irish hero. Stephens uses the fairy-tale form to articulate his vision of how a nationalist childhood could produce an ideal dutiful citizen.

Edmund Leamy published his collection of *Irish Fairy Tales* in 1890. Unlike Stephens, Leamy wrote with a child readership in mind, using the fairy-tale form to bring old stories to a new audience, and in doing so, repurposing them. Though his stories featured mythological elements, they were not direct retellings of the Ulster or Mythological cycles, and as such were closer to traditional fairy tales. Leamy placed a sustained emphasis on the landscapes of Ireland throughout the collection, and on the exploration of those landscapes by the child figures featured in his narratives. Such explorations, and the knowledge of myth, time and selfhood the children gain, are often mediated through their relationships with older figures, who possessed the capacity and the knowledge to tell stories. Much is made of the connections between Ireland, or Erin, and the Faery realm, especially in stories like 'The Golden Spears' where Nora and Connla spend seven years under the land of Ireland, 'Princess Fionola and the Dwarf' and 'The Enchanted Cave'. In each, though the Faery realm is accessed through a familiar location, an emphasis is placed on the temporal disparities between the two places, and on the effects these might have on the central figures.[19]

The fact that numerous collections of fairy tales existed together in the same cultural space is important because while Stephens may not have intended his tales to be read by children, the form he chose bore, and bears, traditional and meaningful associations with a child readership.[20] By choosing the fairy-tale form, Stephens was choosing, wittingly or otherwise, a specific audience of child readers, and tapping into a culture of narratives associated with childhood. In reading fairy tales, we evoke the 'cultural experience of the past ... even as we reinterpret and reshape that experience' (Tatar xii) and retell it. The fairy-tale form is a vehicle then for those experiences of the past. If fairy tales were and are 'powerfully formative tales of childhood' (xi) then in choosing the fairy-tale form, these authors engaged with a dynamic form of transmission with the child reader at the core of its meaning-making processes. Out of old stories, child readers are prompted to make new lives and meanings (Heilbrun 109). Neither Leamy nor Stephens included prefaces in their collections, thus there was and is no reason for their tales not to be assigned to a child readership, in accordance with the former's intentions but contradicting the latter's. Without the statements of authorial intent so common in this period in texts for children that engaged with mythological narratives, these collections were subsumed into that category, precisely because of the forms their respective authors choose. There is a resonance then between contemporary perceptions of childhood, reimagined mythological narratives and the fairy-tale form.

Leamy's text contains a series of notes wherein he detailed his inspiration for many of the tales in his collection, namely P. W. Joyce's *Old Celtic Romances* (1879). Unlike Leamy, Joyce included a preface in his collection, which in turn allows us an insight into the underpinnings of Joyce's work. Joyce wrote about the provenance of his tales, citing collections in Trinity College and the Royal Irish Academy containing manuscripts of various ages, from the year 1100 to the twentieth century, on multiple subjects. His text is now held in the Pollard Collection in Trinity College, a representative example of the collection's abiding ethos to preserve narratives produced for children that engaged with Irish culture and heritage. As Joyce himself stated, 'There is scarcely one important event in our early history, or one important native personage or native legend, that has not been made the subject of some fanciful story' (vi). This is an early kind of reimagination; events and figures have been translated into myths and legends so that they might be 'caught up and remembered, and handed down from one generation of story-tellers to another' (v). While these particular tales were 'quite new to the general mass of the reading public' (vii), Joyce acknowledged that 'scraps and fragments' (vii) of some had been published in what he called popular publications produced by writers who, not having had access to the originals, or indeed the ability to read them, had taken their inspiration from books printed in the English language. But

Joyce lamented the treatment of these scraps and fragments, with many having been 'presented in a very unfavourable and unjust light' (vii) despite the originals being 'high and dignified in tone and feeling' (vii). His own collection was Joyce's response to these mistreated fragments, a reclamation not only of the past but also of the present. He was retelling these tales in order to restore them to their former ancient glory.

Leamy then used Joyce's project as inspiration for his own work. Between the first publication of his collection in 1890 and its reprinting in 1906, the Celtic Revival occurred. In his introductory note to the reprint T. P. G.[21] stated that Leamy's *Irish Fairy Tales* was reprinted 'for a race of readers who have appeared since it was written and who ought to be in a mood more appreciative of such literature than the mood which prevailed in that day.'[22] There was an awareness, then, even in such close proximity to the major cultural events of the Revival, that the movement had effected a change in the reading life of the nation. It would be poor logic to assume that T. P. G was referring specifically and exclusively to child readers born since the first publication of *Irish Fairy Tales*, and to those exposed to the trend of retold narratives produced during the Revival, but the prevalence of literature of this nature produced for children during this period strongly suggests that these readers were part of that new nation. In fact, from Joyce and Leamy through to figures like Colum and Stephens, it is possible to trace the progression of pre-Revival, Revival and post-Revival ideas of retrieval, retelling and reimagination, and how these might be articulated in the production of texts for children. Writers like Dease, Young, Russell, Colum and Stephens were concerned not just with stories but also with storytelling, and this necessarily reflected one of the concerns at the heart of the Revival movement itself. John Wilson Foster states that like several writers of the time, Leamy 'ostensibly wrote for children' but that his *Irish Fairy Tales* 'is nonetheless a fine literary treatment of the plots and characters suggested by Irish bardic tales and fairy stories' (Wilson Foster 236). Foster implies here that even though Leamy's collection was produced for an intended child audience, it still achieved literary merit, while simultaneously hinting at a certain ambiguity regarding the readership of *Irish Fairy Tales*. This might display a certain critical bias against the merit of literature produced for children during the period and in a contemporary context, but it also highlights the fact that literature concerning reimagined mythological narratives for children available immediately before the Revival was of a high quality, a quality that would only increase during the movement, and that this literature displayed a depth and scope that allowed new meaning to be produced from old tales.

One of the key episodes in James Stephens's collection, 'The Boyhood of Fionn', focuses on Fionn's childhood and the time he spent with the female druids Boymall and Lia Luachra, deep in the forests of Munster.[23] Placed in hiding as a baby following the death of his father at the hands of the sons of Morna, Fionn is reared as a child of the woods, close to nature and to the women who teach him how to fight, and to negotiate the landscape around him. Stephens creates a distinctive and intriguing narrative voice for this episode, using phrases like 'the hound that can wait will catch a hare at last, and even Mananann sleeps' (*Irish Fairy Tales* 37) to produce a colloquialism that encompasses figures from various mythological cycles. In doing so, Stephens creates a narrator who is also a storyteller. Figures like Mananann, depicted in Ella Young's narratives as godlike and divine, are evoked here as part of the fabric of everyday life. Like Colum, Stephens's narrator occupies, in print, the position of the *seanchaí*, the storyteller to whom these stories are not only known but are both living and contemporary. Stephens makes frequent and sustained use of the techniques of the *seanchaí*, focusing primarily on the power and authority of the narrative voice and using striking images of exploration and action to encapsulate Fionn's childhood. A section about the young boy climbing trees is particularly arresting and, given Stephens's insistence that his was not a children's book, particularly though-provoking. Here, the narrative is focalized through Fionn himself with his perspective emphasized. The child figure becomes the focal point of the narrative:

> It was pleasant to stand on a branch that swayed and sprang, and it was good to stare at an impenetrable roof of leaves and then climb into it. How wonderful was the loneliness up there! When he looked down there was an undulating floor of leaves, green and green and greener to a very blackness of greeniness; and when he looked up there were leaves again, green and less green and not green at all, up to a very snow and blindness of greeniness; and above and below and around there was sway and motion, the whisper of leaf on leaf, and the eternal silence to which one listened and at which one tried to look. (42)

Fionn is intimately connected to the landscape of his boyhood, and the landscape seems to respond to his child body, unfolding itself in 'little snaky paths narrow enough to be filled by his own feet' (37). Stephens's narration of the childhood of a boy who will grow into a warrior becomes an intimate, yet universal childhood; Fionn, as young children do, thinks of 'his own door as the beginning and end of the world' (38). There is, then, an empowering and dynamic emphasis on childhood experience in Stephens's narrative. Fionn explores the landscape around him as any child would, through physical activity, inhabiting his childhood to the limits of his physical capabilities, and following his father's ghost on adventures, 'going step for step with the long-striding hero' (45). He receives his heritage and his history through his guardians' stories, just as Stephens's readers receive images of their heritage through narrative.

As time passes, Fionn grows 'long and straight and tough like a sapling; limber as a willow' (48), connected always to the landscape that shapes his childhood, and that facilitates the secrecy of his existence. But the sons of Morna know that the son of Uail is living, and they know that their own sons will have no peace while Fionn lives 'for they believed … that the son of Uail would be Uail with additions' (50). This notion of living heritage, of both the past and the future being embodied in a single figure, is crucial to Stephens's retelling of Fionn's myths; it is only through remembrance that these tales can be passed on and reimagined. This is encapsulated in the relationship that develops between Fionn and his father's former lieutenant, Fiacuil, a man 'at war with a world that had dared to kill his

Chief' (54), as the older man takes it upon himself to continue the young boy's education, and to teach him the things his father would have known. This new life for Fionn unfolds in a vast cold marsh, a place with 'damp, winding, spidery places to hoard treasure in, or to hide oneself in' (55). Fionn explores this new space and finds knowledge in it through Fiacuil's teaching; 'what tales that man could tell a boy, and what questions a boy could ask' (55). Contemplation and exploration of place creates an awareness 'not only of time but of self and of the evolution of that self, evoking the simultaneous presence of past and present versions of one's identity' (Ryden 259). By drawing attention to the connections between the past and the present in the landscape, Stephens can focus on the relationship between experience and youth, hinting that Fionn's questions are the key to unlocking Fiacuil's store of knowledge. There is 'a whole new life to be learned' (Stephens *Irish Fairy Tales* 56) on the marsh, with its dark and mysterious secrets. Fiacuil is essentially teaching Fionn the folklore of the landscape and connecting this secret knowledge to his knowledge of himself and his physical and mental abilities. Again, an emphasis is placed on the connection between childhood and landscape; Fionn's boyhood is defined and shaped by the places in which he lives, just as Cuchulainn's childhood, and his warriorhood, is tied inextricably, and even tragically, to Ulster.

As he travels alone, Fionn encounters a group of boys at Moy Lifé playing and mock fighting. The boys tolerate his observations, eventually inviting him to join them; such an invitation being 'among boys, a declaration of war' (60). Stephens draws parallels here between the boys' communal play and the band of warriors that Fionn will command as a grown man. It is here that he receives the name that will follow him into that warrior existence; 'he is fair and wellshaped, and thereafter he [is] called Fionn' (60). This encounter with the boys at Moy Lifé is therefore crucial to the shaping of the figure of Fionn the warrior, the heroic figure around which the events of the Fenian cycle turn. But it is significant that Stephens's narrator states that 'his name came from boys, and will, perhaps, be preserved by them' (60). Child figures and child readers will remember Fionn's name, textually and metatextually. Despite maintaining that his collection did not constitute literature for children, Stephens was acknowledging that children are the natural audience for tales such as these, and that new generations of child readers would generate a demand for these narratives to be retold.

The section of the narrative concerning the Salmon of Knowledge arguably marks the end of Fionn's boyhood and his movement into adulthood, though Stephens includes his battle with Aillen during the feast of Samhain at Tara in the episode. Fionn's time with Finegas the poet and prophet is 'a round of timeless time' (68) where the days and nights are uneventful yet filled with interest for the young warrior. Under the poet's guidance, he not only adds to his physical strength but also to his store of knowledge. His education is a holistic one 'and each night sealed the twain' (68), the physical and the mental being intimately connected. It is only when he receives the Salmon of Knowledge, destined for him since the moment of his birth, according to Finegas's prophecy, that 'his education [is] finished and the time … come to test it' (73). It is this test, the battle against a powerful Sídhe figure at Tara, that marks Fionn's entry into adulthood. The focus on Fionn's childhood experiences throughout the episode resonates within Stephens's particular project of retelling. In attempting to create a new version of Fionn's mythology, separate from previous retellings, he not only distinguished his work from Standish O'Grady's, he also made, inadvertently or otherwise, the warrior's story accessible to child readers, primarily by focalizing his narrative so intimately through the child hero's experiences.

Symbolism, narrative and citizenship

Padraic Colum (1881–1972), a poet and novelist, a children's author and collector of folklore, was, like James Stephens, one of the leading figures of the Irish Literary Revival. Colum saw himself as 'a descendant of the ancient Celtic people' (*Selected Poems* xxi) and his sense of identity as a poet was influenced by his awareness of that Celtic past and by his 'sense of his own work as an extension of that heritage' (Sweeney and Morgan 121). Colum's *The King of Ireland's Son* was first published in 1916. It features a series of interconnected stories concerning the adventures of the King of Ireland's Son, and his encounters with figures from ancient Celtic mythology and folklore. One of the episodes concerns the Sword of Light, one of the four treasures brought to Ireland by the Tuatha Dé Danann, and mentioned in the eleventh-century text, the *Book of Invasions*, or *Lebor Gabála Érenn*. Within Colum's narrative, the Sword is used by the King's Son to slay the King of the Land of Mists, with their encounter setting up 'a mythic conflict between light and obscurity' (Ni Chuilleanáin 116) where the sword as a symbol of enlightenment connects the Tuatha Dé Danann with the idea of a civilizing presence in ancient Ireland. The Sword becomes the point around which Colum's narrative turns, bringing the King's Son into contact with the Gobaun Saor, the artificer god, 'and with the ancient creatures of Ireland' (119). The Sword of Light itself 'provides one of the typical images of the Revival' (119). Conradh na Gaeilge's weekly newspaper *An Claideamh Soluis* took its name from the treasure, and it featured as a decoration for Æ's 1903 text *The Nuts of Knowledge*. Its presence here in a text written specifically for children has a certain 'political resonance' (116) in that child readers were exposed to the meaning-making potential of an ancient symbol, and to its capacity to be reimagined into contemporary culture. They were exposed to 'a recreated culture where the act of narration is of central importance' (119).

The works of many writers of the period stood on two unspoken principles – that the old stories of Irish mythology and folklore 'should not merely be translated … but reshaped' and that 'the new-told tales … should promote the cause and redound to the glory of modern Ireland' (Wilson Foster 23).[24] The working of these principles resulted essentially in a transformation of the ancient narrative forms of Ireland's mythological heritage. John Wilson Foster cites Ella Young as being one of the forerunners of Colum and of James Stephens; her narratives 'domesticate the wilder forms of the Gaelic imagination' (236), specifically for a child audience. These same principles operated in the fiction produced for children in the period as well, not least in Colum's work. Foster also notes that the Revival and the Irish folk imagination were concerned with metamorphosis, a theme that resonates throughout *The King of Ireland's Son* (278). Indeed, Ireland's mythological heritage was itself being put through a process of metamorphosis; it was being reimagined and retold. But Foster cautions against seeing Colum's personal and artistic search for new selves in these stories, saying that 'his choice of children as readers for many of his books reined his powers of self-expression' (278).

Yet, *The King of Ireland's Son* and the register Colum adopted within it for that intended readership proved the appropriate vehicle for what he wished to express – the capacity for folk tales and myths to educate new generations (Colum *Storytelling* 14–15). His choice of a child readership for some of his narratives did not limit his powers of self-expression. Rather, it focused them. If Colum was assuming 'the role of the traditional storyteller' (Foster *Story of Ireland* 278) in print, then his intent was to tell stories appropriate to a child audience. Colum's particular project was one of storytelling, using the conventions of oral culture to retell old narratives to a new audience. Wilson states that in writing for children Colum was following a tendency of cultural revival movements 'to turn saga and folk material into children's literature after it has been adapted for adults' (278). But this process was arguably occurring concurrently throughout the Celtic Revival, with authors adapting material specifically for a child readership. The saga and folk material revived during the movement did not have to be turned into children's literature; it merely had to be retold for children.

In *The King of Ireland's Son*, the main tale's embedded narratives draw attention to the form and function as well as the content of the narrative, inviting readers to consider the art of storytelling in the same moment that they choose to endorse it. These embedded narratives speak to the presence of a storytelling tradition in Ireland (Ni Chuilleanáin 117). These stories are woven together to create a whole, with his narrator assuming the tone of a *seanchaí* or traditional Irish storyteller. The episode is about remembering, recalling and retelling, and a dominant thread in Colum's text is the idea that the memories of Ireland might be encapsulated in these stories; metatextual references to the ancient tales of Fionn and others in the Mythological Cycle speak to the notion of oral memory, and to the processes through which cultural heritage is not only retained but also renewed and reimagined. The stories told within the larger narrative of the King's Son and his adventures are also fundamentally connected to the landscape of Ireland, and to the ways in which he journeys through it. Stories are associated both with movement and with knowledge, with insight and with purpose; later in the text the King's Son must find the Unique Tale in order to learn the way to the Land of Mists and save his love Fedelma, and the quest for the Unique Tale leads him to explore the landscape of Ireland, and the stories that map it.

The most significant of the King's Son's adventures, those concerning his discovery of the Sword of Light, engage with a theme or concept of empire similar to that in Young's 'The Earth Shapers' in her *Celtic Wonder Tales*. Colum's protagonist must possess the Sword in order to rule over his father's kingdom. The Sword of Light is therefore not only a symbol of power within the text. It is a symbol of kingship and dominion, and is fundamentally associated with heritage, inheritance and stewardship. The fact that only the Gobaun Saor, the great smith and artificer god, knows where to find the Sword of Light is significant, in that his presence in the narrative recalls the ancient creation myths of Ireland, when the Tuatha Dé Danann shaped the land. The narrative itself is a repository of Irish mythology, with the Sword of Light functioning as a catalyst for Colum's particular project of retelling. As a dominant symbol within the Revival movement, it connects the pasts of Ireland, and the myths that relate those pasts to contemporary culture.

Having gained their freedom from the Enchanter of the Black Back-Lands and having been betrothed by the Little Sage of the Mountain, Fedelma and the King's Son begin a journey. As they are riding across the Meadow of Brightness, Fedelma tells her companion that when they are crossing the field of white flowers ahead of them, he must tell her a story. The King's Son dutifully tells her a story called 'The Ass and the Seal'. In turn, he asks Fedelma to tell him a story when they are crossing a little field of blue flowers. She tells the story of 'The Sending of the Crystal Egg'. This pattern continues along their journey with the King's Son telling a story as they cross fields of white flowers and Fedelema responding with a story for the fields of blue flowers. The stories finish when they reach a nameless waste ground that fills Fedelma with dread, and it is here that she is taken by the King of the Land of Mists. Stories are associated with movement here, and with connection to and safety within the landscape; stories will save the King's Son and Fedelma, just as they keep them on the right track. The King of the Land of Mists sends Colum's protagonist into an enchanted sleep and takes Fedelema away. But crucially, Fedelma manages to communicate to her beloved before she is taken, writing 'The King of the Land of Mists' in Ogham on the ground. It is the landscape that holds the record of her message. When he wakes, the King's Son does not know what direction to take to reach the Land of Mists, and so returns home. Again, the act of storytelling plays an important role in the young man's quest. In listening to the stories of Art, the King's Steward, the King's Son slowly comes to a realization that he must find the Sword of Light in order to do battle with the King of the Land of Mists. The Little Sage of the Mountain tells the King of Ireland's Son where he must go to seek the Gobaun Saor.

Colum's narrator tells the reader that 'it is forbidden to tell where the King of Ireland's Son found the Builder and Shaper for the Gods' (81). He finds the master smith 'in a certain place' (81) working on a shape of iron. Woven throughout the narrative is the notion of secrecy, and the idea that certain knowledge must be earned and kept, not rearticulated and shared.[25] The reader is never made privy to the location of the Gobaon Saor, just as we never learn the King's Son's personal true name.[26] Before telling him where to find the Sword of Light, the Gobaun Saor demands that the King's Son show him first 'your will, your mind, and your purpose' (81). It is only when the young prince is deemed worthy of the knowledge that the sword's location is revealed to him; the Palace of the Ancient Ones can only be found under a remote lake. The wide space of the underground palace recalls the conceit of the *Sídhe* or fairy fort, always located beneath the ground, implying that the King's Son has somehow accessed a space that is simultaneously of Ireland,

and of Faery.[27] However, due to an encounter with the Swallow People, a strange race who inhabit the Island and who do not recognize the authority of the King of Ireland, the Sword of Light is blackened, seemingly beyond repair. Returning to the Gobaun Saor, the King's Son is told that 'the Sword must be bright that will kill the King of the Land of Mists and cut the tress that will awaken the Enchanter's Daughter' (88). Taking the Sword as the symbol of the Revival, this is especially significant. The Sword can only function and create meaning as a symbol if it is recognizable and whole, and if it is carried forward by a knowledgeable bearer.

Part of the King's Son's punishment for allowing the Sword of Light to be blackened by the Swallow People is that he must carry the Sword in its darkened state and endure the shame associated with his actions; 'You have let the Sword be blackened. Carry the blackened Sword with you now' (88). The Smith no longer refers to the sword as the Sword of Light, and from now on it functions as an image of compromised power within the narrative. It speaks, in its blackened state, to the fragility of heritage and identity. It is significant, then, that the Smith will only agree to restore the Sword if the King's Son will find the Unique Tale for him, and not only the Tale but also 'what went before its beginning and what comes after its ending' (88). The Smith does not just want the Tale in isolation. He is also looking for context. This is a consistent message within Colum's narrative; the stories within stories speak to the notion that meaning comes from the relationship between these tales, and from the context in which they were produced, and out of which they have been reimagined.

The King's Son must thus search for a story in order to learn the way to the Land of Mists; he can only find his way to this particular place in the Irish landscape if he first finds a tale that has ostensibly been lost and removed from the contemporary oral culture. The Land of Mists is not necessarily obscured from his vision by mist or fog but rather by the King's Son's own lack of knowledge. Here again mist is associated with perception and with ways of seeing, and specifically with ways of seeing into the landscape.[28] The quest he is forced to embark on marks a connection between narrative and landscape in literature produced for children in Ireland that continued in the aftermath of the Revival period, becoming a pattern in the following decades. Within this pattern, narrative becomes synonymous with knowledge; child figures in the texts considered in here such as Eileen and Seamus from *The Turf-Cutter's Donkey* (1934), Pidge and Brigit from *The Hounds of the Morrigan* (1985) and JJ from *The New Policeman* (2005) can only move successfully through the landscapes of Ireland when they understand those landscapes, and this understanding is usually gained through stories (see Chapters 3 and 4).

Following his meeting with the Gobaun Saor, the King's Son goes far and has 'many journeys' but he finds no one who has any knowledge of the Unique Tale 'or who [knows] any way of coming to the Land of Mists' (89). These journeys are stories in themselves and though they are clearly critical to the quest the young prince undertakes, they are not articulated within the main narrative. It is not that the Unique Tale itself has never been told, rather that the King's Son must find the teller who has knowledge of it. His quest expresses the relationship not only between the teller and the listener but also between the story and the oral culture that supports and sustains it. The Unique Tale is not part of any of the Mythological cycles. It is a contemporary tale produced in the context of Colum's narrative. This is perhaps why the Five Ancient Ones of Ireland, Blackfoot the Elk of Ben Gulban, the Crow of Achill, the Salmon of Fassaroe, the Old Woman of Beare and Laheen the Eagle have no knowledge of it. The Elk tells the King's Son that there may be no other creature in the world more ancient than him. His ancientness is connected to his knowledge of Ireland, and to his knowledge of the stories that have originated there; 'if it was a Tale of Finn or Caelta or Goll, of Oscar or Oisin or Conan' (92) he could tell it, but he knows nothing of the Unique Tale. There is a cautionary note here; Colum was aware of the need for the ancient narratives of Ireland to be retold and reimagined into contemporary culture, but he was also aware of the need for the art of storytelling to be sustained and invigorated. The Unique Tale is a new story, but it must also be remembered. The Tale is not old enough to have passed into myth, or into the collective cultural memory of the nation. It resides in the present, in the living oral culture of the King's Son's Ireland.

It is from a youth like himself that the King's Son gains knowledge of the Tale. Gilly of the Goatskin has received the Tale from an older figure, the Spae Woman, and in eventually passing the tale on to the King's Son, Gilly also engages with the role of the storyteller, and its significance within Irish oral culture. The Tale is not written down anywhere, and there are no records of it. The only way the King's Son can obtain it is to find someone who can tell it and listen to it. Gilly of the Goatskin has received the Unique Tale from the Spae Woman who has dreamed that Gilly must tell it to the Old Woman of Beare and whoever might be in her house. The two converge on the Old Woman's house, the teller and the listener, and in that meeting their stories also merge. This exchange between Gilly of the Goatskin, as he is known before the Spae Woman renames him Flann, and the King of Ireland's Son highlights the importance of narrative in Colum's text:

> 'What have you come here for?'
> 'To get knowledge of the Unique Tale.' (96)
> 'And it was to tell the same Unique Tale that I came here myself. Why do you want to know the Unique Tale?'
> 'That would make a long story. Why do you want to tell it?'
> 'That would make a longer story.' (97)

With a simple coincidence, Colum comments on the nature of oral culture and memory, demonstrating how the telling of a tale must also simultaneously be the hearing of a tale. The two engage in a reciprocal dialogue based on stories, with Gilly telling the Unique Tale and the King's Son listening. The Old Woman of Beare doubts that they will ever find out what happened before or after the Tale. So, the two set out together, but not along the same path. Their stories separate once more, while still remaining part of the overall quest narrative for the Unique Tale. Though Colum's text is called *The King of Ireland's Son*, Gilly of the Goatskin's narrative is at least as important and compelling within the overall context of the comment Colum is making about storytelling and how it functions. This is primarily because Gilly's quest is to find out who he is, and to gain a real name for himself, beyond the name that was given to him when he was found as a child, abandoned and with no record of his origins. It can only be significant that the central characters of Colum's text are youths who must find and tell stories in order to progress, in order to move through the landscapes of Ireland, and in order to reimagine their own identities.

Colum wrote on what he thought of as the 'story-teller's art' (*Storytelling* 21) and what that art might permit or allow the storyteller to do. Through the use of patterns and conventions, the storyteller reaches an accord with his audience; when the hero is set wandering through a wilderness, the audience and the storyteller rest, 'not because there [is] nothing happening, but because what [is] happening [is] regular and anticipated' (21). Though the story might be new, the conventions through which it is told are familiar. Colum's work, then, illustrates the dynamism that existed in the period between retrieval and renewal; between the need to retell the old tales and the desire to reimagine new life into them. The opening to the section of Colum's narrative that follows the parting of the ways between the King's Son and Flann illustrates this. We are told that 'the story is now about Flann' (*King of Ireland's Son* 211); we are alerted to this change in focus, and to the presence of a new protagonist. The young man walks through the evening, that time when,

> as the bard said,
> The blackbird shakes his metal notes
> Against the edge of day,
> And I am left upon the road,
> With one star on my way. (211)

Colum uses storytelling conventions, not only to describe the action of the moment and to mark breaks in that action but also to remind his listener that they are hearing a story. A later exchange between Flann and Morag, the beautiful young woman he falls in love with, articulates the nature of Colum's particular storytelling project. Morag, like many of the characters in the text, is operating under an enchantment, lifted only when Flann gives her the Rowan Berry that proves to be the key to her liberation. ' "You gave me the Rowan Berry," she says to Flann, "... but what good will my beauty be to me if you forget me?" ' (253). Through Morag, Colum is connecting the survival of these stories to the ways in which they are remembered, reimagined and retold. Flann asks, 'But, Morag ... how could I forget you?' (253) having no way of knowing that this is exactly what will happen later in the narrative as he in turn falls into an enchantment. Flann and Morag's story is not only about memory. It is also about the process of remembering, and the ways in which narrative helps us not to forget. Remembering and forgetting are two sides of a process of identity formation that is often employed in children's literature to articulate the child figure's relationship to the wider community and to society. Published ten years earlier than *The King of Ireland's Son*, Rudyard Kipling's *Puck of Pook's Hill* (1906) is a collection of short stories narrated to two children by various figures out of British history, and by Puck himself, one of the oldest things in Britain. From the narrative of Weland the Smith to the signing of the Magna Carta, *Puck of Pook's Hill* presents the Matter of Britain to Dan and Una in a series of historical and fantastic experiences that are not so much a reclamation of something lost but an affirmation of what is known. Crucially, however, when Puck reaches the end of his stories, the children forget their meeting with him but retain a sense of their experiences that subconsciously informs their cultural and national identity. This trope of children's literature expressing the importance of myth, history and culture in identity formation resonates in both Irish and British literature. In Colum's text, remembering and forgetting are fundamental to being, to the ways in which we evolve into the people we are supposed to be, and to the duties we are assigned as citizens, child or otherwise. In Kipling's narrative, though Dan and Una are essentially made to forget, the sense of experience that remains with them serves only to reinforce the essential nature of the stories Puck has been telling to them; these stories are now known to the children, intrinsically connected to the childhood they will continue to live through. In this way, myth, history and culture become the matter of identity, as well as the Matter of Britain.

The 'particular moment' of the Irish Revival was 'favourable to the incorporation of folk tale, mythological and fantastic elements into adult fiction' (Ni Chuilleanáin 119) but with this text, Colum incorporated those same elements into narratives composed specifically for a child audience. His narrative demonstrates that the same incorporation was occurring in fiction produced for children. His conclusion to the King's Son's adventures 'invokes the idea of youthful adventure as a preparation for responsible maturity' (119) and knowledgeable citizenship in a society defined by its sense and awareness of its pasts and futures. He encouraged his child readers to draw that sense into the present, and into their interaction and engagement with cultural and social memory. While he distinguished between history and folk tale, he suggested that 'history may incorporate myth in its seanchas' (119) and into its body of narratives, and that folk tales and mythological cycles may be carriers of history as well as of culture. Running throughout the adventures of the King's Son is the conceit that claiming, or reclaiming, a personal or a national identity or selfhood is a continuous process, one that involves going back to come forward, over and over again, gaining, applying and regaining knowledge as that process unfolds. It is a process that is perhaps never truly completed.

Having lost his love Fedelma to the King of the Land of Mists, the King's Son finds himself in the Wood of Shadows, where strange voices call on him to say his name aloud. He does, but his name is never articulated in the body of the text. Announcing his name to the spirits that govern the Wood is part of series of exchanges that run throughout Colum's text. Knowledge is given in exchange for knowledge or power received. By giving his name to the Woods, the King's Son consolidates the identity he has been building for himself as the text progresses; the manner in which he names himself, responding to the trees, becomes a rite of passage. Moving through the Woods with his identity intact, he re-emerges into the landscape of Ireland ready to pursue his quest to rescue Fedelma. Like the King's Son, the child reader may return to these episodes again 'with greater understanding', having experienced, through narrative, 'a recreated culture where the act of narration is of central importance' (119) and where the act of reimagination is crucial to that narration. There is a sense of urgency to the text's conclusion as well, as Colum's narrator admits that 'there are many things to tell you still … but little time have I to tell you them', because the barnacle geese are flying over the house, and when they are gone, the narrator 'shall have no more to say' (Colum *King of Ireland* 255). The reader might wonder why time runs so short for the narrator, and why, when the geese are gone, his story will be over. The dilemma of Colum's narrator resonates at the core of the Revival movement. It is the awareness that the moment of the movement might pass, the attention of the audience might stray and that these myths might be lost once more. The King of Ireland lived long, we are told, 'but he died while his sons were in their strong manhood' (275), and after his passing, the Island of Destiny, created under the fall of Brigit's mantle, was governed by them. The deeds of one 'are in the histories the shanachies [*sic*] have written in the language of the learned', and the deeds of the other son 'are in the stories the people tell to you and to me' (275). In the closing lines of the narrative, Colum expresses the connections between history, myth and folklore, and in the modes of transmission through which cultural heritage is retrieved, preserved and reimagined.

A tradition of retelling

The Revival was a cultural nationalist project, in terms of the vision and politics of its founders, and in terms of its immediate and subsequent effects (Hutchinson 4). Authors within the movement were concerned with, among other things, nation-building, and with the construction or reconstruction of a national identity. Their ideas and conceptions of mythology, narrative and cultural heritage directly influenced the production of literature for children in Ireland following the Revival period. The works discussed here, through the medium of reimagination and multiple acts of retelling, achieved a 'higher synthesis of tradition and modernity' (Ni Chuilleanáin 119) bringing the past into the present via a series of myths. If the Revival was nothing less than an attempt, through the dynamics of cultural nationalism, to establish 'Ireland's identity in space and time' (119) then these retold myths were the textual and literary manifestations of that attempt, mythological narratives that articulate Ireland's identity through landscape and time. While part of the larger Revival project – and specifically a part of the literary movement that sought to create a distinctive Anglo-Irish nation through 'a literature in English infused with the legends and idioms' (119) of the Gaelic-speaking Western population of the island – these works were written specifically for children. By reimagining the myths of Ireland, the authors discussed here were retrieving and re-presenting the heritage of Ireland to the youth of Ireland and to future generations. The pattern of mythological reimagination that continues to pervade Irish children's literature is thus part of a tradition of retelling that demonstrably came to the fore in the Revival. Successive generations of readers were and 'are always first of all in the situation of heirs' (Ricoeur *Memory, History, Forgetting* 221). In this way, interpretations and reimaginations 'of texts inherited from the past' can be understood as 'exemplary' (221) experiences in relation to our perception of that past. Traditions, then, and, in the context of the texts discussed here, narrative traditions are bearers of meaning in that they 'set every received heritage within the order of the symbolic' (227). Through inherited texts and narratives, 'the succession of generations' (229) can access these heritages.

Chapter 3

REMEMBERING: PATRICIA LYNCH, UNA KELLY, EILÍS DILLON, J. S. ANDREWS

The primacy of memory: Knowing and remembering

On 30 June 1922, during the Irish War of Independence, an explosion occurred at the Four Courts in Dublin, in the basement of the Public Record Office. As a result, the records of the Irish administration from the thirteenth to the nineteenth centuries were almost completely destroyed. Certain records did escape the fire; the 1901 and 1911 census records were housed in the Registrar General's Office, and the records of the Quit Rent Office, the Valuation Office, the Office of Public Works and the Commissioners of National Education had all been transferred to the newly built Public Record Office.[1] But the census records, an essential part of the stories of the nation, were lost. On 8 July that year the *Irish Times* newspaper described the fire as 'a national loss'.[2] The fact that the Record Office was rebuilt at all, by a fledgling state with almost no financial stability, speaks to the effect of that loss. Restoration was deemed not only necessary but also essential. Authors operating in this period were, in many ways, engaging with and writing into an absence, both a physical absence in terms of the documents that were lost and a metatextual one in terms of the stories that were lost. On 3 July, the Provisional Government issued a notice of preservation in the *Irish Times* asking the general public to take care to preserve any pieces of paper or document fragments that they might find throughout the city and to return them to an office that was specially opened for that purpose.[3] The destruction of the records created a gap in the national memory. In looking beyond that gap, and going further back into the mythology, folklore and history of Ireland, the texts considered in this chapter, texts suffused with moments of remembering and forgetting, brought the mythic past closer by demonstrating that it could still be retrieved and remembered.

What, then, does it mean to remember? And what does it mean that the child figures in Patricia Lynch's *The Turf-Cutter's Donkey* (1934), Una Kelly's *Cuchulain and the Leprechaun* (1945), Eilis Dillon's *The Lost Island* (1952) and J. S. Andrews' *The Bell of Nendrum* (1969) are called on so explicitly to remember their cultural heritage? Memory has been described as 'an act of vision of the past' but, conversely, one that is 'situated in the present of the memory' (Bal 147). We remember in the present. Memory is connected to narrative where 'loose elements come to cohere into a story so that they can be remembered and eventually told' (147). Telling a memory, then, either to oneself or to others, is like telling a story. Remembering is like telling a story. But remembering is not the same as perceiving because 'the memory evoked ... can never reassume its original shape' (Iser 278). Just as stories change with every telling, so too do memories with every remembering. The child figures in these texts are called on to remember the things they should know so that they can understand the mythic and historic events unfolding around them. In this way, they establish 'interrelations between past, present and future' (278), pushing at those unfolding events and the mythic figures they meet to reveal their connections to the contemporary domestic Irelands of their childhoods. Here, in the aftermath of the Celtic Revival, the myths that were once retold as narratives in their own right begin to contribute to new narratives centred on child protagonists. The focus now is on these child figures and how they engage with mythic experiences, and on their ability to remember their cultural heritage. This ability to remember the things they have been taught and the myths they have heard allows the child figures in these texts to perceive the connectedness of time and place, and to engage with their own sense of belonging within both. Memory 'provides us with the capacity for experiencing where we are in the temporal flow' (Scanlan 8). Memory takes us into the world (Casey *Remembering* xix) so that remembering allows us to explore it.

This primacy of memory also resonates within the sense of place and community that makes Irish writing in English distinctive. It is often achieved through invocations of oral tradition (Bourke 1). Irish writing in English produced for children is no different. In fact, there is an even greater propensity to turn towards storytelling traditions in writing for children, who have long been considered the rightful inheritors of traditional tales (Ni Chuilleanáin 113). In the mid-twentieth century, from the 1930s to the beginning of the 1970s, the emphasis on myth, folklore and, indeed, history, in literature produced for children in Ireland, begins to change. The focus moves from how myths might function as retold narratives for children to how child figures in reimagined narratives might interact with those myths. Previously, both during and after the Celtic Revival, myths had been related in isolated form, as stories, or as elements in a specific collection.[4] The tendency had been to retrieve myths in their entirety. Now, only a decade or so later, in the 1930s, the myths become elements in narratives of childhood; myths are reimagined into everyday life as lived in Ireland during this period, precisely so that child figures might interact with them through direct experience. In these texts, myth, folklore and history become conduits between those child figures and their cultural heritage. The stories do not change; rather, their emplacement in the landscapes of literary Ireland is reconfigured and they become embedded into the lives of fictional child figures in this period. Thus, they become mediators between these child figures and their perception of Irish identity, and the children's experiences in the Irish landscape.

Community, tradition and national trauma

This means that a transition occurs in literature produced for children in this period, from retold myths to embedded reimagined myths. This period ranges from the 1930s to the 1960s, during which time Ireland experienced a second World War, created a new constitution and declared an official Republic all while recovering from the effects of a Civil War. This was fought over the Anglo-Irish Treaty of 1921 between two opposing groups of Republicans and Nationalists. The former saw the treaty as a betrayal of the idea of the Irish Republic while the latter saw the same document as a stepping stone in the process towards achieving a legitimate Republic. Many of those who fought in the conflict had been members of the Irish Republican Army, fighting for the united cause of Irish freedom during the War of Independence. The Free State forces or the Nationalist side of the conflict eventually won the Civil War, but the repercussions of the schism would leave Irish society divided and traumatized for generations to come. The Civil War is significant by its absence in the literature produced for children examined in this chapter. Its consequences were local, personal and inescapable. Instead of attempting to articulate these consequences, in the period discussed here, emphasis is placed on community and tradition in Irish life, both urban and rural, and on the ways in which knowledge about the ancient past is transmitted from one generation to another. From the outbreak of the Second World War in 1939 to the joining of the European Economic Community in 1973, Ireland would claim and maintain its neutrality in a global conflict, under intense pressure from its former colonizer Great Britain, declare an Irish Republic in 1948 and oversee the fiftieth anniversary of the 1916 Rising in 1966. The fledging state was attempting to establish itself as an independent entity in a world that still perceived its connection to Great Britain to be fundamental to its existence. But in those efforts to legitimize its own independence, Ireland began to look inwards and to define itself in opposition to the UK, to the detriment of its own national identity. In 1953 alone, the Censorship of Publications Board banned almost one hundred publications for indecency and obscenity. In this isolationist atmosphere, the literature produced for children in Ireland during the period tended to focus almost exclusively on the articulation and preservation of Irish life, through the depiction of Irish childhoods.

The transition that occurs in this period also encompasses the deepening reciprocity between the mythic and the folkloric in narratives of Irish childhoods. Patricia Lynch's *The Turf-Cutter's Donkey* articulates the integration of myth into contemporary childhood experiences. Una Kelly's *Cuchulain and the Leprechaun* interrogates the gap between childhood experience and cultural heritage. In Eilís Dillon's *The Lost Island*, myth provides a contextual backdrop to a narrative focused on exploring identity in contemporary Ireland. And in *The Bell of Nendrum* by J. S. Andrews, a child figure is brought to an awareness of the connection between the past and the present in an historical rather than a mythological context. These texts present themselves for analysis here because they have several characteristics in common. They address relationships between child and older figures, in either a mythic context, as in the relationships between Seamus, Eileen and the Leprechaun who befriends them, or Cu and the Leprechaun who challenges him – or in a domestic context, such as the relationships between Michael and Billy or Nial and the Abbot of Aendrum. The transfer of knowledge concerning cultural and mythological heritage that occurs in these relationships is facilitated through the intratextual act of storytelling and the communication of stories.

Folklore and intergenerational memory

This concept of knowledge transfer resonates within one of the earliest critical definitions of folklore. In 1846, William Thomas wrote that folklore is 'the oral, inherited, popular wisdom and customs of generations of people in a particular place or cultural community' (886–7). The key component of that definition, especially in the context of the narratives considered here, is the idea of oral inheritance, that stories can be passed down from generation to generation within a specific community. Stories can be inherited, and once heard by a new generation, they can be assimilated and reinvented. Most folk tales come into existence as oral compositions, entering the oral stream, and continue that existence by being retold and heard by storytellers and engaged audiences (Sullivan 13), because while 'folklore is expressed by individuals', it also comprises 'a substantive body of collective and shared belief and custom' (Markey and O'Connor 5). As such, folklore narratives offer the individual a transhistorical place within a larger traditional community. They are simultaneously 'the whole body of traditional culture' (Steele Boggs 3) and individual storytelling performances within that culture; they are both the memory of generations and the memory of an individual listener or teller. As Alver writes, in the performance of a song or a tale, 'those who are listening are all related to each other as a component of a single continuum' (49). This is also the process of folklore, 'an artistic and creative communicative process' that needs 'contact between at least two people' (49) to occur. The communications among Eileen, Seamus and the Leprechaun, as well as Cu and the Leprechaun he encounters, are instances of this kind of productive contact. Moments of communication and interaction produce new experiences for these child figures that are simultaneously mythic and folkloric. It is the former because these experiences engage with ancient mythic narratives, and the latter because those experiences are situated in the local and the domestic. The engagement with folklore and folk tradition, and especially, in Cu's case, the idea of patterns and repetition, of treading the same path as those who have gone before, allows these authors to examine issues of place, identity and the cultural value of the past as communicated through retold stories.

Folklore and folk tradition offer these authors and others writing in this period 'fiction-making possibilities' (Butler 183). An example of this, and of the attempt in this period to articulate the centrality of folk tales in everyday life, is Mairin Cregan's *Old John* (1936). The text stages a dialogue between the intimate domestic space of rural village life in Ireland and the presence of folklore in the landscape of that rural life. Cregan engages with the orality and specific locality of folklore narratives, creating a domestic story that is embedded in a local landscape, depicting ordinary people encountering the extraordinary elements of the Faery world. This is why Cregan chooses the intimate register that structures her narrative; she is not engaging with myth, nor are her characters having mythic experiences. Her central character, Old John, embodies that engagement with folk culture; he is a Leprechaun figure himself, operating within his village as a cobbler with almost preternatural talents, situated firmly within that domestic space, yet communicating with and understanding the Faery world. He is linked by his artificer status to the Goban Saor, discussed in relation to *The King of Ireland's Son* (1916), Chapter 2, as both are creative and productive craftsmen figures. The Gabon Saor is central to the King of Ireland's Son's destiny and to the way in which he will progress through his quest in Colum's text. In Cregan's narrative, Old John is central to the community in which he resides; the items he produces are essential to the life of the people he lives among. Cregan uses the resonances between Old John and his mythological antecedent the Goban Saor to interrogate the ways in which folklore articulates the relationship between the domestic sphere and the Faery world in Irish culture. Sally Mitchell writes that fiction 'that becomes very popular and then fades into obscurity draws on the values, interests and concerns of a specific group of readers at a particular time' (5). Susan Cahill maintains that this statement is applicable to writers like Cregan (70) and that the representations of childhood and of Ireland that her fiction presents resonate within a very particular moment of Irish culture. Cahill goes so far as to argue that Cregan's children's literature promotes the agricultural policies of the time, which insisted on 'a rural, self-sufficient nation' populated with 'clear-eyed, happy-hearted children'[5] to whom, as Cahill suggests, Cregan's books must appeal 'in order to preserve such a vision' (71).

The following is an extract from a 1939 review of Irish children's books in which Cregan articulates her thoughts on the function and purpose of literature for children, focusing particularly on the adaptation and retelling of national and local folk tales. In this way she speaks back to the aims of the Revival writers in their attempts to link national myths and folk tales to a revitalization of Irish identity:[6]

> But this precious wheat from our own mountains and plains must be carefully selected, the flour kneaded with the lightest of touches and the loaf served with lots of jam and honey and marmalade so that little eyes may be attracted. (Cregan, 'A Child's Book' 146)

She writes here of the potential for retold narratives to nourish a sense of cultural wholeness in a new generation and posits the idea that Ireland itself functions as a point of origin for these stories. But her use of metaphor here speaks to a holistic vision of Ireland as a nurturing environment for children, in both physical and intellectual terms. The loaf that must be served with jam and honey and marmalade is a product of the landscape in which the children of the nation will grow; they will be nourished and sustained by the agricultural produce of the land, the mountains and the plains. The bread itself must be skilfully made and this is a reference not only to the craft of storytelling but also to the management of Ireland's natural resources for its future citizens. Cregan speaks here to the vision of a nation that can sustain its children with physical and intellectual nourishment, with its produce and its heritage. This should come as no surprise for as Cahill points out, the Free State, within which and of which Cregan writes, 'values children primarily in terms of their relationship to the nation as future citizens' (71).[7] Contemporary reviews of *Old John* cite the central character's 'quiet humour, innate culture and gentle kindliness' as being 'characteristic especially of those parts of Ireland where the old traditions are loved' (*Cork Examiner* July 1938). The implication here is that the text not only highlights these characteristics but also goes some way towards preserving them for a new generation. The story is, in essence, a domestic fairy tale, with almost no engagement with the narratives of Irish mythology. Rather, the emphasis and focus in the stories of Old John and his little family is placed on community, on local landscape and on the power of folkloric culture to retain and communicate knowledge.

Against such a background, and a focus on myth, folklore, landscape and time, it seems appropriate to explore the ways in which mythology and folklore manifest themselves in children's literature produced in the middle of the twentieth century in Ireland, and how the connections made between both mythology and folklore promote a series of ongoing engagements with cultural heritage. These engagements are fundamentally situated within the realm and experience of childhood, focalized through child figures who reside at the heart of the texts discussed here. This allows the authors of these texts to explore not only the realities of childhood in Ireland during this period but also the capacity of childhoods lived out in the rural communities of the island to engage with and draw fulfilment from the past. Through culture, we create 'a temporal framework' (A. Assmann 97) that transcends not only the life of the individual but also the borders between past, present and future. The texts examined here mark points within that framework that allow access into cultural memory. And if, as Assmann writes, the 'dynamics of individual memory consist in a perpetual interaction between remembering and forgetting' (97) and this interaction is the means through which the individual creates a sense of self, then cultural memory might operate in the same way. In the space between forgetting and remembering, the child figures in these texts engage in mythic experiences, learning as they go. If the canon, or in this case, the body of literature produced for children in Ireland, stands for 'the active working memory of a society' (106) or specific community, and is by its nature limited and exclusive, then the archive stands for the 'reference memory' (106) or heritage of a society. The instances of child figures forgetting and not knowing that dominate literature produced for children in Ireland in the middle and late twentieth century become, in this context, a metaphor for the relationship between culture and heritage.

In the texts explored in this chapter (with the exception of Mairin Cregan's *Old John* which does not feature a central child figure but places Old John himself at the centre of the lives of the village children), the child figures at the centre of each narrative are aware of the cultural and mythological heritage that is often fundamental to their particular community's identity and way of life. Awareness does not, however, correspond to engagement. Though Eileen and Seamus, Cu and Michael know the ancient stories and have listened to the older figures in their lives, myth and folklore are not part of their lived experiences. This changes in the course of their respective narratives – for Eileen, Seamus and Cu when they meet a Leprechaun figure who interprets their culture and heritage for them, and for Michael when he embarks on a journey that is essentially inspired by myth. In Nial's case, his awareness of his own place in history is dramatically awakened when he finds himself lost in the past, interacting with individuals whose lives he has learned about in school. Knowledge is transferred between older and younger figures through stories, and in these texts, through shared mythic and historic experiences. In later texts produced for children (to be examined in Chapter 4) these knowledge relationships between generations become empowering for child figures who must negotiate mythic experiences in order to assimilate cultural and mythological knowledge. In these later texts the latent knowledge held by the child figures is gone. It cannot be remembered because it has not been forgotten; it has never been learned. It must thus be gained through mythic experiences in order to enrich contemporary life or to restore a balance that has been lost. Within the anamnestic time associated with cultural memory, events transcend entrenched habits (Harth 85). If, through anamnesis, learning is actually the rediscovery of knowledge from the past, then myths and folk tales function as cultural memories, and, in this context at least, as memory aids to new generations of child readers. Nial's movement back in time looks forward to this part of the pattern in Irish children's books, as the time-slip narrative becomes the medium through which authors explore the relationship between Ireland's ancient pasts and its contemporary identities.

Time-slip narratives, and specifically those where children from contemporary modern times find themselves transported into a recognizably historic or mythic period, had been a staple of British children's literature for some decades at this point, often used as a metaphor or device through which to engage with the trauma and destruction of First and Second World Wars. Displacement out of one time into another was used by British authors to explore the chaos engendered by conflict on personal and national levels. Lucy M. Boston's *Green Knowe* series (1954–76) chronicles the history of the house at Green Knowe, and of succeeding generations of the Oldknow family as the house itself becomes an interface for different time experiences. The series centres largely on Tolly, the latest in a line of descendants to return, in one way or another, to the house, and his relationship with his great-grandmother, Mrs Oldknow. Boston's particular project with the *Green Knowe* series was to centre a wide-ranging account of British history in one particular locality, focalized through the experiences and childhoods of individual protagonists. Tolly's feelings of intense displacement at the beginning of the series speak to a national crisis of belonging in British life and society following the Second World War. Boston uses the time-slip device to not only connect Tolly to his ancestors, who wander through the house and through time freely, but also to explore the ideas of lineage and heritage and how knowing one's origins in the past creates a sense of stability in the present. The time-slip narrative, in British children's literature at least, functions largely as a way in which to reconnect a new generation of children to a sense of belonging. These literary developments occur at somewhat of a remove in Irish children's literature, and in response to very specific national and local concerns, and to the sense of an ancient past that remains contested and traumatic. In the aftermath of the War of Independence and the Civil War, Ireland's isolationist policies engendered a kind of inward reflection in cultural and social terms. The Censorship of Publications Act of 1929 which established the Censorship Board would lead to an atmosphere of cultural and intellectual stagnation in the coming decades. Literature produced for children in Ireland, while remaining conservative, became a site wherein questions concerning national and personal identity could be explored through engagement with the past, however contested that past might be.

This is evident in the change in register that occurs within the literature produced for children in Ireland in this period as it attempts to engage with mythic, folkloric and domestic experiences. It is important to note that this does not mean a movement away from myth and into folklore but rather a movement towards a synergy between the two forms and the experiences they can articulate. Exploring this synergy allows the reader to question what constitutes cultural heritage for children in this period, and to interrogate the extent to which an emphasis is placed on consolidating or reclaiming Irish identity through images of Ireland presented to child readers in texts such as these. In this period, mythic narratives merge with folkloric narratives, the latter told in a more domestic register that speaks to the everyday experiences of childhood. The mythic resonances within the articulations of national identity change. If knowledge of the past is related to a concept of identity, it 'acquires the properties and functions of memory' (Assmann Cultural Heritage 113). This is because any conception of selfhood, of a self existing continuously from a personal past into the present moment, is a key component in any individual identity. This connection between knowledge of the past, memory and selfhood allows the authors here, and those who will be examined in the next chapter, to explore the ways in which the childhoods of the child figures at the centre of their narratives are influenced and shaped by the presence or lack of cultural heritage in their lives. Just as memory reaches back into the past, it shapes perception in the present and carries cultural beliefs forwards into the future (Alderman and Inwood 187).

Patricia Lynch: Landscape and the act of remembering

The Turf-Cutter's Donkey (1934) by Patricia Lynch is the story of Seamus, his sister Eileen and their adventures with their donkey, Long-ears. Living on the edge of a bog in the west of Ireland, in sight of a mysterious flat-topped mountain, the children encounter figures out of folklore and myth as Lynch's narrative moves out of a domestic scenario towards a mythic revelation. Eileen and Seamus's father the turf-cutter seems to know the mythic significance of the bog and the flat-topped mountain.[8] He tells his children that he 'wouldn't be surprised to learn that there was a great highway across these parts in ancient times' going 'from that side of the mountain ... across the centre of the bog' (Lynch 153). The possible existence of this ancient road is posited as an explanation for some of the incidents that occur within the bog, particularly the arrival of a stranger who bears gifts for the children. The turf-cutter knows that there are 'strange tales told of that self-same mountain, even in these times' (153), a statement that connects the pasts of the bog to the children's present through oral tradition and folklore, and the passing on of stories. Yet, the children do not hear these stories from their father within Lynch's narrative. They experience the pasts of the bog themselves and its mythic significance as it begins to resonate within their everyday lives.

The central adventure in the narrative begins to unfold as summer arrives in the bog, and the men commence the cutting of the turf. This is a summer ritual, an intrinsic part of the rural community's life in the Irish countryside. The lengthening days take on a seemingly endless quality, as the bog becomes charged with the physical energy of the communal turf-cutting enterprise and reaches the zenith of its productive capacity. The routine of everyday life is lived out in profane, continuous time while sacred, mythical time (Eliade *Sacred and Profane* xi, 68) is accessed through the repetition of myths, that is, through the reimagination of traditional narratives. Neither time is more meaningful than the other and meaning is produced and experienced differently in each. Profane time is associated with physical experiences, and with the physical connections we make to each other, and to the landscape in which we are emplaced. Eileen and Seamus's childhoods are structured by this profane time as it passes in the bog. Sacred, mythical time is associated with existential experiences, with the connections we make to the metanarratives that govern the ways in which we understand the world. The journey the children make to an ancient forest and their encounter with figures out of Irish mythology occur in sacred, or mythical, time. Thus, the physical and existential are also 'modalities of experience' (Eliade 14) in the landscapes of Ireland as depicted in Lynch's text. They are 'modes of being in the world' (14). These modalities fuse into an engagement with a mythological heritage when the children embark on an imaginative exploration into the bog, even as the physical and metaphorical dimensions of the landscape itself become what Spirn calls 'one country' (119). For Lynch's child figures, then, emplacement in the landscape is connected to the ways in which they experience time, both profane and sacred. Eileen and Seamus's interaction with the landscape is influenced by the temporality of their actions and experiences in it. This is expressed here in a conscious or unconscious acknowledgement of the universal foundation myth cycle through the ritual of the turf harvest.[9]

Each turf harvest not only recalls the harvests that have occurred before but also lays another template for the harvests that will occur in the future. Even as layers of turf are removed from the bog, layers of meaning are added to the community's store of cultural heritage and memory; the turf that is harvested becomes a product of the bog to be used in domestic spaces, just as the stories the bog retains are remembered to be retold. Because acts of reimagination and re-enactment repeat a mythical or exemplary model, their meanings are connected to that model, and within it, through repetition and reimagination, those meanings are perpetuated. Within the patterns of reimagination that influence the production of cultural heritage in Irish children's literature, Eliade's 'gestures of consecration' (3) become gestures of reimagination. In the same way that the re-enactment of mythical examples results in an initiation into sacred time, reimagination in the landscapes of Ireland effects the transformation of 'concrete time into mythical time' (13). Through 'the paradox of rite' and through the commemoration and reimagination of traditional narratives, 'profane time and duration are suspended' (21). In this way, sacred time is experienced in the bog. By undertaking the process of turf-cutting again, just as it has been undertaken before, the men and the children of the rural community are engaging in the larger ritual or ceremony of harvesting that has been preserved, transmitted, and perpetuated universally by and for countless generations. Through repetition, sacred or mythic time is invoked. The ritual taps into the temporal potentiality inherent in the bog. As the bog is opened, its layers are exposed by the men and their *sleán*, or traditional spades. While the physical layers of the bog are cut out in the form of turf briquettes, the temporal layers of the bog are also exposed, as the stories associated with the ritual of the harvest are remembered and retold. As more and more of these physical and temporal layers are exposed, the potential for the children to engage imaginatively with the landscape is heightened. Lynch uses the ritual of the harvest, a practice intrinsically connected to Irish life, and yet also one connected to life in communities all over the world, to align Irish myth with universal myth, and with the archetypes that are common to these systems of meaning. Lynch is therefore creating an opportunity for a sophisticated reader to recognize this alignment with universal myth and to engage with the ways in which Irish myth structures experiences in the Irish landscape. By placing the harvest at the centre of an episode that engages with mythic experiences, Lynch highlights the alignment between the quotidian and the eternal in the landscape, and between the domestic and the mythic in the text itself. By following that alignment, the reader can recognize the reciprocity between what is specific to Irish myth and the universal archetypes of world mythology. The harvest is at once a physical marker of summer and a metaphor for transformation, as well as a marker of how Irish mythology also operates within the structure of world mythology as both of these systems use symbols of sowing, reaping and rebirth. What is crucial to Lynch's particular project here is what happens after the harvest, and the manner in which the bog and its store of heritage is transformed.

One morning, after the turf harvest, Seamus and Eileen see a stranger coming across the bog in a straight line, though none of the paths the children know 'go straight from one side of the bog to the other' (Lynch *Turf-Cutter's Donkey* 146). These paths across the bog are 'story lines' (Whiston Spirn 17), connecting the landscape with the community that travels in it, narrative maps which chart the movement of figures in that landscape. But the stranger does not follow any of these paths; he does not travel along the known lines which map the bog. His is a different kind of movement, set apart from the usual activity that occurs there. Most people 'tend to follow a path if there is one' (Whiston Spirn 120) but people can also create paths through the landscape with their movement and actions in that landscape. Just as narratives of place transmit communal knowledge and cultural heritage, so paths through landscapes may convey messages that are both physical and metaphorical in nature (120). A straight path can be perceived as the shortest way between two points, but it can also be interpreted as a sign of a ritualized journey that connects those two points, a desire path or line that visually articulates movement through the landscape, and between zones in that landscape. These zones can be urban or rural, profane or sacred, planned or wild. These ritualized journeys can be undertaken many times, and they symbolize returning as well as going and stepping away from these paths can create new rituals.[10] Given the stranger's identity (he will later be revealed to be a member of the Fianna, a band of warriors from Ireland's mythological past) and the journey he leads the children on, through and into the bog, his path links the physical and metaphorical dimensions of the landscape Lynch depicts.

The stranger reaches the little cabin and is welcomed into the children's home. When he speaks to Seamus, the stranger tells the boy that he is 'tired and hungry' (Lynch *Turf-Cutter's Donkey* 146) and that he needs rest. He speaks into a cultural paradigm, using a traditional dialogue often staged between a traveller asking for hospitality and the homeowner expected to offer it, while receiving a story or a song in return.[11] The children receive neither. Instead, the stranger leaves two figures carved out of bog oak, a dog and an elephant, which seem to move when the children look at them. As part of a cultural transaction that occurs between the stranger and the children, in their wooden states the dog and the elephant become symbols of reimagination within the text; they have been created by the stranger in a transformative act using material from the bog that is crafted and reimagined into new forms. The dog and the elephant come to life in a different paradigm. In the domestic space of the cabin they are wooden objects that move when the children look at them. In the bog itself, as the children begin their journey towards the ancient forest, the figures truly come to life, transcending their wooden forms as they are reimagined into the landscape of the bog on a moonlit night. It is the return to the bog that allows the figures to be transformed, to transition again into their mythic selves, just as the children's movement from the domestic space of their home into the wider landscape of the bog facilitates their mythic experiences.

Once the bog oak dog comes to life, he is no longer referred to as a dog but as a wolfhound. Seamus's growing awareness of the mythological significance of the hound begins to mirror this development in narrative register; he knows that the 'collar of gold' (Lynch *Turf-Cutter's Donkey* 154) around the wolfhound's neck is an icon of a mythological past and heritage, so much so that he is trying to decipher the letters on the collar as the hound leaps from his windowsill to the ground below. What was once a piece of the bog has been transformed from a carved dog into a living animal. It is an act of recognition that further transforms the dog into Bran the wolfhound of Fionn MacCumhail; without Seamus's eventual recognition Bran's presence in the bog as himself would be meaningless. Seamus's recognition also pre-empts or even coincides with the reader's cognition of Bran's significance, or at the very least fills a gap in the reader's mythological knowledge. A double paradigm shift occurs within the evolving register of the narrative; the bog as meaningful landscape provides the backdrop to Bran's mythological reimagination into that landscape. This is what Lynch's text is attempting to do, and specifically during this episode. By articulating the stages of the bog oak dog's transformation, Lynch is giving her readers a template for the way in which mythological narratives can be retrieved and reimagined within the Irish landscape. When the children move into the bog, eventually finding their way to the forest, they are essentially moving back into the past of the bog, while simultaneously engaging with it in their own present. Hannah Arendt writes about the act of going back into the past, 'reaching all the way back into the origin' and how this 'does not pull back but presses forward' and that it is actually the future 'which drives us back into the past' (10–11). It is therefore crucial to consider the catalyst for the children journeying into the bog; Seamus remembers who Bran is. By recalling mythological knowledge, the children engage with the past, in turn allowing their future to be enriched with their heritage.

A thick white mist rises from the bog, as though the landscape itself is responding to the mythological resonances of the wolfhound's presence. The mist functions within the text as a visual symbol of mythical time, made accessible because the children are moving deeper into the pasts contained in the landscape. Again, the mist is associated with ways of seeing and with perception as the children are encouraged by its presence to look deeper into the landscape than they have previously. Seamus can see it 'spreading along the road and creeping in at the gate' (Lynch *Turf-Cutter's Donkey* 154), neutralizing the border between the bogland and the domestic space of the cabin. Lynch's narrator tells us that 'the moonlight [makes] a silver path across the mist' (154) and Seamus's reaction to what he sees, and the manner in which it is articulated illustrates the transition that is occurring in the narrative register. Seamus '[knows] that he must travel that path' (154) as though a *geis* or obligation has been laid on him, and he holds this awareness 'though he [isn't] at all sure he [is] awake yet' (154). The *geis* was a law or institution in Irish legend, the violation or observance of which 'being frequently the turning-point in a tragic narrative' (Rolleston *Myths and Legends of the Celtic Race* 164).[12] In Lynch's story, Seamus feels compelled to follow the moonlit path, and the moment the children move into the bog is a turning point in the narrative. Rolleston also notes that the *geis* was regarded as a kind of sacred obligation, and also as a way to maintain harmonious relations with the other world, the world of Faery. The children's journey to the ancient forest becomes the manifestation of a rapprochement between their world and the world of Faery, between the ancient past and the present.

Here, an allusion to an archetypal heroic situation where the hero recognizes the call of a quest is juxtaposed against a child figure's incredulity and sense of wonder. In this sequence, the narrative is moving from a domestic setting into an expansive mythic landscape. This shift in register makes sense when we consider register to be language 'defined according to situation of use' (Stephens and McCallum 10). Lynch begins to move from a demotic register to an epic one, as the narrative in turn begins to demand a register that can articulate elements of a mythological cycle. The epic register offers Lynch the language she needs to present and articulate the images of cultural heritage this sequence generates. If all languages of heteroglossia are 'forms for conceptualizing [sic] the world in words' (Bakhtin *Dialogic Imagination* 291) then Lynch's language changes precisely because she begins to conceptualize a series of mythic experiences in the world of her narrative.

Lynch's depiction of the bogland as an affective landscape is crucial to the mythic experience the children go through as it engages with the 'intrinsic connectedness of temporal and spatial relationships' (Bakhtin 84) which form the basis of Mikhail Bakhtin's definition of the chronotope. In the context of this specific narrative sequence, then, the bog 'becomes charged and responsive to the movements of time, plot and history' and time itself becomes 'visible' (84). The mist which surrounds the children as they leave the bog, and which plays such an affective role in their journey, and in their return to the cabin, itself constitutes this visible time, and evokes mythical time as it aids them in moving from the bog of their present to the forest of the past. That forest stands at an 'intersection of axes' (84) between landscape and time, and this is where the mythological archetypal image of the Fianna is reimagined into a mythic reality experience by the children. If time is 'the fourth dimension of space' (84) then a forest that is simultaneously of the past and of the present can be termed a 'time-place' (Lynch *What Time is This Place?* 241): a space where the children experience mythic time. In this place 'time ... thickens' (Bakhtin 84) and in this thickened, meaningful time, the children's actions become more weighted, and more significant.

The wolfhound stands with 'the mist flowing over him' (Lynch *Turf-Cutter's Donkey* 154), and in the moonlight the letters on his collar are illuminated to read 'BRAN'. If, as previously stated, the mist from the bog is mythical time made visual then Bran himself becomes a timeless figure, one who has been retrieved out of Ireland's pasts in order to revitalize his own myth and to communicate it to a new generation of readers. It is significant then that Seamus recognizes him now as 'the magic hound of Finn [sic], chief of the Fianna' (154) recalling what he has learned at school about such mythological figures. The fact that Seamus has been educated about the mythic cycle that contains the stories of the Fianna is crucial to the production of cultural heritage the narrative promotes: Seamus is inclined to follow the hound precisely because he eventually recognizes the significance of his presence in the bog, and of his emergence out of the mythic past of Ireland. But the fact that the mythical wolfhound wears a collar that bears his name at all implies that Seamus may not have been able to recognize him without it, and the little boy only realizes who the hound is when he sees his name. Bran himself becomes a living image of the cultural heritage that the tales of his exploits transmit; his appearance, both in the little cabin and in the bog, marks and instigates the beginning of a new cycle of reimagination as the children enter into the mythic past of Ireland. But he is an image that must be glossed before it can be accessed, understood, and reimagined.

Eileen and Seamus's journey from the little cottage to the ancient forest may take place over the course of a single night, but it fuses narrative growth with physical progress (Bakhtin *Dialogic Imagination* 3–40): as they move further into the landscape, they gain more insight into both it and their places in it as children. The children move through space and time and into a mythological experience, and their appearance is altered to reflect the fact that they are moving out of their ordinary lives and towards a momentous event in the landscape: Eileen is now wearing a beautiful lace gown, and Seamus is barefoot, dressed in a short leather tunic. Though the style of these clothes may mean nothing to them initially, when they reach the ancient forest and meet the Fianna, they see the similarity between the warriors' appearance and their own. As the children themselves are reimagined into the mythological context of a traditional narrative, they are literally clothed with meaning. The lace dress and the leather tunic resonate within the narrative register that Lynch now begins to use.

The mist slowly reveals a grey forest, and 'giant trees with great overhanging branches heavy with leaves' (Lynch *Turf-Cutter's Donkey* 160), and from her vantage point on the bog oak elephant's back, Eileen can see everything. The Leprechaun, their companion from previous adventures in the countryside surrounding the flat-topped mountain, tells her that ''twas all a great forest in ancient times': what is the bog itself but 'dead trees and plants' (160). It seems the children have entered a primordial, mythic time. They are moving through an ancient version of the bog, through its past incarnations. The trees from the ancient forest will become, through the passage of millennia, the bog where the children make their home. The cyclical image of the forest and the bog resonates within the pattern of reimagination that dominates the sequence. Surprised at her apparent lack of knowledge of the organic nature of the bog, the Leprechaun asks Eileen if they teach her 'anything at all in that stone school house' (160). Lynch's reference to the stone structure of the school is pointed and specific, especially when contrasted against the organic construction of the cabin the children live in. Their home blends into the landscape of the bog: the cabin is 'so low and the thatch so covered with grass and daisies, that a stranger would never [find] it only that the walls [are] whitewashed' (7). The children are deeply connected to the bog through the cabin. It emplaces their childhood in the rural landscape which surrounds them. What they know of the bog and the stories that are told about it they have learned from their parents, in a cabin that seems to have risen up out of the ground. The knowledge that has been passed down to them within these walls is never questioned, but the information they have learned in the stone schoolhouse is. Seamus's awareness of Bran and the tales that surround him was gained in school, yet it is his father who recognizes the significance of the bog oak dog carving the stranger brings into their house. Seamus only realizes who Bran is when his name is revealed on his collar. It is only when Bran is emplaced in the bog itself, with the mist flowing over him that Seamus can connect the stories he has learned in school with the reality of the mythological figure in front of him. It is the journey through the bog that provides this context, connecting knowledge with experience. A disconnection is articulated here between the transmission of cultural heritage through education in Ireland and an engagement with the landscape that so fundamentally influences and shapes that heritage.

Eileen displays a similar lack of recognition when she fails to connect the forest they are moving through with the bogland of her everyday life. Given that she does not initially perceive the connection between the ancient forest and the present reality of the bog, her reply to the Leprechaun's question is significant within the larger context of the accessibility and transferability of cultural heritage; she tells her friend that he would be surprised 'at all we learn' (160) in the schoolhouse. But she 'can't always be remembering' (160); she cannot operate in a constant state of recall. For Eileen, remembering is a conscious act that takes her outside of profane time, and outside of the realities of life in the rural landscape, and Lynch's use of the Hiberno-English construction points up the observation. Remembering invokes sacred time, but life itself cannot be lived in sacred time. It is not enough that knowledge is learned, and inheritance is gained. That mythological heritage must be reimagined in the midst of that landscape, and lived, as well as remembered. Lynch's imposition of colloquial syntax on Eileen here succinctly expresses the idea that recollection is not and cannot be a continuous process.[13] If memory brings us back to what has already occurred, and imagination brings us forward into what is to come, then a sense of self-continuity in time is mediated through the interaction of cultural memory and imagination (Casey *Back into Place* xix). It is not enough for cultural heritage to be transmitted through archetypal images; it must be remembered, it must be actively recollected, and reimagined.

The Leprechaun himself is not only a central character in this particular adventure. He stands for the relationship that exists between the mythic and the folkloric, providing a bridge for the children between the domestic spaces of their everyday lives and the dynamic mythic reality of the primordial landscape they find themselves moving through. In the Leprechaun's attempt to explain the nature of the forest, he articulates the dialectic that exists between the physical and metaphysical dimensions of this 'other land' (Lynch *Turf-Cutter's Donkey* 160). In a way 'it's real and yet again, in another way it isn't real' (160). The forest exists simultaneously in its own present moment and in a mythic epoch from Ireland's past. And yet, it also exists in the children's present because the bog is both the future and the present manifestation of the forest. In this place, the past, the present and the future converge as 'everything that has been is and maybe everything that will be' (160). It is a liminal space where the past, the present and the future thicken together into mythic, sacred time. The forest becomes a microcosm of the larger pattern which frames it. It is a place where narrative and cultural archetypes are renarrated, and where key moments from Ireland's mythic history are reimagined into Eileen and Seamus's childhood experiences.

The children follow Bran and the Man from the Bog through a gap in the rocks where the path seems to end, and which stands up 'tall and straight like a gateway' (164). According to Lynch's narrator, this corresponds to a movement 'into the past' (146). Bakhtin writes of an 'absolute past ... separated by an unbridgeable gap from the real time of the present day' (218). But here, the forest itself provides the bridge that connects the past to the present. The children do not go back in time, into that absolute past, to meet the Fianna any more than the Fianna come forward in time, into the real time of the present day to meet the children. Rather, they meet in mythical time, in a forest that is simultaneously new and ancient, in a space where a new story involving the Fianna can take place, a story that uses elements reimagined out of traditional narrative. The forest exists simultaneously in the ancient past, in the children's present as the bog, and in the future as an imagined and reimagined landscape. This encounter with figures from Ireland's ancient past unfolds on the flat-topped mountain.[14] When he realizes where they are, Seamus cries, 'I know this place!' (Lynch *Turf-Cutter's Donkey* 164). He is deeply affected by this recognition, even though it soon becomes clear that the summit he remembers and the summit he has now reached are not entirely the same place. He includes his sister in this recognition, and in his remembrance of a past experience, stating that Eileen 'knows it too' (164). Seamus is attempting to emplace himself more securely in a landscape that is at once strange and familiar. Even Seamus's sense of his own continuity in time is affected by the journey across the bog and into the forest. When he recognizes the clearing, he says, 'I came here a long time ago' (164). His and Eileen's adventure on the flat-topped mountain occurred in their recent past and yet it seems that Seamus feels far removed from the experience. This confusion speaks to a breaking down of the temporal borders between past, present and future, and supports the idea that the children have not gone back into the past but are experiencing an expansion of time where the past, the present and the future are experienced simultaneously in sacred or mythic time, in this primordial place.

In another attempt to centre himself, Seamus looks for the Magic Pool, a feature he remembers from his own previous experience on the mountain. But the pool is nowhere to be seen; it has been replaced by a fire of crackling logs. As Seamus watches, the flames rise and sink, rise and sink, in a series of movements that are constantly changing yet which form a certain pattern. The shadows the fire casts '[run] across the grass and [hide] among the bushes, then [spring] up and [return] to the fire' (165). This cyclical movement of going and returning resonates within the pattern of the children's and the Fianna's movements in the landscape and the fire thus becomes a significant image in the pattern of reimagination which dominates the sequence, in the same way that the Magic Pool endlessly reflected the sky above it and the butterflies fluttering over it. Just as lakes and pools 'mirror the landscape', ensuring that 'the world's experience is not lost, but [is] forever reflecting on its future' (Dearing 78–9), the image of the fire performs a similar memorializing function; it is a familiar image that both the children and the Fianna can respond to. Lynch establishes an affinity between the warriors and the fire, and its symbolic potential when Seamus sees a shadow '[rise] and [stay] still' (Lynch *Turf-Cutter's Donkey* 165) – the shadow of a man holding a horn. The shadows on the rocks are redolent of the shadows on the walls of Plato's cave in that they are images which must be interpreted within a context in order for them to generate meaning.[15] Without context, the shadows on the cave wall are just shadows. But in the clearing, the children see both the mythic and the physical reality of the scene before them, the shadow on the rock and the man who casts the shadow. It is as though the shadows of the Fianna have stepped out of the fire, out of the imaginative potentiality it symbolizes. The Fianna themselves are guided by a pattern of familiar actions, and by the remembered narratives of their previous adventures: the horn is sounded in the forest to call the Fianna to the clearing and they respond to it because it is familiar, and because they understand its significance.

The scene described and presented in the clearing becomes an interactive image of cultural heritage as the children engage with archetypal figures from Ireland's mythic past. To Seamus, the warriors are 'just like the picture of the Fianna in the big book at home' (165). He has encountered visual and textual representations of these mythological figures before and now he will encounter the men themselves, as 'representation and reality fuse' (Whiston Spirn 27). The Man from the Bog is standing by himself: though he is one of the Fianna, it is as if his experiences in the present-day landscape of the bog have set him apart from them. He steps forward to explain the children's presence in the clearing. He has brought them 'by the Secret Way across the Road of Dreams' (Lynch *Turf-Cutter's Donkey* 169) because he sometimes fears that the Fianna will be forgotten. Lynch uses his explanation to establish a continuous reality for the Fianna: they have not simply arrived out of the past, rather they have arrived out of an existence that is ongoing and meaningful. The mythic pasts of Ireland remain to be reimagined precisely because they are connected through the landscapes of Ireland to the present. The Man from the Bog brought the children to this meeting with the Fianna to 'teach them that the past makes the present and the present the future' (169). Though he presents the passage of time since the band of warriors disappeared from this landscape as a linear progression, it is in essence a cycle of repeating images, retold and reimagined in different temporal contexts, echoing Yeats's idea of a national reverie comprising many individual streams of thought.[16] It is a journey, a movement through a series of cycles and spirals. They have reached a land that they never actually left. Conal himself articulates this paradox; 'this is a hungry, empty land we have reached' (170). There is a distance alluded to in his words, the Fianna have travelled, and they are far from home, in both a temporal and geographical sense. What is the emptiness he speaks of? Is it related to the fear the Stranger from the Bog harbours about Ireland's mythic past being forgotten? Is the land empty of stories to guide children back into the past, and into engagement with their cultural heritage? The presence of the children in the forest provides Lynch with a catalyst for the transmission of cultural heritage that must occur if the mythological narratives of the Fianna are to be remembered and reimagined. Finn asks Conal if he has 'forgotten the deeds of other days' (170) as though the Fianna have somehow fallen out of their place in the mythic history of Ireland. As it unfolds, Lynch's sequence becomes a commentary on the nature of memory and how it is preserved through images of cultural heritage.

The children's return to the little cabin on the edge of the bog is perhaps the most meaningful movement within the sequence. They return, into the present, with a deepened imaginative knowledge of the mythic past. The forest functions in multiple dimensions, and in multiple subjective realities. Dawn is rising over the flat-topped mountain as the children return to the little cabin. Time has passed while they have been in the forest, as it was the middle of a moonlit night when they departed on their journey. Bakhtin writes that 'when there is no passage of time there is also no moment of time' (146). If time does not pass there can be no meaningful moments of time. When time does not pass, the present is disconnected from 'its relationship to past and future' (146). It breaks down into 'isolated phenomena and objects' (146). In the context of a narrative like Lynch's that is episodic in nature and is seemingly comprised of a series of stand-alone stories, this becomes especially relevant as these episodes are enriched with meaning when viewed in relation to each other. The stories of *The Turf-Cutter's Donkey* were initially printed in serial form in *The Irish Press* before it was published as a novel in 1934. This print history means that Lynch's first readers for this text were encouraged to perceive them as both stand-alone and interconnected narratives, echoing the episodic nature of the mythological cycles they reference. Each individual episode can be viewed as a particular part of the pattern of reimagination at work in the narrative which is only fully revealed when the text begins to operate in the higher epic register Lynch uses.

As part of that pattern, the rising dawn marks both a new day in the landscape and a new phase in the children's engagement with it. As a result of their experience, their knowledge of the bog has deepened, as has their awareness of the significance of the mythical reality they have accessed through the landscape. The mist is a connecting border, between sacred and profane zones in the landscape Lynch is depicting, and between the domestic space of the cabin and the rural space of the bog. Its presence in the little cabin is not only an evocation of the adventure the children have just experienced but also a sign that the past is never far away. 'Spears of light [are] flung across the sky' and on the path the children find an 'ancient rusty spearhead' (Lynch *Turf-Cutter's Donkey* 176). The use of such a dynamic verb is notable here as the spears have been flung into the sky as though they have been projected into the future, from a fixed point in the past. The images of the spears in the sky mirrors that of the physical weapon on the ground, a repeating image that evokes the pattern of reimagination that is coming to a culmination. The spear on the ground and the spear in the sky articulate the potential for reimagination that resonates within the landscape Lynch is depicting. The spearhead, an image of the mythical past the children have just engaged with, has been reimagined into the physical landscape of their childhood. Ancient and rusty, it is an artefact from the past, but it is still recognizable in the children's present. Even in its tarnished state, the spear recalls the Blackened Sword from Padraic Colum's *The King of Ireland's Son* (1916) and the capacity for objects and artefacts to carry meaning. The preservation and reimagination of cultural heritage lies in the imaginative potential of archetypal images. Holding the spearhead, Seamus seems surer of the reality of their experiences than before and he tells Eileen that they 'know the way' (176) and that they will see the Fianna again. Cultural inheritance here is explicitly connected to the landscapes of Ireland as the journey the children take into the ancient forest is established as a journey into an engagement with the cultural heritage of the mythic past.

Myth and education in a new state

In 1935, the year after *The Turf-Cutter's Donkey* was published in its entirety, the Irish Folklore Commission (or *Coimisiún Béaloideasa Éireann*) was established by the Irish government of the time to collect and study the folklore and oral traditions of Ireland.[17] It was founded and directed by James Hamilton Delargy (Séamus Ó Duilearga), an Irish folklorist. The commission's life in that form was concluded in 1971 when it was amalgamated into the Department of Irish Folklore in University College Dublin. It operated under the aegis of the Department of Education and one of its first projects was the Schools' Collection Scheme (1937), a voluntary nationwide effort to preserve the oral culture of the nation. Facilitated through the national schools system, the Scheme collected half a million pages of folklore, primarily by asking children to recount stories told to them by older family members. This is significant given that from the late nineteenth century onwards a charge of neglecting the Irish language and Irish culture had been brought against the national school system (see Coolahan 21). It followed then that schools were seen to be the primary agents in 'the revival of the Irish language and native tradition' (38) which the cultural nationalism movement held to be fundamental for an independent state. This ongoing rediscovery of Gaelic heritage necessarily 'led to demands for [its] prominent inclusion in school courses' (38) where myths played a central role, not only in the construction of national identity but also in the education of new generations. In the Irish historical consciousness, 'the deepest layers shade into legend and mythology' (Frehan 25). The consistency with which the aspirations of the nationalist independence movement were linked with the educational system in Ireland is something that cannot be ignored, not least when it comes to the presence of myth and folklore in educational texts produced for children in the early and mid-twentieth century.[18] Padraic Frehan goes so far as to say that 'these mythological tales were the sole vehicle for presenting an Irish identity within ... schoolbooks' and that the 'power of the national message held within them was large' (34). Though essentially categorized as part of the history syllabus, the Literary Readers were particularly focused on mythological tales, which were now employed 'to portray [Ireland's] unique past' (42).[19] This was not just a hearkening back to but a perpetuation of the aims of the Cultural Revival, that is, that Ireland's mythic past would provide a template of virtues, both cultural and civic, for a new generation of citizens.

Within this particular corpus of tales there are a number which refer to or occur in what Frehan calls 'real-time history' which, he argues, establishes 'the authenticity of character and event in the myth and therefore arguably authenticat[es] the characteristics and virtues described in the stories' (36). Una Kelly's *Cuchulain and the Leprechaun* (1945) from the Parkside Children's Series is one of these tales.[20] Featuring a young boy named Phelim Cuchulain [sic] O'Callaghan as its central character, the narrative charts his movement into an awareness of his cultural and mythological heritage through a reimagination of the hero Cuchulain's childhood. While the narrative unfolds in Frehan's 'real-time history', authenticity in Kelly's text, and in the other texts explored here, is connected to the compelling nature of the present moment. Eileen and Seamus's adventures in the forest, Cu's journey to Emain Macha, Michael's voyage of discovery and Nial's movement back in time in the texts discussed here are all facilitated by a construction of connections between the past and the present. For these child figures, the past becomes the present in the present. This renders mythic experience accessible and ultimately knowable, even if it is initially unfamiliar. The authors considered here tap into the sense of authenticity Frehan is arguing for by allowing the childhoods of their central characters to encompass, and oftentimes be defined by, such mythic experiences.

The relationship between temporal experience and authenticity is also expressed in the use of language in educational texts in this period. Frehan notes that the usage evidenced in the tales concerning the concept of time is generic, using phrases such as 'at same time', 'from that time on' and 'throughout that time' (248). This language echoes the use of such narrative phrases as 'once upon a time' which characterize the fairy and folk tale and '[replicate] the orality of the storytelling being mapped upon the expository text' (248) in these schoolbooks. Kelly uses these phrases to open her narrative. The sense of cultural authenticity these texts strive for is strengthened by an engagement with Irish oral and folk culture. By consciously placing their narratives within the tradition of oral storytelling, these authors are accessing the well of cultural belief associated with that tradition.

Una Kelly: Temporality, belief and mythic experience

Irish folk tales, like those in the folk-cultural register from other countries, use several categories of time that are crucial to their structure (Nicolaisen 150). These encompass narration time (the time it takes to tell and listen to a story), narrative and folk narrative time, which distinguishes the time frame of a tale from historical time, and recounted time, which is the total time encapsulated in the tale (151). Irish folk narratives especially show what Wilhelm Nicolaisen calls a 'consistent preoccupation with the day as the unit for the structuring of narrated time' (151). Within this preoccupation is a focus on a small number of days 'strategically placed in the protagonist's life' (151) just as the monumental mythic experience that facilitates Cu's engagement with his cultural heritage takes place over the course of only three days. Seamus in *The Turf-Cutter's Donkey* still believes in the mythology surrounding Bran and the Fianna once he recognizes the resonance of the mythic figures he encounters, but just over a decade later Cu actively disbelieves the mythology and folklore he is exposed to in the day-to-day experiences of his childhood. The old stories seem to mean nothing to him; he is a child figure very much concerned with the contemporary moment. This lack of connection to and belief in the mythological narratives of Ireland can only be resolved or restored by a mythic experience that is akin to yet different from that which Seamus and Eileen experience in the bog; Cu's physical body changes during this experience, whereas Eileen and Seamus's clothes are the only things that change. In both narratives, and in both mythic experiences, the Leprechaun figure acts as a mediator, not only between quotidian life and that mythic or primordial time but also between myth and folklore. In Kelly's text he is a figure from Faery that walks between modern and mythic Ireland. He is also mindful of the importance of mythological heritage to Cu's world and to his childhood. It is crucial, therefore, that once every hundred years it is a young boy who is called on to experience Cuchulain's life, and not a grown man.

As previously stated, the opening of Kelly's narrative evokes the fairy-tale form, as the reader is told that 'once upon a time there was a boy whose name was Phelim Cuchulain O'Callaghan' (Kelly 1). As the narrative unfolds, Kelly weaves fairy-tale motifs, such as the use of patterns of three,[21] into a story that operates in dual registers – a domestic folkloric register and a mythic register. Within this opening section, Kelly's narrator engages with the everyday experiences of Cu's childhood. He is described as 'a short-sized lad' with 'blue eyes and a mop of yellowish hair that would never lie down beneath comb or brush' (1). There is, initially at least, nothing remarkable about Cu, except his name, and the hero he is named for. It is telling, though, that his school friends shorten his name from Phelim Cuchulain O'Callaghan to 'just Cu' (1), not only giving him a nickname but also veiling the significance of the name he has been given, that of the warrior Cuchulain, and taking that name out of its mythological context. It becomes a young boy's name, just like any other. Kelly's narrator is keen to impress upon the reader the importance of names. Cu's nickname leads 'to the name that was put on his sister' Eileen 'by the people of Kilmoley' (1). Searching for her brother at mealtimes, Eileen is known to go along the roadsides looking for him and calling 'Cu! Cu … are you there?' (1). She consequently becomes known as Cuckoo O'Callaghan. Her name is, as the narrator states, put on her by the people of the town – put on her, in the sense of Hiberno-English, as though it is a garment of clothing, just as Cu's new identity will be placed upon him later in the narrative, through the regaining of his full name and a change of clothing. This speaks back to the moment in *The Turf-Cutter's Donkey* when Eileen and Seamus realize that their clothes have changed, signalling their imminent meeting with the Fianna. Like Lynch, Kelly uses Hiberno-English here for a specific purpose – not only to draw attention to the importance of names but also to the idea that names are like mantles that we take upon ourselves.

In the village of Kilmoley, the place fundamentally associated with Cu's childhood, 'the people would sit talking over their fires' (2) as soon as the evening lamps are lighted. In 'small houses and large houses' (2) the village community becomes many smaller communities; communities of tellers and listeners are connected by stories.[22] The things the community talks most about define it – 'the fairies and the elves, the Banshee, and all the queer creatures that men called the Good People' (2). These storytelling communities are sustained, night after night, by the oral culture that constitutes their folkloric memory. Cu even goes so far as to call them 'a superstitious lot' with 'never a thought in their heads but those old stories' (2). Kelly uses Cu's vehement denouncement of these old stories to establish, even at the outset of her narrative, a dichotomy between the past and the present, and between heritage and contemporary culture. The fact that this denouncement is made by a child, the central figure in the story, is all the more significant as childhood, and particularly Cu's experience of it, is set at odds with the traditional oral storytelling culture of the village.

The narrator initially seems to endorse Cu's opinion of the people of Kilmoley, telling the reader that 'it was true what he said about the people. Kilmoley was a superstitious place' (2). The old stories are 'what its people busied themselves with most of the time' (2). In other words, the old stories are very much part of the everyday life of the community, part of their present. The narrator's confirmation of Cu's opinion lacks his judgement; Cu may be right about the people, but it is the town itself that is a 'superstitious place' (2). Thus, the place that Cu calls home is connected to the stories that are told by the people who inhabit it. But Cu himself is 'a different kind of person' (2); he is marked out from the other members of the community, isolated almost by the way in which he engages with the world around him. He is 'a boy of to-day' thinking 'more of the things that are happening to-day' and the things that 'will be happening tomorrow' (2). To him, these practical, pragmatic things are 'more wonderful than ancient tales of … the Pooka or the Leprechaun who knew where the Crock of Gold was buried' (2). The narrator's choice of words is significant here; everyday things are more wonderful to Cu, not more important. The old stories hold no wonder for the boy. It will take a mythic experience even more immersive than what Eileen and Seamus experience in the primordial forest to instil or awaken that sense of wonder in Cu. For he has not lost that sense of wonder – he has never experienced it. Cu's mythic experience occurs when 'he least expect[s] it' (2), when he meets the Leprechaun in person.

When that meeting occurs, the Leprechaun addresses Cu in a very specific manner, using only his second name and his surname, shouting, 'Ho, there Cuchulain O'Callaghan, you that bear the name of one of the great heroes of Erin!' (2) Not only does the Leprechaun discount Cu's given name, Phelim, he makes a direct connection between his second name and the hero figure Cuchulain. This is the first time this occurs in the text. When the Leprechaun calls out, Cu is 'just meandering along' (2) reading a book of stories about aeroplanes as he walks. He does not take his eyes from the book as he answers – he still has no connection to the world of Faery the Leprechaun represents. Cu refuses to engage with the Leprechaun, even when he identifies himself as 'the Leprechaun of Ireland' and states that he wants to speak with Cu 'by reason of the noble name you bear' (3). Again and again Kelly draws attention to Cu's indifference to the culture and heritage the Leprechaun represents and to the significance of his own name. He continues to actively ignore the supernatural presence of the Leprechaun, convinced that it is one of his friends playing a trick on him while he is reading. But as darkness falls, Cu can no longer read the printed words on the pages in front of him, and as this connection to the modern world is lost, the Leprechaun identifies himself again, calling himself 'the Fairy Cobbler, the only one who knows where the Crock of Gold is hid' (4), speaking to his place in the corpus of stories that define the life of the Kilmoley community. Cu stands on the bridge, a pebble in his hand ready to throw down to the owner of the voice who he still cannot see, and unwittingly recreates a moment from the myth of his namesake, when Cuchulain stood ready with a pebble to defend himself against the Hound of Cullen. The boy tells the voice in the darkness that he is not afraid, 'no more than the Cuchulain in that old fairy tale you're talking about' (5). This is the first time Cu reveals any knowledge of Cuchulain 'for many were the stories he had heard about the mighty Cuchulain, champion of Ulster and of all Erin' (5). Cu calls these stories fairy tales, oblivious to their mythological significance, something the Leprechaun takes issue with, stating, 'Indeed and they're no fairy-tales!' (5). Kelly consciously uses this Hiberno-English syntax throughout the narrative to draw attention to the traditional oral heritage of the community Cu is growing up in. This is the language of stories. In this moment, the connections and boundaries between folkloric and mythic culture are acknowledged within the text; Cu has equated the stories of the Good Folk the village people tell with the ancient myths of Cuchulain, believing them to be part of the same cultural register. When he throws the pebble into the darkness, again evoking imagery of Cuchulain, Cu is in fact symbolically expressing his lack of connection to these oral cultures, and his simultaneous embodiment of them. Despite himself, however, Cu begins to engage with the voice of the Leprechaun, if only to tell him that 'I don't believe in fairies … I don't believe in yourself, Leprechaun' (5) and the boy challenges the voice to show itself. In response, the Leprechaun demonstrates the power he holds over nature itself, sending a gale of wind swirling at Cu. This is the first moment the boy feels fear, and the beginnings of the belief he has previously denied.

Kelly's narrative now begins to engage with the fairy-tale register again as a sequence of three misfortunes befall Cu. These three events foreshadow the three battles he will participate in later in his adventure with the Leprechaun. When he begins to realize the error of his actions he 'put[s] the thought of his book out of his mind' (9) and begins to walk away from the village, hoping for an encounter with the Leprechaun. The mental action of putting the thought of his book out of his mind is crucial in the context of the mythic awakening he will experience later; Kelly has set Cu up as a modern child who does not believe in fairy tales, and who does not recognize the significance of myth. Here, with a conscious decision, he sets aside the stories of today that have always interested him and begins to actively seek out an encounter with one of the Good People, and with the world of Faery, even though he does not yet understand the distinction between that world and his.

Cu's faith or belief in the Leprechaun functions, initially at least, on sight, on his own vision. The second time he meets the little man he knows it is not his friend Michael D'arcy because 'he [has] seen Michael not a half an hour before' (9). The first time Cu sees the Leprechaun is also the first time the figure is described within the text. He is a 'tiny man dressed in brown … [with] a long white beard and a wizened face' (9). When Cu sees him, he is performing the Leprechaun's traditional function, hammering nails into the soles of a little shoe. Even though the night is dark, Cu can 'see him clearly by reason of the ring of light that surround[s] the cobbler' (9) as though the Leprechaun is aware of Cu's need to see what he is to believe in. We are told that 'quite suddenly Cu remember[s] the tales he [has] heard from the story-tellers' (10) and that if you could only catch the Leprechaun, he would tell you where the Crock of Gold was hidden. This moment of remembrance is crucial within the larger dialogue Kelly is staging between tradition and modernity, in that Cu displays an ability to not only retain but also recall culturally significant information, information received through oral transmission. Cu tries and fails to catch the Leprechaun but the fact that he tries signifies the beginning of a basic engagement with the idea that the fairy cobbler is real. The Leprechaun now begins to question Cu's non-belief in his own existence, asking him, 'Do you still not believe in fairies … even after looking at myself?' (12) When Cu replies that he doesn't, the Leprechaun questions him further, asking him, 'Who do you think I am then?' (12). Cu isn't sure. This is a pivotal moment for the development of his character and for the dialogue between belief and scepticism that Kelly places him within. He does not reply to the Leprechaun's questioning, because he is 'not very sure whether he [is] right or not' (12). Having firmly established that Cu is too concerned with the modern stories in his book and that his 'disbelief in the things of the fairy world' (13) is something to be rectified, the Leprechaun proceeds to give Cu a golden ball, another image in Kelly's narrative that resonates intertextually within the fairy-tale register the text plays with.[23] Instructing Cu to bowl the ball eastwards and to follow it wherever it leads, the Leprechaun tells him that 'you shall see what you shall see' (13). Once again, the Leprechaun calls attention to the connection between seeing and believing, between perception and experience and between playing and becoming. The mythic experience Cu is about to enter into, during which he will fight and lose three battles, will allow the young boy to engage with a cultural and mythological heritage that has been absent from his life up to this point, not due to a lack of accessibility, since stories are told in his village every night, but because he did not recognize the significance of it.

The boy follows the golden ball all night and Kelly's narrator uses his full name here, Phelim Cuchulain, to denote the fact that he is still the same boy who left the bridge where he spoke to the Leprechaun but also foreshadowing the changes that will occur as he moves deeper into the mythic experience that is unfolding. Again, his movement through a night-time landscape, 'across grassy plains and treacherous bogs where the white cotton fluffs blew like snow around his heels' (14), is structured by fairy-tale principles; when he comes to the edge of a sea, the ball turns into a boat of glass which sails throughout the day, and he feels no hunger or thirst. On another shore, the boat vanishes and is replaced by a silver cord that stretches out into the foothills. It is here on the shore that space and time coalesce in the narrative for the shore 'is not only a tangible, observable boundary … it is also the limit of temporal existence' (Nicolaisen 157). Usually, the island of Tir na nÓg lies across the water but in this context, for Cu, it is Ireland's mythic past made present in the landscape. It is clear that Cu is meant to follow the cord; 'there [is] no question of making up his mind what [is] to be done' (Kelly 14). As he moves deeper into this strange landscape, Cu seems to gradually lose his connection to the modern world that is so important to him. He even walks 'with a queer feeling of excitement in his chest' (14). On the morning of the third day, again the number three being a common trope in fairy tales and folklore, the silver cord vanishes at the edge of a blue lake where cranes are fishing. Cranes are common in Celtic, Asian and North American mythologies, denoting happiness and eternal youth due to their fabled lifespan of a thousand years.[24] The presence of the cranes is significant at this particular juncture in the narrative, signifying the change in register that will occur as the story moves from the fairy-tale and folklore world into the world of myth. It is only here, in sight of the cranes and after three days' travel, that Cu sleeps, immersing himself completely into the landscape wherein his mythic experience will unfold.

When Cu enters mythic or sacred time and begins to operate in Emain Macha as Cuchulain, a change in the narrative register of the text occurs, similar to that of *The Turf-Cutter's Donkey* when Eileen and Seamus cross over the Road of Dreams. This change clearly occurs in similar circumstances too; a child figure experiences a movement out of the everyday landscape contemporary to his childhood, and into a mythic landscape where his own body responds to that change. Yet, the myth which begins to be re-enacted still retains elements of a folkloric narrative, even within that elevated register. The three battles that Cu must fight and lose while he is still himself, still a child, and the reappearance of the Leprechaun or guide figure at the end of his adventure are evidence of this. The motif of three continues, as he encounters the three battles the Leprechaun promised – a wild boar, a man bearing a spear in one hand and a shield in the other and a serpent. He throws a stone at the boar, again, just as Cuchulain threw a stone at the Hound of Cullen, but to no avail, and the boar bests him. He breaks a branch from an oak tree to use against the champion, advances bravely but misses his mark. He ends the battle with his back against that same tree and the champion's sword at his throat. The champion vanishes. The serpent comes at him so fast he cannot find a weapon. He struggles in the water but once it bests him the serpent vanishes too. Cu does not succeed against the odds. He fulfils the Leprechaun's prophecy by virtue of being roundly defeated. He appreciates the significance of his three defeats, and the danger he has experienced, saying, 'For if something had not saved me each time I'd surely have been killed' (17). This is when the subtle transformation that lies at the heart of Kelly's narrative begins to stir. Cu realizes that 'it's only a small boy I am, for all my talk and reading' (17), and it is with this realization, this grounding in his own child state that his connection to Cuchulain is forged. A 'picture of the hero Cuchulain, after whom he had been named' (17), comes into his head, and Cu begins to compare himself to his namesake, who would not, he reasons, 'have allowed himself to be overcome' (17). Again, Cu displays the ability to recall information about Cuchulain and his exploits, and his comparison of his own actions and the actions of the warrior marks an awakening into mythological knowledge that had previously been denied or discarded.

The moment of Cu's transformation from Phelim Cuchulain O'Callaghan to Cuchulain the boy warrior is not explicitly articulated within the text. It is the Leprechaun who announces it to the reader, signalling the change that has occurred in the young boy he met at the bridge. He hails him as 'Cuchulain, mighty champion of Erin!' (17), bowing as Cu comes towards him, and from this moment on, the boy is no longer named as Cu by Kelly's narrator. The Leprechaun calls him 'Little Setanta, who was renamed the Hound of Culainn' (17), evoking again the myth of Cuchulain's childhood and specifically the episode in which he took on the mantle of child warrior. Cu himself has not noticed the change. It is only when the Leprechaun urges him to look at his reflection in the lake that he realizes what has occurred. It is no longer a boy that looks back at him 'but a tall and beautiful youth' (18). His clothing has changed completely, just as Eileen and Seamus's appearances respond to the mythic experience they participate in. He now wears a silken tunic, a purple cloak embroidered with gold and a pair of leather sandals. He carries a shield of leather and a light spear. But Cu's physical body has changed as well; 'I'm grown older ... and bigger ... all of a sudden' (18). Kelly's narrator tells us that this statement is muttered by Phelim Cuchulain. It is the boy who asks, 'Why have I changed? Amn't I still Phelim O'Callaghan?' (18). Significantly, as a figure who represents the presence of folkloric culture within the text, it is the Leprechaun that finally articulates the transformation that has occurred; 'Phelim O'Callaghan you are no longer ... but the mighty Cuchulain himself, terror of all Erin' (18). The fairy cobbler even bows to Cu as though to imbue his words with legitimacy. Cu has not simply assumed the mantle or even the appearance of the Ulster warrior, he has become him.

Once the change has been articulated the narrative begins to support it totally. Now it is not Cu who toys with the spear he finds in his hand but the warrior youth he has become. And the next time he speaks, he speaks as Cuchulain. Mircea Eliade writes that the history of the Cosmos and of humanity is 'preserved and transmitted through myths' (xiv). This history can be repeated indefinitely because the myths serve as ritual models that 'reactualise ... events that occurred at the beginning of time' (xiv). By knowing the myths and the exemplary models they preserve, we can re-experience the mythical times they narrate. Eliade even goes so far as to say that this re-experience only occurs when the individual is truly himself, 'on the occasion of rituals or important acts' (36). In these moments, the individual enters sacred time; the rest of his life 'is passed in profane time ... in the state of becoming' (36). This concept of sacred and profane time in the context of myth applies to Cu's movement into the past. Initially through imitation of the hero Cuchulain, Cu 'seeks to approach this archetypal model as closely as possible' (37). The imitation becomes meaningful and transformative when he picks up Cuchulain's spear. As Eliade writes, 'He who produces the exemplary gesture thus finds himself transported into the mythical epoch in which its revelation takes place' (36).

The Leprechaun states that once every hundred years 'it is given to a mortal boy to become Cuchulain for twelve hours' (Kelly 19). In these twelve hours, the chosen boy 'can do many of the things that the greatest Cuchulain did himself' (19). This sets up a complicated engagement with ideas of ritual, re-enactment and temporal experience, mediated through the new perspective of Cu's changed self. He is now Cuchulain, and because he bears 'the Christian name of the hero' (19) he is eligible for the transformation he has undergone. This is a ritual that has been undertaken by boys before him, and will, the Leprechaun intimates, be undertaken by boys who come after him, always providing that the name of Cuchulain survives in

Irish oral culture. The boy who is chosen, and who makes the choice to become the mythic hero (though Cu himself seems to have little choice in the matter), can do many of the deeds Cuchulain himself performed. Is this merely a repetition of those deeds, or, by re-enacting them as both Cuchulain and as a child of modern Ireland, is the chosen boy investing those deeds with new meaning?

The very fact that this transformation occurs every hundred years implies that it is a meaning-making ritual, a pattern of re-enactment that produces an energy of its own, independent of the original moment the deeds were performed.[25] But the slippages between Cu's selfhood and his incarnation as Cuchulain create gaps, not just in the narrative but in the ritual itself. The Leprechaun begins to tell the new Cuchulain that farther off, in the Province of Ulster, lies Emain Macha, 'the place of Conacher, King of Ulster, who is your uncle' (20). Though Cu has become Cuchulain in physical form, he has none of the knowledge or experience of the hero. He is still himself, then, just in a different form. Rather than limiting the meaning the episode can produce, the duality of Cu's presence in Cuchulain's landscape enhances the meaning-making potential of the mythic experience he is engaging in. Just as the Man from the Bog brings Eileen and Seamus to the clearing in the primordial forest so that they can recognize the connections between the past, the present and the future, so Cu's innate selfhood is preserved even as he operates in Cuchulain's physical form. He can retain the memory of his experiences, even as he repeats the hero's deeds, so that those memories might influence the ways in which he engages with his cultural heritage in his everyday life. It is significant then that it is a physical action that precipitates Cu's movement into the mythic experience that awaits him. Hefting the spear that he now holds, the young boy in the warrior's body casts it northwards, 'a mighty cast that [sends] it out of sight beyond the edge of a distant hill' (20), and he sets off running after it. Not only does this physical act engage with the mythic deeds of Cuchulain (this spear evokes the infamous Gae Bolg that Cuchulain will bear as an older warrior[26]), the movement of the spear also recalls the spears that signal the end of Eileen and Seamus's time with the Fianna.

The temporality of Cu's experience is just as complex as Eileen and Seamus's movement into primordial time in the forest. He runs towards the province of Ulster and Kelly's narrator states that the way is clear before him 'for in those days the countryside of Erin had no hedges and walls around the fields' (20). Has Cu gone back in time then? Back to the mythic past of Ireland? Or is it rather that his journey of three days and nights across land and water has allowed him to access a moment outside of time? Just as Eileen and Seamus met the Fianna in a space outside of both the past and the present, Cu has entered the continuous mythic time of Ireland. This is further complicated when Cu reaches a shepherd's camp and stops to pass the night with them. When 'the noble youth walk[s] in … the light [is] so dim that they [do] not know him' (20). Kelly's narrator wonders at this, musing that 'surely they should have known the great Cuchulain!' (20). Cu himself complicates the situation even further by asking the shepherds how the hero Cuchulain got his name, for he has been 'told that in the beginning he was named Setanta' (20). The narrator's voice is now distanced from Cu; it refers only to Cuchulain's physical appearance, and not to the perceptions of the boy operating within that physical manifestation. It is Cu who is asking to be told about Cuchulain; it is Cu who has become aware that there are gaps in his knowledge. When the shepherd proceeds to retell the story of the Hound of Cullen, stating that Setanta was only 8 years old when it occurred, close to Cu's own age, Cuchulain's status in the oral culture of the time becomes apparent. If Cu is the Cuchulain of that moment, the noble youth who is not quite yet a man, then Cuchulain's childhood belongs to the recent past. Yet it has already passed into the oral storytelling culture of Ireland. The shepherd can retell the story of how Cuchulain got his name because it has already been told before. In asking to be told a story about the hero he has become, Cu is engaging with the deeper meaning of the chance he has been given to connect with the cultural and mythological heritage that has been so lacking in his childhood to date.

Cu now engages with one of the significant moments in Cuchulain's early youth, the day he takes arms after hearing the prophecy of Cathbad the Druid who says, 'That if any young man takes up his sword and shield for the first time to-day his name will become the greatest in Erin' (21). The Druid also says that the youth's life will be a short one, just as Cu's time as Cuchulain has a finite limit. It is during this particular moment in the episode that Cu himself seems to disappear completely and the narrative begins to totally support his transformation into Cuchulain. Kelly's narrator tells us that 'the listening Cuchulain look[s] at the spear and other weapons' (21) he acquired at the lakeside, telling himself that 'they [are] only boys' weapons ... only fit for practice' (21). There is no sense of Cu here, and the register that the narrative begins to move into supports Cuchulain's presence in it totally, both in physical and psychological contexts. Phrases like 'without another thought Cuchualin set[s] off in search of his uncle' (21) further endorse this. The narrative now begins to move into a retelling of some of the key moments in Cuchulain's early warriorhood.

The king presents Cuchulain with his own royal weapons, telling him, 'You are armed now as a champion among champions' (22). We are told that Cuchulain is still only a youth, 'though already he [has] shown that he [is] no ordinary one' (22). Again, the distance between Cu and Cuchulain is now much more pronounced, with very little interiority from the youthful warrior articulated within the narrative. Even when the warriors of Emain Macha declare that 'this noble youth is no ordinary boy' (22), they are referring to his physical prowess and not to any discrepancy that might betray his true self. The chariot master tells Cuchulain, when he asks, that the road out of Emain Macha leads to Ath na Foraire, to the Watcher's Ford in Sliabh Fuad, and that the place where the river is crossed 'is one of the entrances to the Province' (22). A constant watch is kept at this entrance point by 'some champion ... there to challenge those who try to enter' (22). This particular set-up foreshadows a moment later in Cuchulain's warriorhood when he stands against Queen Maeve's army in order to defend Ulster, with all of the province at his back. On this day Conall Mac Amargin, also known as Cearnach the Victorious, is standing watch. When Cuchulain addresses Conall, his speech is markedly different from Cu's; Cuchulain is operating fully within the mythic register that Kelly's narrative has adopted. He says, 'Well you know who I am Conall Cearnach ... and these are no longer the King's weapons but my own. I have taken them this day from his hand' (25). Again, attention is drawn to and focused on Cuchulain himself, on the authenticity of his appearance and presence in the landscape. Cuchulain asks Conall to retire for the day so that he might stand in his place but Conall laughs and refuses. Angered, Cuchulain sets off towards Leinster with Conall in pursuit, until Cuchulain destroys his chariot. This reckless and violent behaviour in pursuit of a challenge is a hallmark of the youthful warrior's character and Cu/Cuchulain's actions reiterate this.

This particular adventure, an encounter with the Sons of Nechtan at Nechtan's Dun, again evokes the fairy-tale pattern Kelly uses earlier in the narrative as Cuchulain battles with three warriors. Now, however, as Cuchulain and not as Cu, the noble youth defeats all three of his opponents. In Cuchulain's myth, a message is written on a pillar that stands at the front of the Dun, and this particular retelling is no different. The message reads, 'All those who read these words ... must call to those within the dun to come and meet them in battle' (26). When Cuchulain reads this, he uproots the pillar from the ground and flings it into the river. His charioteer Jubair laments that 'you will now get what you have been looking for – and that is a quick death!' (26). Again, Cuchulain's reckless and impulsive character is to the fore in his actions and there is no trace at all of the disbelieving boy from the village of Kilmooley. He fights the three sons of Nechtan, killing them all. In this way, 'the first day of hero Cuchulain's taking of man's arms' (29) ends in violence and in victory. The twelve hours of the re-enactment have come to an end. As Cuchulain lashes his horses towards the king's palace, he sees the structure itself fading in front of him, and the trees around it, even the people who are gathered to welcome him home. In a matter of moments, it has vanished, 'leaving only a high grassy mound, peaceful in the gathering dusk' (29). Now, at the end of the adventure, and of the ritual, the narrative's register begins to change again, as Kelly's protagonist re-enters the world of modern Ireland, and of his childhood. Stopping the horses, we are told that 'the boy [leaps] down from the chariot' (29) only just having time to wave to his charioteer before the chariot, the man and the horses vanish even as he watches. He is no longer Cuchulain, but he has not yet become Cu again. He is, at this moment, a boy in a landscape that has just undergone a profound change.

The Leprechaun is waiting for him, and is, we are told, 'grinning at Phelim Cuchulain O'Callaghan' (29), the boy who has returned from being Cuchulain, and is standing before him in traditional schoolboy dress, 'in his boots, short trousers, and home-knitted jersey and stockings' (29). Kelly's narrator has now confirmed that the transformation has come full circle. The fairy cobbler wants to hear about Cu's adventures. In stark contrast to his earlier hubris, Cu's answer makes it clear that his mythic experience has changed him; 'to tell you the truth, Leprechaun, I don't know' (29). The fairy man tells the boy that it will be some time before he is able to think clearly and to remember all that has happened to him. He will be remembering mythic events as his own personal experience. The Leprechaun is now sure that Cu 'won't be jeering any more about the stories you hear of ancient Erin and the fairy people' (29). Kelly's narrator confirms that 'the Leprechaun's words were to come true' (29), validating the mythic experience Cu has engaged with and reinforcing its value in his own childhood.

Marie-Louise von Franz uses Jung's concept of the collective unconscious in her analysis and interpretation of fairy tales, arguing that invasions of that consciousness into 'the field of experience of a single individual' generate 'new nuclei of stories' (24), keeping the already existing material vital and relevant. This model can also be applied to the experiences of Seamus, Eileen and Cu. A greater mythic consciousness pushes into their everyday experiences, creating a new and contemporary development in an ancient narrative. These texts are representative of the merging of myth and folklore within the literature produced for children during this period. The concerns of myth resonate in fairy and folk tales with the myth standing as 'something national' and the tales representing 'local saga[s]' (Von Franz 26). The former represents continuity, and the latter authenticity for the participants in a national culture (Foster and Tolbert 1). In terms of identity, personal, cultural and national, finding one's place in a nation's past, or at least a place occupied by a relatable figure, can be crucial to asserting that one belongs, and that one should have access to certain stories or myths (Alderman and Inwood 187). Cu does this by briefly occupying the position of a figure from Irish myth.

Eilís Dillon: The mythic in the domestic in rural Ireland

Eilís Dillon's *The Lost Island* (1952) marks a further evolution in the synergy that develops between the mythic and the domestic in this period of Irish children's literature production. In an adventure story centred on two young boys who must set out to find a mythical island, the focus is placed firmly on the rural Irish way of life; on the rituals, routines and practices of that life; and on the images of Ireland it produces. This is a contemporary Irish childhood, lived out within the rigours and structures of country life in the Ireland of the 1950s, where the gaining of knowledge is no longer mediated through mythic experience but through domestic experience and personal growth. Michael's father has been missing for four years, absent on a quest for a mythical island, and when a stranger comes with news of him, Michael and his friend Joe set off to find the island, with the myth of its existence as their guide. The myth or legend of Manannan is cited throughout the narrative as a context for the adventure that is taking place. But the actual presence of myth is much less dominant in the text than in *The Turf-Cutter's Donkey* or *Cuchulain and the Leprechaun*. Here, the myth does not offer an interactive experience. Rather, it is part of a repository of older beliefs. There is a distance between mythology and everyday life that is absent from the other texts. Here, life is centred on the patterns and cycles of nature, on the land and on the stories of the community rather than on the narratives of the mythic past. However, though the principal characters of Dillon's narrative seem not to engage with the deeper mythic realities of the Irish mythological cycles in the manner that characters from *The Turf-Cutter's Donkey* and *Cuchulain and the Leprechaun* do, the text itself is structured by both myth and folklore, even as both are retold and reinterpreted within the narrative. Dillon blends the folkloric and the mythic with the modern, using folklore to make specific statements about Ireland's culture and way of life (Ni Chuilleanáin 126). Consequently, the text marks a movement on the spectrum of concern with myth and folklore towards domestic rural life and adventure.

This is a first-person narrative, with the central protagonist Michael recalling an adventure that began one spring morning when he was 14 years old. His narrative is already a retelling and an act of remembering. His voice and the story he tells articulate a specific set of realities for a young boy in the rural Ireland of the mid-twentieth century. His life is structured by practicalities and by routines. The morning he opens his story with is one of many similar early mornings when he travels with the pony into the Saturday market in the town. Through Michael's observations of what is familiar to him, the reader gains an insight into a particular vision of Ireland that Dillon is trying to represent. Michael's description of the stream of carts heading to market provides an image from that vision. He tells the reader that 'mountainous old women in patterned fawn-coloured shawls [sit] in the donkey-cars' while the men drive big horse carts, 'some with high loads of turf, thatched on the top to keep them dry' (Dillon *The Lost Island* 8). There is a sense of community even in this moving crowd, with the spring sunlight casting their shadows before them as they move 'along companionable together' (8). This narrative is focused on contemporary experience. There is no sense here at the beginning, or later as the adventure progresses, that Michael is looking to the ancient past for knowledge or enlightenment. Myth and folklore are now embedded into the oral culture of communities such as the one Michael and his family are a part of; myth structures the origins of the landscape, providing the name for the lost island at the heart of the adventure; folklore is interwoven into the daily routines of the community, explaining the eccentricities and foibles of rural life. As a writer, Dillon was fascinated with the nuances of communication, and with the ways in which communities remembered their history through story. She writes of the Galway landscape she remembers that 'adults and children were always together, and conversation was uninhibited' ('A Writer in Cork' 35). This influenced her vision of how children's literature should function in that, 'because of the structure of our society, fictional adults and children will be together in the community, just as they are in real life' ('Unclouded Vision' 65–6). Through communities, often rural communities, Dillon engages with the traditional structures of contemporary Irish life, and far from dismantling them, endorses them; the protagonists within her texts, just like Michael and Joe, may plan to leave their communities, but usually return, having gained new experiences (Rahn 365).

At the market Michael meets Joe, a boy of his own age, standing initially on the edge of the crowd. He is smaller than Michael and much thinner with 'big dark brown eyes like bog holes' (*The Lost Island* 10). This seems to connote intelligence and awareness; in *The Turf-Cutter's Donkey* the bog is a repository of culture, history and myth. The boy is described by Michael in an almost otherworldly fashion, with his slight frame and larger eyes recalling the appearance of a member of the Faery folk or Good People. This is never expanded on within the text but the allusion to folklore stories where people meet Faery figures at fairs and markets is undeniable.[27] Michael agrees to go with him once he has sold his vegetables, and when they leave together the boy offers him his name, Joe Clancy. As though seeking it in return, he asks Michael for his. When Michael tells him, he repeats this over and over; 'Michael Farrell, Michael Farrell – that suits you' (10). This exchange of names also feeds into the otherworldly description of Joe and lends the weight of tradition to his offer of hospitality to Michael. An individual's true name is a powerful thing in Faery folklore and once the exchange occurs, the boys' friendship is secured.[28] Dillon is engaging here with the idea of border crossings, moments within the narrative, that allow her text to operate within the adventure genre and also within the folk or fairy-tale genre, where not everything is quite what it seems. The quest the boys will embark on operates similarly within multiple paradigms; metaphorically the quest to find the island becomes a quest to restore Michael's relationship with his father while in cultural terms they must enter into a new way of engaging with the landscape and with their own perceptions of it in order to follow the story that will lead them to it.

Michael's childhood has been radically affected by his father's absence, so much so that he states he has 'lived the life of a grown man with very little time for play' and that he must 'learn to think and act like a grown man also' (12). The adventure he undertakes with Joe in order to find his father and the lost island is thus a movement back into the childhood he has been denied. Undertaking the journey itself is not only a statement of faith in the island's existence but also in the myth of Manannan that surrounds it. Michael follows Joe initially because he does not want to refuse his offer of hospitality. Life in this rural region is structured by traditional beliefs and systems of etiquette. Michael longs for friends more than anything else but because both his father and mother are 'strangers to the place' (12) he hardly knows anyone in the town. He is more connected to the rural landscapes than the more urban space of the town. But, significantly, he finds a welcome in Joe's house. The text is studded with images of domestic spaces, and of the women who generate and sustain them, and the kitchen in Joe's house is no exception. With its open fireplace, earthen floor and the three-legged pot hung over the large turf fire, it is the quintessential image of a rural Irish hearth, the heart of the home. There is a woman there, watching the fish that are cooking on the fire; she and her fisherman husband are Joe's guardians. She wears 'the long red skirt and cross-over plaid shawl that all the fishermen's wives wore in those days' (12), Michael tells us. Through Michael's narration and his ability to observe the life and the people around him, Dillon is glossing the images she is presenting to the reader, even as the narrative is producing them, just as Patricia Lynch glosses the images of life in the rural west of Ireland in *The Turf-Cutter's Donkey*.

The islands off the west coast are a source of mystery within the text, especially to Michael who has so little knowledge of the sea. Pete, Joe's guardian, points out some of the island boats to him, which the men live on when they come into town. Michael remembers seeing these island men in the town on market days, always dressed 'in dark blue homespun and the rawhide shoes that they made at home'

(16). They come, it seems, from another world entirely, a world that generates its own mythologies and traditions. The three islands in question lie across the mouth of the bay and on a clear day they can 'be seen from the town, floating dimly on the horizon' (16). They look, Michael muses, like 'the world's end' and it seems impossible to him 'that people like myself should be living on them' (16). The fact that Michael and Joe will go further than this world's end on their adventure speaks, it seems, to the need for young people to engage with what appears strange to them. It is only because of the voyage that Michael interacts with the people of the islands and gains an insight into their community structures and values.

This theme of cultural education, or how childhood is influenced by cultural education, is one that these texts share. Eileen is asked by the Leprechaun what she learns in the stone schoolhouse, implying that the education she is receiving there is somehow lacking. Cu is an extremely well-educated young boy, constantly reading, engaged in contemporary culture, yet he lacks a knowledge of and a respect for traditional stories. In Dillon's text, the focus on education is different. Michael himself states that he craves schooling but because of his family circumstances, he hasn't received it. Throughout the text, Michael is instead educated through stories. Billy, the man who works the farm for his mother, engages him in evening discourses, 'mentioning some far off part of the globe' and proceeding to 'describe the people, their dress and habits, their food, their religions, and their history' (22). These stories expand Michael's horizons and thinking; it is from Billy that he has learned his reverence and respect for books, and it is through him that he has 'read a fair number of the world's classics' (22). Stories then become a medium of experience for Michael. Though mythology and folklore are less prominent in his education than Eileen, Seamus and Cu's, it is only through mythology and through a folkloric model of education that he ultimately reaches his father. The idea that Michael finds his father by re-enacting a myth is a compelling one and it is something that Dillon uses deliberately to explore the meaning that is produced at the intersection between oral tradition and modern experience. The focus of her narrative and Michael's life is initially domestic and inward, with that focus placed on the home and the community. Michael's journey into myth allows Dillon to explore how communities create meaning through stories by using them to chart the movement from the domestic to the universal, the home to the world. Jan Assmann makes a distinction between communicative and cultural memory, linking it to the difference between 'the everyday and the festive, the profane and the sacred, the ephemeral and the lasting, the particular and the general' (*Cultural Memory* 43). Communicative memory can include 'the passing-on of narrative patterns between generations' (Erll 56) and storytelling is one means through which these memories can be passed on. Storytelling is also one of the means through which communicative memory can pass into cultural memory – how stories can become myths. So, the distinction between communicative and cultural memory can also be linked to the difference between story and myth. The transition from communicative to cultural memory is mirrored in the movement from the domestic to the universal that Dillon seeks to chart in her narrative. This is expressly articulated in the exchange between Bartley Connolly and the two boys where, through the act of storytelling, the old man communicates a series of cultural memories to them.

It emerges that one of the old men of the village community told Michael's father the story that changed all their lives and sent him on his voyage of discovery. As Michael's mother recalls, the old man told him about Inishmanann, 'the lost island of Manannan, the old god of the sea' (Dillon *The Lost Island* 38). Two aspects of this sentence are significant. The first is that the island of Manannan has been lost. The island itself has passed out of living memory. It is no longer a part of the stories that shape the community and it resides only in the memory of an old man who can no longer fish. The second is that Manannan himself is described as the 'old god of the sea' (38). This implies that he is obsolete, even redundant, and that the sea no longer has such gods, at least in the culture of the men who now sail it. No other gods from the pantheon of Irish mythology are mentioned within the text, only Manannan, and this only in a context that highlights how close he has come to the periphery of Irish life and culture. Michael's mother tells her son how the old man told his father that 'no one who ever went to the island had ever come back' but 'according to the story, anyone who succeeded' in both finding the island and returning 'would bring back something rare and valuable with him' (38). Upon hearing this, and for most of the adventure, Michael is convinced that there is treasure on the island, but arguably what Michael, Joe and his father bring back from the island is a revitalization, not only of Michael's family life but also of the idea of the myth itself. The island has been recovered. It is no longer lost, and it has been proven to exist. Therefore, the myth that surrounds it has been authenticated. Michael's father says as much himself before he goes, as his wife tells him 'that there was never a god of the sea called Manannan' (38). He reasons that there must be a real island 'or else the story would not have lasted so long' (38). Dillon is using this dialectic between mythological narrative and physical reality to examine the nature of belief in Michael's rural community, and the ability of that community to connect with the ancient past as well as the recent.

Michael goes to see Bartley Connolly himself, the man who told his father the story. In this way he enters into a pattern of telling and retelling that Bartley has been engaging in for years, telling the young men the stories he first heard when he himself was a young man. His own daughter in-law tells the boys, 'Don't you believe all you hear from him, or this place will get too small for you and you'll have to go roaming the world' (47). Bartley's retellings of the myths that chart the development of the landscape open up the world for a new generation of listeners. He tells the boys that 'the stories say that Inishmanann was the last stronghold of Manannan, the old god of the sea' (48). He connects the god to the Isle of Man, another island that once belonged to him. There is no mystery to that island because it is inhabited, 'people live there, and boats go in and out every day' (48). But because no one lives on Inishmanann, 'no one seems to know exactly where it is' (48). The very location of the island is known only through the stories that are told about it. Some sailors even say that it is 'Hy-Brazil, the fairy island that floats on the edge of the world, between the sea and sky' (48). This fairy island has been described in Irish mythology as an island cloaked in mist for years at a time;

even when the mist lifts, it cannot usually be reached. Again, the trope of mist is connected to ways of seeing, and particularly here to concealment and revelation. Here, Bartley's stories forge connections between the geographical realities of the sea surrounding Ireland and the metaphysical realities of the myths that have been told about it.[29]

Bartley admits that he doesn't know how the story about the treasure began. He knows of an old story about a prince who went to the island to ask for Manannan's help in battle 'and perhaps it was he who told about the treasure' (48). Bartley consistently associates the stories he tells with truth, and with different kinds of reality, be they mythic or metaphorical. He is a storyteller; his knowledge of old stories lends his retelling voice a certain kind of authority. It seems that he alone remembers these stories and that by retelling them he is preserving them. Another of his old stories implies that Manannan still lives on the island and to avoid staying there forever, anyone who came to that place would have to know the right spells to make themselves invisible. It is clear to both boys 'from the way the old man [speaks] that he more than half believe[s] these stories' (48) and through Michael's narration, Dillon posits the idea that there are many like him, 'who spend long winter evenings exchanging stories of fairies and witches, giants with three heads and eight legs, beautiful maidens and the King of Ireland's Son' (48).[30] These storytellers would 'sit in the dark kitchen with no light but the glow of the turf fire … and recall old tales they had heard from their grandfathers' (48). Just as in Cu's rural community of Kilmoley where the villagers gather around their hearths to share stories, stories in Michael's community do not necessarily belong to the older generation but are remembered and passed on by them. Michael has experience of such storytellers, and he recognizes that 'Bartley's yarns about the island [follow] a similar pattern' (48). Perhaps then, the stories about the island have survived not only because the island really does exist but also because they have been told in such a way that they have become part of the storytelling stock of the area.

Bartley tells the boys that when the prince from the story sailed for Inishmannan, 'he went to a sage of his acquaintance to ask him how to get here – just as you have come to me' (51). The boys are thus implicated in a re-enactment of the story Bartley is retelling once again, a story that speaks back to the myth of Manannan and the Tuatha Dé Danann. In the story, the Prince is told to 'set the stern of his boat against the Eagle's Rock when the tide [is] full' and to then 'sail north of south and south of north for seven days and seven nights' (51) after which time he would reach the island. These are precisely the directions Michael and Joe follow when they eventually set out on their adventure, in a boat they name the Wave-Rider, after the Prince's boat in the story. Again, they are re-enacting the adventure and the return of the old story. The boys find the island and rescue Michael's father, who has found a treasure of sorts, in the form of sea pearls. As they embark on the journey home, the island, 'ringed with gold', is slowly covered in mist, and as they watch they see it 'floating between the sea and the sky' (170), just as Bartley himself said. Then, despite the strong sun, the island is suddenly covered completely in mist, rendering it invisible. They cannot even see 'a thickness in the mist where it had been' (170). Just as the bog mist lifts to reveal the primordial forest to Eileen and Seamus in *The Turf-Cutter's Donkey*, here the island that has been revealed is concealed again in a mist that becomes a visual embodiment of the myth which narrates its existence. Though they continue to watch, the island does not reappear, as the myth of Manannan's island is brought to a close again. Michael and his father return to their community, and ultimately, their family home, having restored a sense of equilibrium to that domestic space.

J. S. Andrews: Agency and history in the time-slip narrative

Whereas *The Lost Island* deals with a community's sense of and connection with a mythological past, J. S. Andrews's *The Bell of Nendrum* (1969) engages with the idea of an individual's interactions with and influence on history, and on the capacity of human experience to transcend temporal boundaries. From texts that have articulated mythic and folkloric realities, Andrews's text deals exclusively with historical contexts, and with the time-slip narrative, which allows him to send his teenage protagonist Nial back in time to 974. Andrews's 'Author's Note' harkens back to the tradition of prefaces that was so common in early twentieth-century literature for children in Ireland, especially those narratives that concerned themselves with mythology. Here, Andrews deliberately aligns his text with history, calling the book 'the result of an actual happening' (7). What the reader cannot know is whether Andrews is referring to the historical authenticity of the sacking of the Abbey at Nendrum or to the moment when Nial slips back in time. He tells his readers that in 974, the monastery on the island of Mahee in Strangford Lough, County Down, was attacked and destroyed, and that almost without exception 'the greater part of the site has remained uninhabited from that time' (7) so that the ruins of the Abbey still remain to be seen. Unlike the other texts examined in this chapter, this narrative is explicitly emplaced in a specific location, in a specific time and in a specific cultural and historical context. Andrews even cites his historical sources within his author's note, again adding to the authenticity of the historical past he describes as part of Nial's time-slip experience.[31] Closing the note, Andrews tells his readers that 'Nendrum is there for all to see' meaning the ruins that Nial looks at in his own time, and 'so, sailing from time to time on the blue waters of the lough, is Cuan' (7). Because the boat Cuan has sailed on the waters both in Nial's time and in Cailan's time, this could be an implication that the past is always continually present in the present, not a repetition but a continuous enactment, each perpetuating the other.

Opening the narrative, Andrews's narrator informs the reader that Strangford Lough received its name from Viking invaders who settled on its western shore. On the other hand, 'the Irish at that time called it simply 'Cuan', the Harbour Lough' (9). Nial has named his twelve-foot dinghy Cuan because somehow 'the ancient name went well with her traditional construction' (9). The boat is part of Nial's boyhood, a modern piece of sailing equipment that is also traditional and echoes the construction of boats far more ancient. It is a modern version of an ancient thing. This is significant in that the boat will function later in the text as the means by which Nial will move into the past, and back into the present again. The boat, even within the Northern Irish countryside, is the only common element in both Nial's present and Cailan's present, moving through the waters common to both, again symbolizing the synergy between past and present. During his explorations of the surrounding coastline, Nial has always lamented a lack of time; 'always, long before the day's end, time ran out, prematurely shortening the distance he could cover, limiting the places he could see or sail around' (11). He wishes, in fact, for more time, for the chance to 'just stay, living nearby for a mere week' (11). This is, ironically, exactly what occurs after Nial finds himself in the past.

The moment just before Nial moves through time is a moment of stillness. The wind suddenly drops, and the boat glides to a standstill 'about mid-way between the two islands' (17), at a point of intersection, just as Cuan itself provides a point of intersection between the past and the present. The sky begins to darken above Nial's head, and he finds it difficult to breathe 'with the sheer weight of the atmosphere' (17) pressing down on him, as though he is being focused into a specific space. Then, 'with the violence of an explosion' there is a 'sudden terrifying instant of back-pressure' (17) and a squall that threatens to take the boat from under him. Each of the child or young adult figures in these texts experiences a time-slip or time-change moment in that they move into different experiences of time, but Nial's differs considerably from the temporal transitions the other figures encounter. Eileen and Seamus are fully in control of their physical bodies during their journey across the Road of Dreams and into the forest of the bog. Cu physically travels for three days and nights to reach the time of Emain Macha, and though Michael and Joe do not move into another world or time, they do journey, with great physical hardship, towards an unknown destination, with a myth as their only guidance, and the fact that their transposition is in real time and a real place is in keeping with the mapping of myth on to reality that characterizes Dillon's text, as discussed above. Nial, however, is physically displaced out of one time and into another, with the landscape as the only constant throughout. He has almost no agency within this seemingly random movement. He can only gain agency by engaging with the community he finds himself a part of. Subjectivity is shaped not only by time but by space as well, in that we need time to fix ourselves in space (Campbell *Past, Self, Space* 31–2). Once Nial fixes himself in time as well as in space, he can begin to fully engage with his own actions in that time. This comes full circle when he brings his own subjective memories of history forwards into the future.

The first person he meets in the past, or, rather, in his new present, proves to be the most important connection he makes. Cailan greets him as a friend, and Nial responds, 'somehow [knowing] that he [has] not spoken in English' (21). He finds himself communicating suddenly in Erse, what he himself perceives to be 'the ancient Irish language', a 'tongue he [has] never learnt' (21) but that he is now able to understand. Just as Eileen, Seamus and Cu find themselves responding to their mythic experiences, Nial is responding to the new reality of the situation he finds himself in. Asking Nial to 'tell me about yourself as we go' (24), Cailan brings the boy up to Aendrum. It is at this moment that the strangeness of his predicament overwhelms Niall, and he attempts to articulate the fact that he has never heard of this place and does not know what to do; 'I don't understand! Who are you? And, well – where am I?' (24) When Cailan asks if Nial is lost, the idea begins to occur to him that he is lost in a place he knows but in a time that is strange to him.

He realizes that Strangford Lough is known here as Cuan, even though 'the lough [has] not commonly been called Cuan for centuries' (26). He begins to wonder if 'time [has] slipped back in some way, carrying him with it?' (26). Again, there is an emphasis on the fact that Nial has no agency or choice in the movement out of his own time and into another, just as for Eileen, Seamus and Cu a Leprechaun figure mediates between them and their mythic experiences, and for Michael and Joe the choice they make to undertake the voyage and the myth that guides them facilitates their agency. For Nial, it is seemingly a random event that has brought him to this point in time. Andrews sets up an idea about the ways in which individuals can engage with history, suggesting that personal experience and engagement with the past can result not only in a gaining of knowledge but also a sense of reflection about one's relation to that past as well. Nial's lack of historical knowledge works against him as the adventure unfolds. It occurs to him at one point that when Cailan refers to the Danes, he probably means the Vikings 'but he [can't] remember enough from his history classes to know if this is a Viking period or not' (34). Just like Eileen, Seamus, Cu and to a certain extent Michael and Joe, there is a lack of knowledge or awareness at the core of Nial's interaction with the past that is only resolved through direct experience of that past. It is only when Nial can connect the landscape of his present-past, the moment in time in which he finds himself, with his own present that the connection between history and personal experience begins to reveal itself to him. Looking out over the wooded hills beyond Reagh Bay, he sees 'the solid and unmistakable outlines of Cave Hill, Divis, and the Black Mountain', the landscape he sees 'rising over the city when in the morning he [throws] back the bedroom curtains of his Belfast home' (43). Andrews is drawing particular attention here to Nial's perspective on the rural and urban spaces that dominate his county. From this moment in time he looks out over a rural landscape from a rural landscape. In his own time, he looks out from the urban into the rural. In both times Nial gains a perspective on his own life by looking at the rural spaces that surround his home. Andrews makes a fundamental connection between Nial's domestic everyday life and the lived history he experiences in Cailan's time by suggesting that the landscape, even though it changes between each time, supports that connection.

With the adventure moving towards its climax, Nial and Cailan sight an approaching Viking ship, preparing to land near the Aendrum, as the Abbey is known in 974. As Nial realizes what this means for the religious community, his presence in the abbey becomes essential to the preservation of its relics. The Abbot shows Nial these treasures, explaining their significance and impressing upon him the necessity for the Chalice to be saved from destruction. The Abbot's charge to Nial is significant within the context of the argument Andrews makes about personal connections to and involvement with history. The older man implores him that 'if ever ... it should be in your power ... to make it possible for the cup to be preserved for other men – perhaps in other times – to see, to wonder at' (91), Nial should do all he can. The Abbot is essentially asking him to ensure that the Abbey itself will not be forgotten, and Niall is ultimately promising to remember the history he is living through. As Nial escapes the destruction of the Abbey with Cailan and one of the other monks, the Abbot's words are paramount in his mind. This is the moment where the time-slip occurs again, returning him to his own present. As he crosses a tangle of driftwood at the high-water mark, following Cailan, he feels his foot catch under something and as he falls, 'the world [bursts] into a great explosion of brilliant, dazzling, intermingling lights, all colour, dancing, flickering, fading' (188). He wakes into consciousness on the beach with Cuan present with him, 'her tall mast tilting' (188) as though she has undergone a journey as well.

During his time in the abbey, the monks give Nial some of their own clothes to wear. These are gone upon his arrival back in his own time, but a brooch that he was wearing in Cailan's time is still here. Crucially, the narrator states that he remembers it had been pinned into his woven belt. He is remembering not only history now, but, simultaneously, his own immediate past experience. He looks around for Cailan and sees only the proof that he is back in his own present, 'the clean, white rectangular shape of a cottage on the distant shore' (189). It is the landscape that shows him this proof, allowing him to centre himself once more in his own time. Catching the bus home, Nial realizes that he is 'seeing the familiar passing landscape with new eyes' that observe the changes in that landscape, 'brick and concrete houses, the metalled road, telegraph poles, the bus windows, cars, a motor-bike' and the things that haven't changed at all, 'birds and a brown scurrying rat, trees, grass' (191). Andrews is positing the idea that having engaged so deeply with the past, Nial's present is now infused with it, and consciously so. For other people, this can be achieved through interaction with artefacts, with objects from the past that have survived. Believing Nial's story, his parents take him to the museum where he is told that the chalice Cailan and himself were trying to protect was found 'in a circular earthwork ... away down in the middle of Ireland' (200). To Nial, this means something beyond the preservation of heritage and culture; it means that his friend also survived. He wonders was it 'last night? Or all but a thousand years ago?' (199) and in having Nial contemplate this, and in making it clear to the reader that his sojourn in the past has deeply affected him even after he has returned to his own present, Andrews asks the reader to consider whether the relationship between the historical past, the mythological past and the present can be accurately measured or expressed through concepts of time or whether a paradigm that allows for simultaneity of experience might be considered.

The text looks forward to the development of the time-slip narrative in Irish children's literature, which, especially in a fantasy context, often deals with Ireland's ancient mythic past, as well as exploring the duality of the metaphysical relationship between Ireland and Tir na nÓg. Here, the time-slip device is used to explore a specific period in Irish and Northern Irish history but there is also an emphasis placed on the supernatural and the otherworldly as well as a particular focus on the capacity for landscape to function as a repository for communal memory and culture. There is even a reference to a more ancient past within the narrative; one of the Abbey's guards is known as Lugh, and carries a spear, an image which resonates within the Cuchualinn saga, as Lugh, the God of Light, comes to aid Cuchulainn at the Battle of the Ford against his foster brother Ferdia. Nial's movement into the past and his return out of it are never fully explained. Rather, the reader is encouraged to view the development of his character as a result of his experiences as a comment on the necessity to engage with the past in order to more fully understand the present. Nial gains a greater connection to his native landscape, the landscape of his childhood and young adulthood through his experiences of that landscape in a different temporal context. Because an emphasis is placed on the ability of an individual to interact with and gain personal experience from the past, and that agency can be gained through retelling the narrative of that experience (which Nial gains when he tells his parents what has happened to him), *The Bell of Nendrum* resonates within the larger pattern of retrieval and remembering that dominates Irish children's literature in Ireland in the twentieth and twenty-first centuries.

Conclusion: The national past and the national identity

Anthony D. Smith posits that the enduring relationship between the national past, present and future of a country can be examined under three headings: recurrence, continuity and reappropriation (11). Recurrence refers to the idea of the nation as a 'recurrent form of social organization [sic] [and a] mode of cultural belonging' (11), expressed in various forms which facilitate communal experience. In the context of Irish children's literature, one of these forms is narrative, and specifically mythological and folkloric narrative. The existence of mythological narratives contributes to the continuity of the nation (11) – literally how far back in time its origins can be traced. For Smith, continuity represents the reaching forward of the ethnic past into the national present, whereas reappropriation signifies a reaching backward into the past, in an attempt to authenticate the existence of the nation (12). The texts discussed here articulate the synergy that exists between continuity and reappropriation, when for these authors, the authenticity of the nation is linked to cultural and mythological heritage. In this context, what Smith calls ethnoscapes become especially meaningful – 'landscapes endowed with poetic ethnic meaning' (16) through the narrativization of history and memory. The bog Eileen and Seamus journey into is one of these ethnoscapes, as is the Emain Macha Cu visits, and the lost island Michael rediscovers. The nation stands as a 'stratified or layered structure of social, political and cultural experiences and traditions' laid down by 'successive generations of an identifiable community' (171). These texts, and the texts that follow in later decades, provide access points into experiences that are cultural, mythologic and folkloric, where myth is available to be experienced in a way that explains the present for the child figures concerned. Moving from that moment of reimagination in the forest in *The Turf-Cutter's Donkey* when Eileen and Seamus come to a greater understanding of their cultural heritage through mythic experience, to the articulation of folk culture in *Old John*, Cu's re-engagement with oral culture in *Cuchulain and the Leprechaun*, Michael and Joe's re-enactment of a mythic journey, through to *The Bell of Nendrum* where the emphasis is on Nial's place in and ability to engage with history, these texts mark an expansion of the ways in which Irish children's literature communicates experiences of childhood, usually through an engagement with remembering.

The pervasive twentieth-century representation of Ireland 'as a troubled but authentically romantic folk culture' (Hedges Deroy and Caulkin 73) proves to be a productive one for the writers considered here. In these texts, the emphasis on stories and on storytelling that dominates Irish children's literature in the twentieth century is placed not only on child figures receiving experiences and narratives from mythic figures but also on older adult figures recounting community narratives in the oral tradition. The trouble, in the context of these texts, is the disconnection between contemporary childhoods and the cultural heritage of the nation. The authenticity of the folk culture that must be engaged with and preserved provides a wealth of narratives to be retold to a new child audience. These texts articulate the reality that 'Gaelic culture meant different things to different people' (Ferriter 340). The child figures at the centre of these texts reflect this idea. Eileen and Seamus represent the rural working class, Michael the small farmer. Even Cu speaks to the 'continuous demand for English publications and English modes of entertainment' (340) so prevalent at the time, with his penchant for non-fiction information books. But within these texts, Gaelic culture, or, rather, Gaelic heritage, comes to mean aspects of the same thing or comes to facilitate similar experiences. For myth and folklore become the means through which these children come to know themselves as citizens of a modern Ireland, and the language through which they come to understand their duty to the preservation and revitalization of that heritage.

By examining these texts, it is possible to investigate not only how a culture remembers and how it forgets but also what this might mean for narratives of cultural and mythological heritage. The child figures in these texts are placed at the heart of a discourse between forgetting and remembering, in the liminal space between operating without knowledge and the gaining or retrieval of that knowledge. Their journeys back into awareness become larger metaphors for the regaining of cultural awareness in Irish society. In these texts, that awareness or mythological knowledge is only a generation or so removed. In fact, Cu's sister is more aware of the Good Folk than he is, and Eileen and Seamus's father still retains the knowledge of stories about the flat-topped mountain, just as Michael's father has faith enough in a myth to follow it out to open sea. In later texts, that knowledge is even further removed, so much so that it cannot be regained, it must be learned for the first time. Cultural and mythological memory become, as children's literature in Ireland moves towards the end of the twentieth century, narratives that facilitate contemporary mythic experiences. If cultural memories are 'constructed as they are recollected [because] memory is a form of interpretation' (Hua 139), then the child figures at the centres of the texts discussed here, and in later texts produced for children in Ireland, are contributing to the cultural memory of the nation through their experiences.

Chapter 4

REIMAGINING: PAT O'SHEA, ORLA MELLING, JIM O'LEARY, KATE THOMPSON, SIOBHAN DOWD

Myth, place and identity

In 1996, the Irish Children's Book Trust, which would merge with the Children's Literature Association of Ireland in the following year to create Children's Books Ireland, published *The Big Guide to Irish Children's Books: Mórtheroraí Do Leabhair Éireannacha don Óige*. Its editors, Celia Keenan and Valerie Coghlan, called the publication 'a celebration of the recent dramatic growth in Irish publishing for children and young adults' (11). It was the first publication of its kind that examined, in detail, the contemporary state of publishing and books produced for young people in Ireland. In her foreword, the then president of Ireland Mary Robinson highlighted 'the remarkable revival' in the area of 'writing, illustrating and book production for children' (10). It is significant that she chose the word 'revival' to speak about the production of literature for children in Ireland, recalling the aims and values of the Cultural Revival, almost one hundred years later. Also significant is the acknowledgement within this collection of the importance of Irish myths, legends and folk tales to this new revival (Kennedy 81; Dunbar 40).

One year later, in 1997, Michael Scott referred to collections of Irish folklore and myth assembled by authors such as Standish O'Grady, Patrick Kennedy, William Allingham, T. Crofton Croke, Augusta Gregory and W. B. Yeats in the late nineteenth and early twentieth centuries[1] as 'the earliest fantasy fiction for children' (322) in Ireland.[2] This description, far from fallaciously equating myth and folklore with fantasy, engages with the relationship between these narrative forms and that particular genre. Using that relationship as a touchstone, this chapter explores the capacity for the fantasy genre to augment mythic and folkloric narratives, and to widen the scope within which these narratives function, using an analysis of Pat O'Shea's *The Hounds of the Morrigan* (1985), Orla Melling's *The Singing Stone* (1986), Jim O'Leary's *The Fuchsia Stone* (1993), Siobhan Dowd's *Bog Child* (2005) and Kate Thompson's *The New Policeman* (2008). These texts are representative of a relationship between the fantasy genre and Irish myth that develops and deepens in the latter half of the twentieth century. In this period Irish mythology and folklore are increasingly expressed within fantasy narratives that allow authors to not only retell those myths and folk tales but to also reimagine them, and to expand them beyond the borders of their original narratives. The reimagination of myth in each of these selected texts is expressed through representations of the

Irish landscape, and through interrogations of the effects of these representations on identity and selfhood. This chapter will explore representations of landscape in Irish children's fantasy and the degree to which these texts speak to a broader cultural concern with issues of space and place in Ireland during this period.

As literature for children produced in Ireland, this fantasy material is, if not unique among bodies of children's literature in a global sense, remarkable in its sustained engagement with tradition, folklore, landscape and identity, and in the ways in which that engagement is influenced by myth as 'a form of thinking that remains interpretively open to both the past and the present' (Lloyd 4). By terming those early collections and the expanded narratives that emerged after them 'fantasy fiction', Michael Scott acknowledges the synergy that exists between children's fantasy literature and myth. As Lillian Smith writes in *The Unreluctant Years* (1953), 'fantasy uses a metaphorical approach to the perception of universal truth' (150), which is, fundamentally, what myth attempts to communicate. Smith goes on to observe that the word 'fantasy' finds its origins in the Greek language 'and literally translated', means 'a making visible' (150). In this particular period in the production of Irish children's literature, in the latter part of the twentieth century, the fantasy genre becomes the predominant means through which myth and folklore are articulated and made visible in the landscapes of Ireland. This occurs as authors engage more and more with traditional narratives, and, in pushing the boundaries of those narratives, open them out to a new generation of readers.

Between the publication of Orla Melling's *The Singing Stone* in 1984 and Kate Thompson's *The New Policeman* almost twenty-five years later in 2008, Ireland would see hunger strikes begin in Northern Ireland, bear witness to over three thousand deaths as a direct result of the Troubles, elect its first female president in Mary Robinson and see the Good Friday Agreement signed into law by British and Irish politicians. The country would emerge from the grip of recession in the 1980s into a period of increasing prosperity and social and cultural confidence in the 1990s and 2000s. Events like the funeral held by the Irish government in Glasnevin Cemetery for eight IRA men killed during the War of Independence in 2001 would demonstrate starkly the tension that had always existed between the atemporality of myth and the specificity of historical moments in Irish society. In their own ways, each of the texts examined here engage with that tension, either through the time-slip device, the observation of the parallels and differences between Ireland and Tir na Óg or the observance of borders, both geographical and metaphysical.

In Ireland in the late twentieth century, literature produced for children that engages with Irish mythology begins 'to let the myth cross over into the children's lives' while simultaneously letting 'the lives pass over to the myth' (Dunbar 42). The children to whom Robert Dunbar refers are the child figures at the centre of the texts considered in this chapter, and in the wider body of fantasy texts available at this time for young Irish readers. As the myth and the lives of these children merge, a new story is created. This same merging is also occurring in British literature produced for children during this period. Jenny Nimmo's *Snow Spider* trilogy (1986-9) is set in twentieth-century Wales and focuses on the experiences of Gwyn Griffiths, a young boy descended from magicians. The trilogy draws inspiration from Welsh mythology and writes back to and reimagines elements of the *Mabinogion*. On Gwyn's ninth birthday his grandmother gives him five strange gifts. Collectively, these gifts are the catalyst for a quest that will help Gwyn to discover whether or not he is an authentic magician. Like Susan Cooper's *The Dark Is Rising* sequence, landscape and specifically the storied landscape of Wales features prominently in the trilogy, where myth and modernity meet. Gwyn is an ordinary boy facing extraordinary experiences and Nimmo uses this sense of conflict to explore the tensions between tradition and modernity that exist for children attempting to negotiate a balance between both. In this period, the negotiation of that balance becomes a common theme across both Irish and British literature for children that engages with and reimagines national mythology. In these narratives, which operate at certain points beyond what Alan Garner calls 'linear oral memory', the central figures access mythic time, 'where everything is simultaneously present' (205) allowing mythology and modernity to coexist through reimagination.

Myth, memory and community

The movement of myth into life and life into myth that Dunbar writes about becomes intrinsically and fundamentally linked to knowing and remembering. Because they cannot remember or recall what they do not already know, the child figures considered here cannot remember or recognize the significance of the mythic characters and events they encounter. Like Phelim Cu, they must first live through mythic experiences in order to gain the capacity to remember them. While there is a disconnection between these child figures and their mythological heritage, each of them operates within a society or community that retains the cultural knowledge or memory of that mythological heritage. Within these communities there is always someone who remembers. As anamnesis is experienced, these memories become available to be rediscovered, either through narrative or through emplacement in the landscapes of Ireland. Aristotle marks a difference between memory, the ability to retain and preserve the past, and recollection or anamnesis, the ability to recall the past.[3] For Plato, preservation and recollection are merged in anamnesis; human beings possess knowledge or memory from past lives and learning means rediscovering that knowledge within us.[4] In this way, knowing is the same thing as remembering. Though the child figures in these texts cannot initially remember what they do not know, their movement into experience and discovery functions as a rediscovering of knowledge, and of 'mythical memory' (Vernant 134).

As part of the examination of the ways in which the disconnection between the contemporary lives of these child figures and their mythological heritage is reconciled, this chapter investigates the function of the concepts of imagination and memory, especially in the context of reimagination. Imagination 'defines the experienced reality of memory' so that our sense of belonging to the past depends 'on not only remembering how things were, but constantly reworking that memory in the present' (Trigg xxv–xxvi). Imagination, then, is connected to the way in which we remember. The functions of memory and of the imagination can overlap (Warnock viii). In either imagination or recollection, 'we are thinking of something that is not before our eyes and ears' (75) so that in the act of recalling a memory or in the act of creating an image, imagining is linked to recalling and vice versa. Imagination and memory may both be thought of 'in terms of a kind of imagery or as a kind of knowledge or understanding' (75).[5] Paul Ricoeur notes the interconnectedness that exists between memories and images, asking, 'Do we not speak of what we remember, even of memory as an image we have of the past?' (44). It follows that reimagining is also connected to remembering because to reimagine something is to imagine it again, and, potentially, to remember it anew. The connection between memory and imagination and between memories and images allows for what is remembered to also be reimagined. The reimagined mythological narratives that structure these texts thus articulate the connection between memory and imagination. The mythic experiences these child figures live through have already been reimagined; each of the narratives from Irish mythology engaged with in these texts has been expanded through reimagination. So as authors in the late twentieth and early twenty-first centuries expand Irish myths beyond their original narratives, the child figures in these texts rediscover mythological and cultural knowledge. When this occurs, the jeopardized relationships between myth, selfhood, time and landscape addressed by more recent retellers of myth often find a new harmony, or at least a new resonance, through the treatment the authors attempt. The culmination of this project of recuperation more often than not takes the form of reciprocity of one kind or another.

Reciprocity, in social, civic, economic and cultural terms, is 'the principle and practise [sic] of voluntary requital, of benefit for benefit … or harm for harm' (Seaford 1). It concerns 'mutual dependence, action, or influence'[6] and often involves a recognition by one of two or more parties of the nature of the usually beneficial relationship between them. In ancient Greece it is to be found 'as an ethical value, as a factor in interpersonal relations … [and] as shaping the pattern of epic and historical narrative' (Seaford 1). By its nature, reciprocity is 'at the same time, one and many' (Bruni ix). It functions not only in multiple ways but also on multiple levels, in bonds and relationships that are 'joined with giving-and-receiving, taking-and-giving, going-and-returning' (ix). The Latin etymology of the word supports this; *reciprocal* comes from *reciprocus* or *reciprocaitate*, which means 'returning the same way, alternating'.[7] The word's association with going and returning is especially relevant to the analysis of the texts in this chapter, and the relationship between the past and the present in Irish children's literature. Within these texts reciprocal relationships exist between knowing and remembering, between landscape and culture, between the ancient Celtic world of Tír na nÓg and the modern Irish world, between mythic heroes and child figures and between myth and fantasy. Each reciprocal relationship offers the reader a structure through which to engage with these texts, and with the ways in which

Irish children's literature has engaged with mythology since the Cultural Revival. This is because, in a broader sense, the reciprocity between then and now, between the past and the present, has always structured the production of texts that engage with Ireland's mythological past.

Though Ireland is an old country replete with myths, it is also a country that is constantly changing. The modern experience, not just in Ireland but globally as well, encompasses the sense of a great distance from the past, a separation even. In their own ways, each of the texts examined here interrogates, confronts and attempts to resolve or reconcile a separation from the past. That resolution or reconciliation usually occurs as a result of an engagement with knowledge of the past, mediated through the physical and the cultural paradigms of the landscapes represented in these texts. To know the myths 'is to learn the secret of the origin of things' (Eliade *Myth and Reality* 14) so that knowledge 'means learning the central myth and endeavouring never to forget it' (107). If knowledge in the context of how Irish myths function in texts produced for children means learning and never forgetting, then the concept of memory becomes fundamentally important to the child figures in these texts; in these landscapes of Ireland, 'memory is the joint between space and time' (Bal 147). It is especially significant that the central figures in these texts are children or young adults as youth culture often functions as a kind of measure of the rate of separation from the past, as well as of 'the rate of erosion of traditional norms, values and memory characterised by modernisation' (Corcoran 93). Where memory is 'always embodied in living societies and as such in permanent evolution' (Nora 18), child characters and child readers alike need access points into the cultural narratives of those societies. In the texts examined in this chapter, such points are accessed as a direct result of movement through the landscapes of Ireland. The representations of landscape in these texts are connected to that idea of tradition and memory so that by endorsing the concept of landscape as a repository of meaning, these authors can use the experiences of their protagonists to make evocative statements about the nature of identity, culture and heritage in the Irish context.

These experiences are articulated through a series of movements between Ireland and Tir na nÓg, a series of movements that express the reciprocal nature of the relationship between these two spaces in Irish children's literature. In *The Hounds of the Morrigan*, Pidge and Bridget move sideways from the Galway they know into Tir na nÓg; they access the Faery world through a portal in a familiar landscape. In *The Singing Stone*, Kay moves back in time through a similar portal, finding herself in an Ireland where her knowledge of mythic history allows her to affect a dramatic course of events. In *The Fuchsia Stone*, the rural landscape of the west of Ireland holds both historic and mythic meaning as manifested in Cori's encounters with a supernatural race. In *Bog Child*, Fergus's movements up and down the mountain create a ritual pattern that allows him to access a primordial time, focused through the presence in the landscape of Mel, the bog child brought up out of the peat and out of the past. In *The New Policeman*, JJ's movement through a subterranean portal between the Ireland he knows and Tir na nÓg facilitates an exploration not only of temporality but also of the ways in which tradition and myth resonate in modern life. The reciprocal relationship between Ireland and Tir na nÓg deepens and complicates the ways in which these child figures engage with ideas and experiences of identity, memory and heritage. Landscape, then, is connected to experiences of time through mythic and folkloric realities.

Wilhelm Nicolaisen writes extensively on the notion and function of recounted time in folk tales, and specifically in Irish folktales. While recounted time must, by its nature, be 'removed into a past whose attributes … make it different from the present' (154), it is usually the future that concerns the protagonists in the folk tales in question, and the child figures in the texts considered here. These protagonists need what Nicolaisen calls 'anticipatory advice' (154) which will prepare them for that imminent future, and for the ways in which they must act in order to survive and achieve their goals. It is precisely this 'intensive prophetic rehearsal of the future' (156) that enables the central figure in most folk tales to deal with that future. By knowing in advance 'and by remembering that knowledge well at the right time' (156) the future may be encountered safely. Temporal and cultural knowledge then is fundamental to the success of the individual in folklore narratives. While the authors here engage, to some extent, with both mythological and folkloric traditions and with that idea of foreknowledge, the protagonists of their texts each suffer, at some point, from a lack of knowledge, from an inability to remember or to make connections between the modern world and the world of Faery or Tir na nÓg. This is despite the fact that the imagined landscapes of mythic Ireland interact with the geographic realities of the modern island most of these characters are growing up in. The imagined and the real landscapes that support these narratives become storied landscapes, shaped and influenced by the myths in which they feature so strongly. Fictional landscapes and the characters that interact with them 'allow readers the possibility of vicarious … experiences of … events that have profound effects' (Hua 135–6). Those fictional characters 'whose stories and memories are presented as part of an imaginary geography' (136) can further a communal understanding of past events. In this context, these events are mythological events which unfold in landscapes that are simultaneously real and imagined. In these texts, the child figures at the centre of each narrative are lacking a specific knowledge of Ireland's mythic past. This knowledge must be assimilated through mythic experiences, which occur either in contemporary Ireland or in Tir na nÓg. This means that this knowledge is mediated through the landscapes of Ireland.

The landscape of Irish myths and folk tales, 'whether in this world or the other … is the landscapes of the roads of Ireland' (Nicolaisen 156). This is precisely because, in a continual reprise of the universal hero's journey, in so many myths and folk tales the central protagonists must leave home in order to complete their quests and discover their real or true identities. Therefore, they must journey through Ireland, or, depending on the narrative, move into the Faery world of Ireland, Tir na nÓg. The landscape, the folk tale and the myth are intimately connected, and because children's literature very often concerns itself with the journey into identity or knowledge, in literature produced for children in Ireland, this connection becomes even more visible.[8] Within Irish mythology and folklore, then, 'spatial relationships are such that they create a familiar landscape immediately recognisable by Irish audiences' (156). In other words, readers recognize the landscapes of home in narratives that have been told for generations. In these landscapes of Ireland, layers of time are accessed through narrative. Within these texts place is continuous; Ireland itself is the common factor, a landscape that contains not only narratives of myth and folklore but their retellings as well. Myth and folklore, often mediated through childhood experiences and sensibilities, are expressed in this layering of time in one place.

This chapter focuses on the ways in which the landscapes of Ireland are represented in texts which engage with mythological and folkloric narratives, and which foster a reciprocity between mythic experiences and experiences of childhood. It also explores how these landscapes support the projects of preservation, recovery and reimagination of cultural heritage these narratives articulate. In these texts, key sequences of reimagination occur in which the central figures experience an engagement with a heritage that is simultaneously cultural, mythological and imaginative. In each narrative these sequences are emplaced in and draw meaning from the landscapes of Ireland, as represented and articulated by each author. These texts each engage with the reciprocal nature of the relationship between Ireland and Tir na nÓg, and the ways in which this reciprocity is expressed in the reordering and rebalancing of the lived realities of tradition and modernity. Out of different cultural contexts, and in different ways, these authors use the Irish landscape, in its physical, mythological and cultural paradigms, to preserve, recover and reimagine Irish mythological heritage. This is manifested in the ways in which landscape functions in literature produced for children in the late twentieth century, specifically literature that concerns itself with mythology and cultural heritage. In this period, an emphasis is placed, once again, on regaining lost cultural knowledge, and how this cultural knowledge becomes, once properly engaged with, a form of inheritance.

Pat O'Shea: Remembering, knowing and forgetting

The Hounds of the Morrigan by Pat O'Shea is a fantasy adventure set in Ireland and Tir na nÓg and centres on Pidge and Brigit, a brother and sister who must leave behind the Galway they know to journey into the Faery world and defeat the ancient Irish Goddess of War, The Morrigan, and her second and third parts, Macha and Bodbh. The text is significant within the larger discussion on the primacy of place in Irish children's literature in that O'Shea uses the relationship between Ireland and Tir na nÓg and the structure of the fantasy genre to explore issues of memory, identity and culture in Irish childhoods. A fantasy text is coherent that usually charts a movement from bondage through recognition to healing, where bondage represents a problem to be solved or overcome, recognition involves perceiving and understanding what has been revealed through the course of the narrative and how that may affect the protagonist and the fantasy world and where healing represents the resolution of the initial problem (Clute and Grant 338–9). Pidge and Brigit's journey into knowledge follows this movement from bondage through recognition to healing, and in doing so comments on the ways in which mythological heritage can be accessed through experience and through oral tradition. The children's passage into Tír na nÓg recalls the moment Seamus and Eileen witness the arrival of the mist from the bog into their garden before they begin their journey into the timeless space of the bog, past and present in *The Turf-Cutter's Donkey*.[9] In each case, the presence of the mist indicates transition, liminality and the capacity of the landscape it enshrouds to support mythic experiences. In fact, in both cases, the mist eases the transition between the landscape the children know and the temporal space they are entering. In this way, then, elements of the landscape support the movement from quotidian time into sacred time. Brigit even likes 'the way the mist roll[s] away in little puffs from her face as she breath[es] out' (O'Shea *The Hounds of the Morrigan* 134). Seamus and Eileen are aided by the Leprechaun who has befriended them, as well as a host of animals from the bog. Pidge and Brigit are initially guided by Serena the donkey (who recalls Long Ears the donkey from Lynch's text) and later by candles that appear and disappear as the children pass them. It is obvious to Pidge that 'the candles [are] there to guide them only; but not to guide anyone following after' (134). The landscape then and what the children identify as the natural magic of nature recognize the children and the integrity of the quest they have embarked on. Brigit asks Pidge if they are still in Ireland and Pidge 'wonder[s] before replying' (136). It is this moment of wondering that expresses the distance between the Ireland they know and the Ireland they find themselves moving through. Pidge says, 'I think we are; we must be I think' (136), but he cannot be certain.

In the early stages of the novel, Pidge and Brigit encounter an old angler who has previously hailed Pidge on the road to his home. He asks the two children about the name of Shancreg, the village they are heading towards and something about his question implies to Pidge that the old man has a knowledge of the area and knows that it is named for the 'old, old rock standing in the middle of one of the fields' (121). O'Shea's narrator informs us that once, they all stood upright in a pattern with one or two arranged as capstones, 'so the old people said' (121). Once then, these stones 'had a purpose and a meaning … but the knowledge of these things was now lost' (121). Though the stones are recognized as objects that have meaning, the community has been separated from that meaning through a breakdown in communal memory. The older people in the community hold knowledge about these stones. Were the stories that explained the stones' existence passed on? Or were they lost out of living memory? Why do children like Pidge and Brigit who are clearly engaged in the community not know more about them? What is significant here is that the implied criticism of children for not knowing their heritage that featured strongly in earlier texts such as *The Turf-Cutter's Donkey* (1934) and *Cuchulain and the Leprechaun* (1945) (see Chapter 3) has now shifted into a criticism of the wider community of people for not facilitating the transfer of knowledge effectively.

This seemingly innocuous exchange between the children and the angler foreshadows the children's engagement with the mythological figures they encounter in Tir na nÓg later in the narrative. Pidge and Brigit have been taught about these figures in school[10] and are thus capable of recognizing them but they do not understand their significance in Irish culture or how their myths function in relation to that culture. Just as they know the old stones signify something, the children know these figures are meaningful, but they do not know why. Though it is O'Shea's omniscient narrator who informs the reader of the stones' history, the information is framed within Pidge's own thought process, so we know that he himself is aware of what the old people say. And though Pidge and Brigit never regain the knowledge of what the stones once meant, arguably by interacting with the figures from Irish mythology they meet in Tir na nÓg, they re-establish contact with those 'ancient times' (121). Old knowledge may not be regained but new paths back into the past are forged, and the old stories are reimagined. In this way, they experience a recollection, through anamnesis of mythological heritage.

Before he leaves them, the angler muses wistfully, 'Could it be ... that you have ever heard of the name of Cuchulainn?' (123). This is a directly intertextual moment that looks back to the moment in *Cuchulain and the Leprechaun* when Cu as Cuchulain asks the shepherds gathered around the fire to tell him of his own heroic exploits. Pidge is able to tell the angler that Cuchulainn 'the Great Hero ... lived long ago in olden times' (123). Pidge and Brigit even know of Cuchulainn's prowess with weapons, and his skills as a warrior. The angler is delighted and quotes a prophecy he realizes has come true; that on the first day Cuchulainn took arms 'it was said that his life would be short, but his name would be greater than any other in Ireland' (123). Cuchulainn's name has been remembered and it is known now even to children who struggle with the significance of other figures in the canon of Irish mythology. Pidge tells the angler that he has often heard stories of the hero and that 'there are some in my schoolbooks as well' (123). Just like Seamus's education in Patricia Lynch's *The Turf-Cutter's Donkey*, Pidge's school life is influenced by the mythological narratives that structure Ireland's cultural heritage. Cuchulainn is the only figure in Irish mythology that both Pidge and Brigit have heard of before their journey into Tir na nÓg commences, yet they (and O'Shea's readers) have no way of knowing that the old angler is really the warrior from the stories they have heard. The old man narrates part of his story to the children, telling them that 'Cuchulainn spilled three drops of The Morrigan's blood' (123). Here it is Cuchulainn himself who tells his own story, again evoking the scene in Kelly's *Cuchulain and the Leprechaun* (1945) where Cu as Cuchulain [*sic*] hears his own history around a campfire. Cuchulainn exists now outside of his own myth. The children must move through their own story in order to gain an understanding of who the old angler really is. This movement, physically into Tir na nÓg and existentially into memory and imagination, is not only necessary for Pidge and Brigit to grow in understanding of their cultural heritage. It is a movement that allows O'Shea to chart the distance between the cultural memory of Irish myths contained within communities such as the one Pidge and Brigit are growing up in and the cultural resonance of those myths within the childhoods of Irish children.

As a goddess, the Morrigan is fundamentally associated with war and fate. She stands not only as a symbol of death but also as an active influencer of the outcome of war.[11]

The Morrigan makes her earliest appearance as an individual character in the stories of the Ulster Cycle within which she has a complex and often violent relationship with Cuchulainn. In the *Táin Bó Regamna* or *The Cattle Raid of Regamain*, Cuchulainn encounters the Morrigan as she steals a heifer from his territory, but he does not recognize her. Not realizing who she is, the warrior insults her. It is only when she transforms into a black crow that Cuchulainn perceives her true identity. He tells her then that had he known who she was he would have acted differently. Cuchulainn's lack of recognition has direct consequences for him. The Morrigan then foretells a coming battle in which Cuchulainn will be killed, telling him, 'It is at the guarding of thy death I am; and I shall be.'[12] In saying this, the Morrigan evokes sacred time and the present and the future are conflated. O'Shea engages with this idea of mythic sacred time in her narrative when Cuchulainn confronts the Morrigan in the Third Valley, the place to which she has pursued the children.

The two meet again during the Cattle Raid of Cooley where the Morrigan offers her help to Cuchulainn in the battle against Queen Medb's [sic] forces. When she is rejected by Cuchulainn she intervenes three times in three different animal forms in his combat against the invading army and is injured three times by the warrior. Later, she appears to him as an old woman and he heals her wounds, again without realizing who she is. As she thanks him for healing her, he says, 'Had I known it was you … I never would have.'[13]

These two instances speak to a traditional lack of recognition of the Morrigan's true identity, and of the consequences of not knowing or seeing correctly. The authors considered here all engage with this recurring trope of non-recognition to varying degrees, but O'Shea in particular uses it to demonstrate the complex meaning-making potential of the ways in which Irish mythology operates in Irish children's literature. Layers of ever-deepening interaction finally result in Pidge and Brigit realizing the full significance of the events they witness and the figures they encounter; experience leads to knowledge and remembrance. This realization reaches its zenith when they meet the Morrigan in the Third Valley.

The Valley itself is 'wild and broken and rocky' with 'waves and curls and writhings in the grey stone' (400) so that the physical surface of the landscape seems to both reflect and signify a deep-seated tension within the space. It is a 'blighted, savage and fantastic place' (400). Among the definitions of 'fantastic' is the idea of something not only originating in the imagination but being 'remote from reality'.[14] O'Shea uses the fantastic nature of the Third Valley to stage the final meeting between the children and the Morrigan, precisely because it is a liminal space, removed from reality and yet influenced by the mythic resonances that reverberate through Tir na nÓg. It is a heterotopia, a space that because of its barren otherness prompts the disguised figures who move into it to reveal themselves. Michel Foucault uses the term 'heterotopia' to describe places that are not only multilayered in meaning but also complex in their relationship to other spaces ('Other Spaces' 24). The Third Valley is a 'counter-site' within the larger space of Tir na nÓg where the connections that inform the relationship between that space and modern Ireland are 'simultaneously represented, contested, and inverted' (25). In the heterotopia the Third Valley represents, the children are threatened, not just by the Morrigan and her forces but also by the very landscape itself.[15] When the Morrigan and her second and third parts Macha and Bodbh appear, they have shed their real-world disguises and assumed their full mythological aesthetics. Their hair falls 'in great waves over their crimson-cloaked shoulders ... to ripple with strange life about their knees' (O'Shea 413). The language O'Shea's narrator uses in this section is elevated to an almost epic register as though to carry the weight of the women's mythological significance within the text. A cry of victory breaks from the Morrigan and the 'echoes of these cries fill[s] the second cavern and seem[s] never-ending' (413). The events which unfold in the Third Valley as the children are aided in their confrontation by the figures from mythology they have encountered and recognized on their journey demand to be related in the elevated register O'Shea uses. From this point on, until the children leave Tir na nÓg and return to their own world, the text essentially takes on the appearance and structure of a myth. The Seven Maines reappear to aid the children and they are 'comely and full of life and dressed in princely clothes' (413), in stark contrast to the more comical moment of their initial meeting with the children in a muddy field earlier in the text.[16]

The Valley becomes a transformative site as figures on both sides of the battle cast off their ordinary disguises or ways of being and assume the full mantel of their mythological selfhoods. The tension embodied in the physical geography of the location is also manifested in the conflict that rises between the Morrigan and the children's supporters, because in this space, things that have been hidden are made apparent as disguises are shed and true identities are revealed. When the children initially meet Queen Maeve of Connaught, she is lost in the form of the Poor Woman, an eccentric figure who has no memory of who she is, only that she has lost her sons and her heritage.[17] Her husband Ailill is her Gander who follows her everywhere. It is only in the Valley in the face of an old enemy that the warrior queen is restored to her true self. This speaks to the dialogue O'Shea stages among memory, selfhood and heritage. When the Poor Woman cannot remember who she is, she is ineffectual in her actions, and earns the children's pity. In the face of the ultimate threat from the Morrigan, she is brought back to herself, and to full knowledge of her heroic heritage. The children learn, and Maeve remembers, because learning and remembering are both part of the same process of engaging with mythological heritage. As the Poor Woman and her Gander run towards the children, their appearances change, and the Poor Woman becomes 'a tall proud one ... wonderful in her speed ... a straight red spear in her hand' (416). Again and again, characters that have interacted with the children in domestic, even ordinary settings and appearances are revealed in their full mythological contexts. The Valley itself, as a space that is hostile towards the children, seems to provoke transformation from the mythological figures they have interacted with. But there is more to these transformations than the simple shedding of disguises. O'Shea makes an explicit statement about the multiple ways in which mythology resonates in Irish culture and society. By having her central characters interact with mythological figures in a domestic and familiar context as well as in Tir na nÓg in an epic and formal register, O'Shea articulates the vitality of the mythological narratives she draws on. Cuchulainn walks the bog roads of Connemara even as he recalls the nature of his ancient relationship with the Morrigan. Though the warrior assumes the form of an old man, and the god and goddess of Love and the Hearth, Angus Óg and Bridget, respectively, disguise themselves as wandering vagrants, they are not diminished. They merely operate outside their mythic registers. In order to engage and communicate with the children, these mythological characters adapt and evolve. These are living myths, expanding and evolving within the structures of everyday life in Ireland.

The Old Angler is the last figure to transform in the Third Valley. His transformation is linked to his movement through the landscape of Tir na nÓg. As the children watch him in the smoke of a fire burning in front of them, he is 'running swiftly over vast distances towards them' (418) and the nearer he comes to the Valley and the confrontation with the Morrigan, the more he changes. As he runs, he becomes younger, until he is a youth in a white tunic carrying two spears, as well as a sword and sling in his hands, all evocative images of his position as the Hound of Ulster in his myth. O'Shea's narrator explicitly states that when Cuchulainn leaps out of the fire and into the Valley, there are seven lights shining in each of his eyes, and that there are 'seven lights shining around his head' (418). This is a direct reference to the idea of the hero light, the battle rage that shines above Cuchulainn's head in the heat of combat.[18] This reference is never fully explained or glossed within the text but the presence of the hero light resonates within the mythic register the narrative is operating in at that moment, and the reader is invited, like Pidge and Brigit, to recognize that the moment is significant.[19] The presence of the hero light still produces meaning within the text as it marks Cuchulainn out from the rest of the warriors in the battle regardless of whether the reader is aware of its connection to his myth. Cuchulainn is truly his mythological self, assuming the full extent of his heritage as he casts his disguise away. This is the only way he can meet the Morrigan in the Third Valley, in this hostile space within which the children are essentially trapped. It is Cuchulainn then who articulates the nature of the relationship between myth and reimagination in O'Shea's text, and in the wider context of children's literature produced in this period. When he tells the Morrigan that 'I am your enemy ... I was your enemy in the past ... I am still your enemy' (418), O'Shea encourages the reader to understand Cuchulainn's myth and the myths of others in the text as living texts. Because he has become part of Pidge and Brigit's story, his own myth lives on. It exists beyond and outside of the ways in which it has been told and retold. Just like the Seven Maines who are restored to their mother and, in coming back, move beyond their original myth, so too Cuchulainn finds a place in a new story.

The child figures at the centre of *The Hounds of the Morrigan* embark on a traditional quest to recover something that has been lost and to frustrate the return of an evil mythic force. While Pidge and Brigit display a certain knowledge of and a capacity to recognize the mythological figures they encounter in the course of that quest, their knowledge is far from comprehensive. The knowledge they hold seems to come either from books that Pidge has read or from their education in school. Their experiences in Tir na nÓg augment the knowledge they already hold, allowing them to not only complete their quest but also to appreciate their connection to the mythic past of Ireland. Because they engage with mythological figures who are, in essence, operating outside of their own myths yet still within the reality created by those myths, their quest speaks to the relationship between memory and imagination O'Shea is attempting to articulate, and to the idea that this relationship is expressed through reimagination and through the presence and resonance of myth in everyday life. Yet, for all that it is a narrative concerned with individual and communal memory, *The Hounds of the Morrigan* concludes with an act of forgetting.

Pidge and Brigit are the only characters in the texts considered here who do not retain the memory of their experiences when they return out of Tir na nÓg into their own world. When their quest is over and the Morrigan has been defeated, Angus Óg, the God of Love, makes the children forget. After Cuchulainn returns them to the Ireland they had left behind, the two look into Angus Óg's eyes so that his gaze holds them 'and with a wonderful, tender love he gently [makes] them forget' (460). The children do not remember but they retain a sense of what they have learned and experienced. O'Shea's narrator tells us that sometimes Pidge 'would see a frown of concentration on Brigit's face as she tried hard to remember something she couldn't name' and he would 'frown and try to remember with her' (461). The fact that O'Shea makes them forget but leaves them with a sense of knowing is a direct comment on the ways in which cultural and mythological heritage operates in contemporary society. The children retain 'feelings of *knowing*' (461) (emphasis in original) that they cannot explain but it is in this sense of knowing that the potential for their experiences to be recovered again abides. Through anamnesis, because they knew once, because they always knew, they cannot truly forget. If a 'dialogue of the spirit extended across history' can be conceived of, it then 'collapses the distance of separation in time' (Walsh *Anamnesis* 16). In this context, anamnesis becomes not the recovery of a past but a recovery 'of the present of a conversation that is perpetually available' (17). The capacity for recollection involves 'an awareness of what is already present as the possibility of the encounter itself' (17). If a similar dialogue across experience can be conceived of, then Pidge and Brigit's quest through Tir na nÓg becomes an evocation of Eric Voeglin's notion that 'we remain in the "in-between", in a temporal flow of experience in which eternity is nevertheless present' (326). Through anamnesis, through knowing, they remember, though they have been made to forget. The cycle of not knowing, of learning, of remembering, of forgetting and of remembering again turns in tandem with the resonance of heritage and mythology in Irish culture. The children are made to forget, so they can remember again at some point in the future; the feelings of knowing they hold indicate that a way back into memory is available for them. But just like Eileen in *The Turf-Cutter's Donkey*, they cannot always be remembering. Rather, the sense of knowing that remains with them not only augments their lives but also instils in them the urge to look beyond the everyday. They are made to forget but they 'try to remember' (O'Shea 461). O'Shea is not alone in using this conceit of mythic experience proving too much for mortal children to remember in full. In the conclusion to Susan Cooper's *The Dark Is Rising* sequence (1965–77), *Silver on the Tree* (1977), Will Stanton is the only one of the child characters in the series who retains a memory of the battle they have fought between the forces of Light and Dark. Even Bran Davies who is revealed to be King Arthur's son loses his memory of these events once he chooses mortality. He and the other children retain a sense of knowing, just like Pidge and Brigit, and a knowledge of a memory that is now gone. Once the conflict between good and evil is resolved, usually with the help of mortal children, the balance between the mythic and the domestic must also be resolved, though the former may still find ways to resonate within the latter. Pidge and Brigit's sense of knowing, even though it cannot be explained, becomes indicative of an impulse to look back into the past in order to understand the present, an impulse that influences the literature produced for children in Ireland in the latter half of the twentieth century. It becomes indicative of an impulse to remember.

Orla Melling: Time-slip, landscape and identity

This impulse to look back in order to move forward or to regain lost knowledge is a common trope in Irish fantasy literature for children in this period. It has been noted that British fantasy, and especially fantasy produced for children, has demonstrated 'an increasing awareness of the archaeology of Britain' and 'the age of its culture' (Levy and Mendlesohn 123). What is essentially 'the rise of the Matter of Britain' (124) functions as an enriching element in children's fantasy and also highlights the extent to which folklore and mythology have come to influence the genre. And just as British authors produce fantasy texts concerned with British mythology, Irish authors similarly engaging with mythology are attempting to articulate the Matter of Ireland. Orla Melling's *The Singing Stone* is part of a loosely connected series of novels engaging with Ireland's mythological past. Kay, the central figure, journeys back into Ireland's ancient past in order to discover her true identity. It is preceded by *The Druid's Tune* (1983), another time-slip narrative in which two teenagers from modern Ireland find themselves in Ireland's Iron Age where they encounter figures from Irish myth such as Cuchulainn, the Hound of Ulster and Maeve, Queen of Connaught. Melling addresses her readers directly in a preface that takes the form of an historical note. Here she bills *The Singing Stone* as 'a journey into the deep past of Cuchulainn's tribe, a tale of his Gaedil ancestors and the Danann gods of his people' (7). The idea of a deep mythic past is particularly compelling, especially in the context of an evolving body of literature that increasingly uses time-slip to interrogate issues of identity and heritage. Melling is essentially taking her readers beyond Cuchulainn's myth, into a past before it existed.

Melling goes on to say that 'history and myth are vague about when the Tuatha Dé Danann rule in Ireland' (7), acknowledging that some scholars maintain that the divine tribe never existed at all. She talks about her decision to set the last days of the tribe in the Bronze Age *c.* 1500 BCE to correspond with the fall of the acropolis of Los Millares in Southern Spain. Melling believes that this is the city, near Almeria, from which the Milesians, the sons of Milidh, sailed for Ireland. Many of the names and places that appear in Melling's narrative are taken from *Lebor Gabala*, the *Book of the Invasions*, which, according to Melling, 'records the pre-history of Ireland which had been passed down through oral tradition' (7). In this way, the preface speaks back to the ways in which authors such as Standish O'Grady, Augusta Gregory, Violet Russell and others used prefaces or historical notes to directly address their readers and provide a context for their specific retellings of mythological narratives (see Chapters 1 and 2). Like these authors, while acknowledging that hers is a fantasy narrative that engages with mythological elements, Melling claims a certain authenticity for the content of her tale, pointing specifically to her use of places and place names. Landscape then, and particularly the ancient landscape of Ireland, becomes a carrier of meaning and culture in this narrative. As Kay herself states during the opening section of the text, 'Each story is set around these ancient stone monuments … and then, at the heart of every story is something called "The Singing Stone"' (15). The stories she refers to here are myths from different countries, and the ancient monuments are megaliths, tombs and standing stones. These are, by their nature, embedded in the landscape, as Kay discovers when she begins to explore the rural countryside of Ireland. In this way, the Singing Stone, while standing as a symbol of Ireland's mythic past, and an access point to that past, also speaks to the capacity for landscape to communicate meaning and retain memory. As Edward Casey writes, 'Place itself aids remembering [by] being well suited to contain memories – to hold and preserve them' (*Remembering* 186). Kay asks herself 'could ancient stories answer [her] questions' (Melling 18) and in doing so speaks directly to the message Melling seeks to communicate through her narrative – that the past holds answers that are essential to the creation and experience of identity, both personal and national, in the present, and that through narrative, the past can be accessed and engaged with. Primitive rocks like the Stone are 'a kind of anachronism, an eruption from the past, resistant to change or evolution' (Trower 58). This is why the Stone itself is the only unchanging element in landscape Kay finds herself in once she moves into the past. Since the nineteenth century and before, geologists, folklorists and anthropologists have perceived that ancient stones and fossils 'provided a means to extend the imagined past back through time' (Knell and Taylor 94). Melling is not just attempting to set the stories Kay is seeking within a tradition, she is also seeking to set the Singing Stone itself within a wider geographical context that stages a dialogue about these kinds of monuments and their cultural associations. Megalithic monuments feature heavily in narratives of Ireland's ancient past, functioning as they did as 'social and cultural centres in Neolithic societies' (Freeland Thompson 49).

Having arrived in Ireland from America, Kay walks along the seafront in Bray, Count Wicklow, looking for a sign to direct her search through the Irish countryside. A sudden wave sprays the pavement under her feet with pebbles. Looking down she discerns an unmistakable pattern, 'a triple spiral whirling outwards' (Melling 21). This pattern is crucial within the context of Kay's specific quest, since she has drawn it herself on one of her maps as the outline of a trek through the mountains, and one of the possible paths she might take in search of the Stone. But the spiral itself is also a symbol associated with the Tuatha Dé Danann, with Celtic Ireland, and with the production of metaphysical meaning.[20] The spiralling path that Kay takes through the Irish landscape becomes a metaphor for the connection that exists between landscape and meaning in the text. Kay's journey towards knowledge is a movement that echoes Northrop Frye's assertion that the direction of meaning is inward. When we read, our attention moves outward, in a centrifugal direction as we go outside our reading, 'from the individual words to the things they mean' (Frye *Anatomy of Criticism* 73) or to our memory of what they mean. Our attention also moves inward, in a centripetal direction, where we try to discern the larger verbal pattern the words we are reading make. Kay's spiralling movement through the landscape mirrors the direction of meaning her reading has produced, inward and outward. As the spiral of her path tightens, Kay's senses become confused: 'Buffeted by the winds of the uplands, blinded by the dappled light of the river glen, smothered by the scent of green profusion she wander[s] in a daze' (Melling 23). Her physical state is viscerally affected by the landscape through which she travels, precisely because the purpose of this journey is to learn to read the landscape for knowledge. Melling's narrator states that as she moves deeper into the landscape, 'the silence of the hills [is] in her heart' and she is 'moving into timeless space as the endless flow of life eddie[s] around her' (23). Through the landscape of Ireland, that is simultaneously strange and familiar to her, she is beginning to access sacred time. Kay will go back in time and become part of a mythic reality because human beings access reality by re-enacting myths; 'for archaic man, reality is a function of the imitation of a celestial archetype' (Eliade *Myth and Reality* xiv).

Kay's movement back into Ireland's ancient past expresses the relationship between time and place that features so strongly in literature produced for children in this period, especially because she accesses that past through a portal embedded in the landscape itself. That portal stands 'stone upon stone … a massive dolmen, a colossal archway … a giant doorway' (Melling 25). She can tell 'immediately that she [is] in a different place' (25), just as Nial in *The Bell of Nendrum* instantly realizes that the landscape around him has changed. Yet again, for Kay, it is the time that is different, and this is expressed in the changes in the landscape around her. The 'same mountains [shadow] the landscape' but she now faces 'a vast and impenetrable forest' (26). The sudden presence of this forest not only indicates that Kay is now in a different time in the same place, it recalls the moment in Patricia Lynch's *The Turf-Cutter's Donkey* when Eileen and Seamus enter the primordial forest that stands where the bog will lie in their own time. In this new place, Kay has no choice but to explore and attempt to centre herself. In doing so, she meets

Aherne, a vulnerable young girl with no memory of her past or who she is. The two find themselves at a strange tower, where they meet a man known as Fintan Tuan, the keeper of the tower and the memories it holds.

Fintan Tuan is an example of a character in a fantasy text produced for children who operates with the weight of mythological heritage behind him. But while the existence of his textual and literary history provides his character with exactly that authenticity, Melling chooses to reveal very little of his true identity. Though her readers may or may not be aware of the significance of Fintan's place in Irish folklore and mythology, his presence lends a depth of meaning to Kay's story, hinting at a repository of meaning behind it, in the pasts of Ireland; his presence in her story speaks to the significance of the past in Irish culture and heritage. Kay herself recognizes Fintan from the books she has been reading, asking him directly if he is Fintan Tuan; her recognition speaks to his presence in the ancient literature of Ireland. The old man replies that this is but one of his names, implying that identity, like landscape, is multiple.

Indeed, Fintan Tuan features in James Stephens's *Irish Fairy Tales* as Tuan Mac Cairill, a man who remembers the first days of Ireland. In a sequence entitled 'The Story of Tuan Mac Cairill', Tuan recalls his past to an elderly man named Finnian who makes an explicit connection between the past and personal identity, saying 'a man is his past and is to be known by it' (Stephens *Irish Fairy Tales* 8). Though Finnian is asking Fintan for the story of his own past, the nature of Fintan's existence and the scope and depth of his memory mean that the story he relates encompasses the pasts of Ireland as well. Kay too is searching for the story of her past, and must journey back in time to understand it, just as Fintan does when he relates his memories in Stephens's tale. In this way, and in the fact that Fintan relates the history of the Tuatha Dé Danann to Kay and her companion Aherne, his character, both in Melling's text and in Stephens's, engages with the act of storytelling, and with the meaning produced by it, and by recollection. When Finnian asks Fintan to 'tell me of the beginning of time in Ireland' (Stephens *Irish Fairy Tales* 11), he is asking him for the story of his own past, which only he can tell, through memory. He 'remember[s] backwards through incredible ages to the beginning of the world and the first days of Eire' (13). In Melling's narrative, Fintan tells Kay about the trouble with time and its non-linear nature, explaining that he knows her both in the past and in the future, and that he cannot be sure who she is, because she is still in the process of becoming who she is. His presence in Melling's narrative allows the text to question the ways in which we engage with the past, and the ways in which we remember it.

Stephens ends his account of Tuan by stating that no one knows if he died 'in those distant ages' (31) when Finnian was the abbot of Movilla, or if he still keeps his fort in Ulster, 'watching all things, and remembering them for the glory of God and the honour of Ireland' (31). He represents then, not only in Stephens's tale and Melling's fantasy narrative, but in Irish mythology itself, the relationship between time, memory and place; he is, ultimately, one man recounting the entire history of Ireland as a story. As John Wilson Foster points out, the animal shapes Tuan inhabited are 'the chief animals in the bestiary of Irish mythology and denizens of earth, sea, and sky' (249). Within these shapes he retains a sense of himself and his memory but yet, 'he is at the same time not himself' (249), a figure both within time and outside of it, doomed perhaps to remember all that he sees. If, as Foster posits, he is both Ireland, 'the ancient and heroic nation … doomed always to remember', and also the 'adaptive nation transmogrified by successive incursions' (249), then his presence in Melling's narrative can only encourage the reader to question the experience of temporality, and the ways in which the past can affect the present.

When Kay and Aherne return to the tower, near the completion of their quest, they find it changed utterly. This change is linked to Fintan's own revitalized appearance; because his memory has been clarified, the structure that contains it, the tower, is now 'bright and alive' (Melling 166). The tapestries no longer hang lifeless from the walls, rather they flow 'like liquid colour, scene after scene breathed with life and sight and sound' (166). The hall is filled with the murmur of voices as the figures from the rejuvenated tapestries move 'within the clothes like actors across a stage' (166). The girls now begin to experience the narrative of the Dé Danann Fintan has already told them. As they step into the tapestries, they enter sacred time, moving back towards the beginning of the tribe's history, returning to the origin of things (Eliade *Sacred and Profane* 14). Kay calls the scenes the tapestries depict 'living pictures of reality' (166) but Fintan corrects her, saying, 'This is reality … in my tower all that unfolds in the passing of the ages exists here in unity … here the past, present, and future are one' (167), just as in the ancient forest Seamus and Eileen find themselves moving through in *The Turf-Cutter's Donkey*.

The three begin their journey through the cities of the Dé Danann tribe in Findias, 'the White City of the Hyperborean Lands' (167) where the Spear of Lug is forged.[21] On the sandy shores of seaside Murias they witness the turning of the Dagda's Cauldron, 'the treasure of charity and generosity' (169). In fiery, warlike Gorias, Nuada forges the Sword of War, the one treasure that was never lost by the tribe, and the weak link in its collection of creations.[22] In Failias, the race's central city, the girls and Fintan are part of a procession, 'all treading with quiet purpose' (172). For Aherne, a member of the Dé Danann tribe, it is a homecoming; she finds herself in the midst of 'her heritage and ancestry' (172) walking beside the leading figures from Irish mythology: Brigit the poetess, Niamh of the Golden Hair, the sea god Mannanan mac Lir (whose lost island features in Eilís Dillon 1952 text), Aengus the Ever-Young and his swans (Angus Óg) and Iarbonnel the White, prophet and poet, and Melling's narrator states that Aherne knows them all. During this moment of recognition, she comes to a realization about her own place in her heritage as she regains her true identity. She remembers who she is. Unlike Kay, who spends the narrative seeking knowledge, Aherne operates under a kind of amnesia throughout the quest. But crucially, it is only when she reconnects to her Danann heritage and culture that she can regain control over her own selfhood, just as Kay must look to the past in order to understand her present. In this place, Kay perceives the connection between 'every dolmen, menhir and henge, every mound and cairn, every temple and tomb raised up in the far-flung lands' (173). That connection manifests itself in a vast network of stone encompassing the world, 'a city beyond imagining' (174) so that Failias itself is everywhere, in all places. As Aherne realizes how her heritage resonates within her selfhood, Kay experiences a sense of the reciprocity that resonates between these landscapes, the memories of disparate communities and the experience of identity.

Jim O'Leary: Cultural memory and contemporary experience

The reciprocity between landscape and cultural memory is one that permeates the literature for children produced in Ireland during this period, especially in the 1990s when the country was beginning to experience a respite from the economic crisis of the previous decade and a surge in national and cultural pride.[23] Jim O'Leary's *The Fuchsia Stone* takes place over the course of a summer in the Dingle Peninsula where the novel's protagonist, Cori Duignam, is visiting her grandparents while her parents work abroad. The text is unusual in that it not only engages with and reimagines elements of Irish mythology, it stages a conversation between it and global culture, specifically the cultural mythology and history of Peru, and of the Inca civilization. It does so against a backdrop of modern-day rural Ireland, juxtaposing the historical against the mythological and against the contemporary, in a Dingle where ancient cultural sites are jeopardized by the arrival of film crews and tourists. Against this backdrop, O'Leary writes a fantasy narrative that works against the idea of a global heritage industry that 'sells the past to promote tourism and development, feeding … an appetite for things … restored and re-enacted' (Alderman and Inwood 186). Cori meets a host of Faery figures, the Tir Runians, the people of the Hidden Land, a race of people clearly connected, if not related, to the Tuatha Dé Danann, and their land, Tir Rune to Tir na nÓg. By staging Cori's adventure in terms of a dialogue or exchange between cultures, O'Leary is able to tap into the reciprocity that exists between myth and fantasy, this being one of 'one of interrelation and entwinement' (Fimi 5). This is because mythology and modern fantasy share structural and aesthetic elements, including but not limited to landscapes, characters and motifs (5). Fantasy then can be described as 'a modern genre … very much in dialogue with ancient and medieval mythological texts' (6). In order to comment on the relationship between culture and mythology in contemporary Ireland, O'Leary uses fantasy as precisely such a modern genre, operating within the context of ancient texts and artefacts.

The Fuchsia Stone of the title is an ancient artefact from the Inca Empire and its connection to Irish myth and to the Irish landscape is revealed as the narrative unfolds. O'Leary uses the Stone not only to interrogate the relationship between the past and the present in Irish culture but also to examine the role of youth and childhood in the preservation of that relationship. This is illustrated early in the text, when Cori initially discovers the Fuchsia Stone in her grandparents' barn. The Stone reacts in an unprecedented manner when Cori makes contact with it. This strange behaviour is observed by one of the central characters in the narrative, an owl gifted with the power of speech. He connects the Stone's new behaviour with the fact that Cori is a child, as though a new generation might elicit new meaning from the Stone, distinct from the meaning produced by previous generations. This idea of meaning being created through the presence of artefacts connected to the landscape runs throughout the text, reinforcing the connections between past and present in Irish life. Generations are connected through mythic experiences. Cori's grandfather maintains that he saw one of the Sídhe, the fairy folk of Ireland, when he was younger, as did Cori's father. There is a heritage within Cori's family, a heritage constituted by these mythic experiences and by moments of contact with the Faery world. It is also worth noting that each of these generational encounters occur during childhood. O'Leary is clearly making a connection between childhood and mythic encounters and this is crucial to the message that this narrative and others considered here support; that child figures not only benefit from the influence of the mythological past in the present in Irish life, they, by engaging with that past through objects such as the Fuchsia Stone, enrich their own present with new meaning.

The Celtic calendar structures many of the mythic experiences that occur in these texts; the passing of time in the Faery worlds accessed by these child figures tends to follow that particular seasonal structure and often, festivals or key dates in this ancient system have significant meaning or consequence in the Irelands these children call home. Cori discovers the Fuchsia Stone on the eve of Beltain, a festival she has never heard of; she must look to her new friends for information about the significance of the festival.[24] She is told that it 'goes back into the past ... long before Christianity' and that there are 'other festivals that birds and animals follow ... they mark the seasons of the year' (O'Leary *Fuchsia Stone* 24). A connection is established here between ancient Celtic Ireland and the natural world, and a reciprocity between the two is continuously articulated as Cori's adventures unfold. Cori's relationship with the owl is indicative of this connection. For her, 'Celtic Ireland was an awful long time ago' (24), a statement which prompts the owl to bluntly tell her that she has a lot to learn, an attitude similar to that of the Leprechaun in Patricia Lynch's *The Turf-Cutter's Donkey* towards Eileen's lack of knowledge about the bog.[25] Like Lynch, O'Leary is using his protagonist's lack of knowledge not only to educate his readers but also to engage with what the notion of knowledge means in the context of cultural and mythological heritage. The owl informs Cori that '[her] education in these matters starts this evening' (24) at the celebrations that mark Beltain. The festival then, for Cori at least, becomes one of initiation into a wider experience of Ireland's mythic past, and its mythic present.

The Beltain celebrations also mark the moment Cori first comes into contact with the Tir Runians, the Faery element of O'Leary's narrative who, while distinct from the Tuatha Dé Danann, clearly recall those mythic figures, from their aesthetic features to their history of exile. At the clearing where the animals have gathered to celebrate, the focus of attention is centred on a rock directly in front of her, but Cori can see nothing. When she makes a flippant comment about the nature of the gathering, a voice asks her 'who speaks of the Wild Geese, heroes of the land called Éireann' (29), and it is only when Cori identifies herself that Shimlyng, one of the Tir Runian princes, 'as though from out of the rock … appear[s] directly in front of her' (29). Not only does this reinforce the connection between the Faery world and the natural world, in that Shimlyng almost literally appears out of the landscape itself, it also highlights the theme of perception. Because Cori does not know what she is looking for, having next to no knowledge of Ireland's mythic past, she cannot see what the animals are waiting for. In the context of Irish history, the Flight of the Wild Geese refers to the departure of Patrick Sarsfield's Jacobite forces from Ireland to France, as agreed in the Treaty of Limerick in 1691. The term 'Wild Geese' also refers to Irish soldiers leaving Ireland to serve in European armies in the sixteenth, seventeenth and eighteenth centuries.[26] It is a significant reference for a Faery character like Shimlyng to make in that it not only displays a knowledge of Irish history but also an awareness of the ways in which Irish culture has been shaped and influenced by such history and emigration. The fact that Shimlyng refers to the Wild Geese as the heroes of the land called Éireann also recalls the soldiers of the Fianna Éireann. As the legend of the Fuchsia Stone is revealed to Cori, it becomes apparent that the connection between myth and history in this narrative is a productive one; O'Leary uses the quest Cori must ultimately embark on to explore this connection and the relationship between the local and the diasporic in Irish culture.

Shimlyng begins to explain the history and origin of the Fuchsia Stone to Cori, expounding at length the legend of the first Incan emperor Manco Capac's brothers Auca and Cachi who represented on the Stone are.[27] According to that legend, both brothers were turned to stone and Cachi was entombed in a mountain.[28] The Stone not only records the legend, it commemorates it. Shimlyng tells Cori that two of Manco's tears, one for each of his brothers, are sealed in a tiny bulb, shaped like an oval pearl, which in turn is sealed in the stone. This looks forward to a moment later on in the text when Cori's tears will save another of the Tir Runian princes, through the power of the Stone. Crucially though, Shimlyng then begins to speak about his own heritage, and how 'long ago [his] people were forced to leave the land of Éireann and find sanctuary elsewhere' (36–7). Again, parallels are drawn with the Tuatha Dé Danann, and their eventual exile from the land they had conquered. According to Shimlyng, the Incas were not as fortunate; 'their land was invaded … their culture destroyed' (37).

This brings the Fuchsia Stone into focus as a relic from a lost civilization that must be interpreted if the heritage it represents is to be preserved and reimagined. Shimlyng himself states that 'to honour the Inca people we revere those items which they once also revered' (37). The Fuchsia Stone is also an artefact, an object of cultural significance. The Tir Runians' reverence of the object constitutes an imaginative engagement with it which holds the potential to return it to its former life. As Neil McGregor writes in his *History of the World in 100 Objects* (2011), engaging with such an object 'as generously, as poetically as we can' offers us the chance to '[win] the insights it may deliver' (xiv). At each of the Celtic festivals of Beltain, Lughnasa, Samhain and Imbolc, at chosen locations the Tir Runians commemorate the Inca nation. O'Leary is working here with the idea that even ancient traditions can be infused with new meaning and experience; essentially the Celtic festivals have no relationship to the Inca civilization, neither temporally nor culturally, yet precisely because these festivals are also rituals, their capacity to commemorate and represent moments of history, be they mythic or not, is magnified. Rituals, by their nature, combine elements of repetition and representation. The more structured the rituals are, the more dominant the aspect of repetition is (Assmann *Cultural Memory* 3). The more freedom the individual participant is allowed within the ritual, the more the idea of representation or re-presentation dominates (3). The Celtic festivals the Tir Runians observe are rituals dominated by representation, allowing them to both commemorate and celebrate not only their own heritage but also that of the Incan civilization. The element of representation also allows Shimlyng to re-present the narrative of that lost civilization to Cori. Ritual then becomes associated with knowledge and with memory. Shimlyng specifically connects the commemoration to the landscape of Ireland and its ability to support and retain moments and images of cultural heritage. He tells Cori that the abundance of the fuchsia shrub in parts of Ireland is a sign that the Inca people are content to have the Fuchsia Stone in the care of the Tir Runians; the fuchsia shrub originated in South America and thereby represents a connection to that lost civilization.

Cori embarks on a journey to Skellig Michael to locate the cell used by Brother Declan, a monk who harboured the Spanish soldier entrusted with the preservation of the Fuchsia Stone. Her quest constitutes an exploration of the connections between myth and history in the Ireland that Cori knows and in a wider national sense of the effect this connection has on the experience of culture in Ireland. O'Leary uses Cori's journey to Skellig Michael to explore these paradigms of myth and history and the ways in which individuals might use these to access cultural heritage. Cori herself states that they are looking for evidence of something that happened almost four hundred years ago but Shimlyng and Ruabawn, another Tir Runian, question her perception of temporality and of the linear nature of time and how it passes. In this way, Cori's journey to Skellig Michael becomes not only a commemoration of previous journeys but an engagement with the past and its capacity to influence the present. The Hermit, an ancient bird who gives Cori and her friends guidance ahead of the journey to the island, advises her to 'consider only the seasons and the inbetween' (O'Leary *Fuchsia Stone* 98). By attempting to move back in time in order to access knowledge, Cori is essentially revering the memory of her antecedents. The moment Cori finds herself in Tir Rune marks the peak of the novel's engagement with the mythic paradigm of the Irish landscape. The Hidden Land is just that, a land hidden within the Ireland Cori knows, existing within it and yet separate from it. It is, in the tradition of a heterotopia, a simultaneously mythic and real representation of the domestic space in which we live (Foucault 'Other Spaces' 25). Her presence in it, her admittance across the threshold that separates Ireland from Tir Rune brings her narrative full circle, and in doing so articulates the capacity for landscape to produce meaning and preserve knowledge in these texts.

Kate Thompson: Tradition, modernity and identity

Landscapes are comprised of palimpsestic layers, where the lived and imagined pasts of a particular community or nation are preserved 'like ... insect[s] in amber' (Carroll 133). The pasts and the presents of such communities can be connected by 'lapsed aspects of the physical landscape' (134), fallen spaces that expose forgotten layers of time in that landscape. These lapsed spaces 'illume the process[es] of history and memory' (Lowenthal xxiii) and are used in some of the texts considered here as points of intersection between the physical and mythic landscapes of Ireland where these processes can be interrogated. The souterrain JJ is led into by Anne Korff in *The New Policeman* is one of these points. Kate Thompson's text follows the adventures of JJ and his quest to recover the time Ireland has been losing by journeying into Tir na nÓg. His quest becomes a larger effort to restore the balance between tradition and experiences of modernity in Ireland. Thompson uses her fantasy narrative to bring what Brian Attebery calls 'the strange, the magical, the numinous into modern life' (4). Thompson can attempt this because fantasy provides both new contexts and new meanings for myth (2). Fantasy is thus a literary form that provides 'a way of reconnecting to traditional myths and the world they generate' (4). Every fantastic narrative 'is engaged in solving a problem or set of problems specific to the time in which it was written' (Tompkins 38). For Thompson, that set of problems involves interrogating the relationship between tradition and modernity, and how it is expressed through the interconnection between Tir na nÓg and Ireland, where each space is aligned with a particular temporal and cultural experience.

A souterrain can refer to an underground chamber or to a passage. It is a subterranean construction that can be both a container and a connection between two spaces, or between two places. In children's literature, 'damaged, submerged, and even subterranean spaces allow characters to reach out towards and to engage with the past' (Carroll 134). JJ reaches out in precisely this way, but instead of engaging with the historical past, he finds himself engaging with another paradigm of Ireland, a mythic paradigm, and with a different experience of time. In this context, the souterrain he enters refutes the linearity of time (Nikolajeva 2–10) by allowing JJ to move out of ordinary profane time, and into mythic sacred time (Eliade *Sacred and Profane* 14) where myth and the experience of everyday life become enmeshed. It is a 'geographically and temporally liminal' space, where the influence of the time-skin that separates Ireland and Tir na nÓg 'resonate[s] backwards and forwards' (Edensor 126) and facilitates a connection between myth and reality. If, within the larger pattern of imagination and reimagination that structures Irish children's literature, we see mythic and cultural heritage and lived experiences of childhood as distinct yet related strands, then spaces like the souterrain mark points at which those strands are spliced together and interwoven to produce a new image in that pattern.

The souterrain is a concealed or even secret space. Anne Korff seems to be the only person who has accessed the chamber for at least two generations.[29] She is more deeply emplaced in the landscapes of Thompson's modern and mythological Ireland than JJ is, even though she is originally from Germany. Because she stands outside the mythical and cultural structures of Ireland, she can perceive them with more clarity; she occupies the ethnographer's place in the landscape.[30] Anne's presence in the narrative articulates the idea that culture is revealed through patterns that are available to be discerned (Assmann *Cultural Memory* 224). Thompson uses Anne's presence in the landscape of Kinvara to decode and recode cultural and mythical 'systems of meaning' (Clifford and Martin 2) and to interrogate the capacity of the landscape to transmit cultural heritage and memory. The subterranean nature of the souterrain speaks to the depth of memory, heritage and history that is preserved within the landscapes Anne has accessed, and from which JJ remains disconnected. JJ is led to the souterrain by Anne and this illustrates the fact that knowledge is needed to negotiate the landscape, be that geographical, historical or cultural knowledge. This is in turn linked to heritage; JJ is disconnected from the deeper meanings the landscape holds because he is lacking the knowledge required to access it.

In the souterrain, Anne tells JJ that 'there used to be thousands of these all over Ireland' (Thompson *New Policeman* 133) but that very few are now left. She supposes that 'most of them are still there, somewhere' (133) but that the entrances have been blocked up and lost: they can no longer be accessed because no one knows they are there. The idea of the souterrains being lost is connected to this lack of access; even though the subterranean spaces themselves still remain, their existence has been overlaid by a veneer of modern reality that now complicates or even compromises experiences of emplacement in JJ's Ireland. There is a disjunction between the meaning held within the landscapes of Ireland and the ways in which these landscapes are engaged with by those who inhabit them. The souterrains exist within narratives of historical and cultural heritage, and yet have been disconnected from the sphere of everyday experience. Anne further tells JJ that some parts of the world house more complicated versions of the souterrain model – 'pyramids, catacombs, henges' (134), evoking the vision Kay has of the global nature of the Dé Danaan city of Findias in *The Singing Stone*. These historical and mythological monuments become points on a metaphorical map of world geography and culture. In this wider global sense, they function as images in a system of universal cultural heritage; they are ways of knowing the landscape. This further resonates with the description of the city of Failias in *The Singing Stone*. These monuments, and the subterranean spaces they house, are primarily associated with rituals of death and rebirth.[31] In this context, JJ's movement into the souterrain and out the other side through the time-skin marks a rebirth into a new engagement with, and a reimagination of, the cultural heritage of Ireland.

JJ can see no way out of the subterranean room, and when Anne points to 'the angle where the two walls [meet]' (Thompson 134) he can perceive nothing but solid stone. Anne then asks JJ if he 'really believe[s] anything is possible?' (134). It is only when he answers in the affirmative that she walks through the wall and disappears, clearly expecting him to follow her. So, JJ's imaginative capabilities and perceptiveness are linked to his ability to pass through the time-skin, which is as much an act of imagination as it is a physical movement. He now finds himself in a mythological time zone, a space he is not culturally equipped to operate in knowledgeably or safely. Anne warns him about the memory losses he is likely to experience, telling him not to stay too long. Before she leaves him, she says, 'Don't forget what happened to Oisin' (140). The wording of this statement is especially significant, given Thompson's emphasis within the text on the importance of cultural heritage, national identity and traditional narratives. Anne does not tell JJ to remember the story of Oisin, she tells him not to forget it, implying that the story should have a place in his everyday life or at least that it should reside in his recent memory. But JJ has either already forgotten the story of Oisin in Tir na nÓg or he never knew it to begin with. Either way, he does not yet realize its significance, either in the canon of Irish mythology or in the context of his own person circumstance. JJ knows three people called Oisin, but he can't see 'what relevance any of them [have] to his current situation' (140). Like other characters examined here, such as Seamus and Cu O'Callaghan, JJ does not understand or recognize the mythic resonances of the name. He is already operating within one of the lapses in memory Anne warned him of, a lapse in cultural memory. Thompson seems to imply that this lapse is endemic in wider Irish society. It does not occur to JJ to look back into Ireland's past, mythic or otherwise, for the knowledge Anne alludes to because he is simply not aware that the knowledge exists.

Like Seamus and Eileen in *The Turf-Cutter's Donkey*, JJ also fails to recognize Bran, the legendary hound of the Fianna's Fionn Mac Cumhail, when he encounters her on the other side of the time zone. The suffering Bran endures as she follows JJ's movements in Tir na nÓg articulates the relationship between bodily experience and emplacement in the landscape that permeates the narrative, as Thompson uses the dog's plight to highlight the breakdown that has occurred in the connections between Aengus's world and JJ's modern Ireland. This is a different incarnation of the mythological hound, and she stands in contrast to the Bran Seamus and Eileen eventually recognize in the bog. This dog is huge, and 'its wiry coat and long, fine muzzle [give] it the appearance of an Irish wolfhound' (149) but JJ has never seen a dog as broad and heavy as this one. The dynamic that existed between the children and the mythological figure in Lynch's narrative has changed in Thompson's text. Eileen and Seamus follow Bran to the ancient forest, but in Tir na nÓg, it is Bran who follows JJ, in a continuous and painful attempt to connect him to his cultural heritage, and to redeem herself out of her own suffering, which symbolizes the disconnection between tradition and modernity or between mythological knowledge and childhood in JJ's Ireland. The dog becomes a symbol of the compromised reciprocity between Tír na nÓg and modern Ireland. She is a familiar, even archetypal image, and one charged with heightened cultural meaning and mythological significance. But she has been damaged, just like the connections between Aengus and JJ's worlds. Unlike Seamus, JJ does not recognize Bran for who or what she is. He does not realize that her gender is a departure from Fionn's original myth where his hound was depicted as a male. Thompson uses this seemingly innocuous detail to highlight the fact that JJ does not know enough about Irish myths to question the ways in which they are reimagined. It is

Bran's injury which captures JJ's attention. The lower part of her leg is 'hanging on by a thin cord of skin and sinew' (149) and as JJ watches, 'a drop of blood [falls] from it and [soaks] into the dust' (149). The complex nature and experience of time in Tír na nÓg is expressed through Bran's suffering. Caught and suspended in sacred, mythic time, she cannot be healed, and she cannot die. Thompson uses her plight to articulate the vulnerability of Irish cultural heritage in the context of modern life and technological advances. Bran's suffering becomes a tangible symbol within the text of the breakdown of sacred time which is slowly beginning to occur.

It is only when Aengus tells him that Bran belongs to Fionn Mac Cumhail that JJ finally begins to recognize her. Despite the fact that he has already passed through the time-skin from his own world into Tír na nÓg, JJ is initially incredulous and states that Fionn is 'not real … just a character in a story' (191). He makes no allusion to Mac Cumhail's status in the mythological cycles and narratives of Ireland's imagined pasts; he can perceive no connection between the legendary warrior and the myths that are coming to life before his eyes. JJ finally cedes that Fionn 'might have been [a real person] once', but that this 'must have been an awful long time ago' (191). In making this statement, JJ unwittingly articulates the distance that stands between Thompson's vision of modern Ireland and the cultural heritage that has influenced and shaped the pasts and presents of the nation.

The direct cultural belief in mythic stories that suffuses *The Turf-Cutter's Donkey* has disappeared in this modern Ireland, and the tales of the Fianna have ceased, for JJ at least, to be myths. Though JJ and the wider cohort of Irish children he represents have forgotten the myths or at least lost their personal and cultural connection to them, Bran continues to follow JJ, limping after him always, attempting to prompt those memories to return. The mythology, in the traumatized and injured body of Bran, remains present, demanding attention even in its diminished state. JJ's apparent lack of cultural and mythological memory, his uninformed movement through the landscape of Tír na nÓg and the knowledge he gains from Aengus's stories prompt the reader to consider the ways in which mythology has evolved within and worked to shape Irish culture. The fact that Bran follows JJ relentlessly is significant in this context; she cannot find release from her suffering until JJ facilitates a rapprochement between the time-spaces of Tír na nÓg and Kinvara by fixing the timeleak. In reconnecting with his cultural and familial heritage, JJ allows Bran to die. As her body disintegrates into dust in the Kinvara souterrain, she becomes an image of the reimagination that must occur if modern Ireland is to be infused and reinvigorated with the creative potential of its imagined pasts. Bran can live a life of eternal suffering in Tír na nÓg or meet a release in death in Kinvara; the two spaces must exist in reciprocity with each other, if the cultural and mythological heritage so fundamental to both can be shared and reimagined. Bran's and Oisín's deaths are not only elements in an exemplary mythological pattern; the traumas their bodies endure articulate the experience of physical and existential emplacement on both sides of the time-skin. Under the immense weight of profane and sacred time, their corporeal bodies collapse and disintegrate into dust when they move out of Tir na nÓg and into Ireland. Oisin, the mythic hero, returns to the land of his birth only to find that hundreds of years have passed, and everything has changed.[32] He knows no one, and no one knows him. He is a stranger in his own land. The moment he touches the soil of Ireland, the Irish landscape, he disintegrates into dust. Beyond the experience of emplacement, the story articulates a particular anxiety relating to Irish identity and connection to the landscape of Ireland, where a concern about losing a connection to the land is augmented by the perceived power of the land to destroy or forget the figures that move through it.

With this remembered knowledge, JJ looks across the plains to the sea on the summit of Eagle Hill and is faced with the possibility of exile from his native land, as he realizes that he has been unwittingly re-enacting Oisin's story. It is only when JJ's awareness of Ireland's mythological pasts is awakened that he can truly begin to engage with the landscape he finds himself moving through; the memorialising capacity of the landscape of Tír na nÓg facilitates, articulates and requires 'the solidarity of memory and imagination' (Bachelard *Poetics of Space* 6).[33] Experiences of reality and imagination are connected within these landscapes by reverie, by the act of imaginative exploration. Emplacement occurs not only through physical emplacement but also through the solidarity of remembering and imagining. If 'imagination augments the values of reality' (3) and if a reciprocity exists between imagination and perception, then a similar reciprocity can be said to exist between Tír na nÓg and modern Ireland, between mythology and reality, a reciprocity that has been compromised by a breaking down of temporal borders. The connection between memory and time breaks down as place proves to be 'the more effective absorber of our past' (Trigg 12). Emplacement in landscape mediates our experience of time.

At the summit, from three directions, JJ and Aengus can see the 'the Burren Hills reaching into the distance, and on the fourth, the green plain with the sea beyond' (Thompson 297). Looking simultaneously in four directions, the group stands at the centre of a kind of compass, at a central point in the landscape. They not only survey a geographical landscape but also a temporal one, and look outwards from the mythological island of Ireland to where the horizon meets the sea. In his own world, in modern Ireland, JJ has visited this place many times. There is a duality then to his gaze; he has seen this vista from the other side of the time-skin as well. The hill of stones is a meaningful place in both time-spaces. In JJ's world, the beacons that stand on the opposing summits, 'both so tall they [can] be seen from the ocean' (297), are burial mounds that have never been excavated. In this world they are cairns, constructed from stones that 'speak of other years' (Basu 120). These monuments keep 'the fame of past heroes alive for future generations, preserving their memory in the landscape' (120). The cairns, standing in both Tír na nÓg and JJ's Ireland, commemorate multiple versions of the past. Just as our bodies 'retain habitualized [sic] patterns' (Trigg 12) produced and mediated through memory, imagination and experience, the landscapes of Ireland and Tír na nÓg reproduce patterns of habitation, mediated through images and sites of cultural heritage and memory. But as the scene on the mountaintop unfolds, it becomes apparent that when monuments become disconnected from their memorial narratives, their capacity to narrate the past is compromised.

JJ notices 'the figure of a man standing on the seaward side' (Thompson 297) of the massive cairn. Gazing out to sea, the man stands with the cairns and the landscape of mythological Ireland at his back. When he speaks about the effects of time in Tír na nÓg, An Dagda states that it is 'contaminating … all this. All that is left of us' (297). The nature of the Tuatha Dé Danann's existence, their eternal youth and their existential perspective, is tied to the landscape of Tír na nÓg; it memorializes their past, while they operate in a continuous sacred time where that past is ever present. An Dagda's presence on the hilltop, at the site of the memorial beacon, becomes a physical symbol of that sacred time; he is remembering the past instead of dreaming about the future. Consequently, the dream of that future is never articulated.[34] JJ asks An Dagda why he stays in that place, knowing as he does that the warriors he led into battle will now never return. The pattern of reimagination and remembrance has been interrupted; the Dagda cannot witness the return of his people, and narratives of their exploits cannot be accessed or retold. The rawness and depth of the emotion the stricken leader displays speaks to the proximity of the events Aengus narrates, though they may have occurred thousands of years ago, and implicitly challenges JJ's chronological view of Ireland's mythological past.

If Tír na nÓg is perceived as the land of eternal youth by the inhabitants of JJ's Ireland, and Aengus and the others refer to Ireland as 'the land of the dying' (Thompson 300), then Thompson is establishing a dialectic between the two time-spaces, a dialectic that is represented by Aengus and JJ's movements across and through the time-skin. The Dagda articulates the potential consequences of the timeleak by stating that the land around him is beginning to die; the inhabitants of Tír na nÓg are slowly beginning to perceive sacred time as profane, ordinary time, as time that is passing. Their temporal experience in the landscape is changing. Sacred time is 'time that does not age, time immortal and imperishable' (Vernant 130). Now, temporal experience must encompass a sense or an awareness of mortality. For Aengus's father, the landscape he surveys has become a 'ruined landscape from which life has ebbed' (Basu 120) but where the memory of the past is perpetually present. Because he is tied to that landscape, he cannot escape the past it commemorates. As Thompson points out, 'A thing is happening that has never happened' before (300); this new paradigm of time in the mythic landscape is conflated with the commencement of a negative pattern of degeneration. The passage of time is connected to dying instead of to living. The moment JJ asks Aengus and his father what happened on this open space atop the mountain is thus a hugely significant one within the narrative as it marks the beginning of a particular cycle of reimagination, for both JJ and Aengus. As the narrative of the Tuatha Dé Danann's defeat is retold, JJ begins to gain a true insight into the way in which time operates in Tír na nÓg, and how a collective cultural memory can continuously situate the past in the present, and in the landscape.

Just as JJ is about to play for him, in response to the narrative he has just heard, the Dagda recognizes that 'there might be a bit of the Sídhe' (300) in JJ after all.

Thompson uses this hypothesis, which will later be proven true, to explore the idea that JJ, because of his fairy lineage and his musical heritage, comes to represent, physically and existentially, the reciprocity between the spaces of modern Ireland and Tír na nÓg. So when he asks JJ to take his fiddle and play a tune for him, and for the lost warriors who constructed the beacon, the Dagda is asking him to play for his own ancestors, and to communicate, through reimagination and re-enactment, with his own heritage. In a way, JJ's upbringing and immersion in traditional Irish music have been a preparation for this moment, and the advent of his greatest challenge, 'to play with the lost tribes of Tír na nÓg and their warrior king' (302). His performance is not only an act of musical reimagination but also of commemoration. In this scene, music becomes a sacred experience as JJ closes his mind down and feels 'his soul respond and send his fingers and his bow to the strings' (302). He plays the slow air he chooses once through before he actually realizes what he is playing and 'remember[s] how it had come down to him, through his mother and his grandmother' (302). In this moment of remembering, his performance accesses the exemplary model of traditional music which has structured his childhood, through memory. As he plays the tune through again and again, heritage and reimagination are connected through his performance, and he gains a certainty that 'the other JJ Liddy, his great-grandfather, had learned it from the Sídhe' (302). The Dagda recognizes and identifies JJ's lineage from his performance, and connects him to his own son, Aengus Óg. It is Aengus's 'coming and going' (302), his crossing of the temporal boundaries between Tír na nÓg and Ireland that have ensured that the mythic heritage of the former is passed on into the latter, even though JJ must be awakened to an awareness of it. This moment in front of the beacon when JJ reimagines, re-enacts and reperforms his musical heritage creates a meaning that resonates throughout the narrative, and within JJ's own existence. He is 'the right boy' (302) that Aengus has brought to the top of the hill, and he is the hero who will save the worlds on both sides of the time-skin. Joseph Campbell writes that the 'composite hero of the monomyth', and the world in which he finds himself, suffer 'from a symbolic deficiency' (Campbell *Hero with Thousand Faces* 37). In JJ's modern Ireland, this deficiency is manifested in a disconnection from the mythological and imagined pasts of the nation. JJ becomes the hero who remedies this deficiency when he brings back through the time-skin 'the means for the regeneration of his society as a whole' (37). In a mythic context, a successful heroic adventure results in 'the unlocking and release again of the flow of life in the body of the world' (40). In this narrative, that flow is represented in temporal terms, and is ultimately capitulated by JJ's return out of Tír na nÓg and back into Kinvara, and the manner in which he fixes the timeleak.

Upon that return, it becomes apparent that JJ has evolved as a player, that 'something [has] happened to his playing while he [has] been away' (Thompson 401). His return, which 'is indispensable to the continuous circulation of spiritual energy into the world' (Campbell 36), into both worlds, in fact, marks the beginning of a new cycle of reimagination and re-enactment. He has gained an independence within the traditional framework the music provides. In the moment JJ begins to play a tune on his own, on his grandfather's fiddle, the musical and cultural heritage he has connected with in Tír na nÓg is reimagined into a modern context. When Aengus tells JJ to believe the things he remembers, even if they do not make sense, he is imbuing the myths of Ireland's imagined pasts with an authenticity and a cultural reality that JJ will consolidate by returning to a modern Ireland that has been restored to a sense of those pasts. He can only see the pattern of connections that exist between the Liddy family and Tír na nÓg in his own world, 'a world with a time scale' (402). It is only when the elements of the pattern are fitted together in a linear narrative that the pattern becomes clear, and the line of his lineage emerges. Memories connect us to specific places in space and time, and the more securely they are fixed in space, the sounder they are. Where a figure experiences or engages with a specific place, topography, memory and identity intersect (Waller 304). A sense of continuity in time then can be linked specifically to emplacement in a landscape, a fixed position in space. There is a relationship then between the way we remember landscapes and the way we remember ourselves in them (303). Bachelard writes that while we may think we 'know ourselves in time', what we actually know is a 'sequence of fixations' in space (*Poetics of Space* 8): what we know is a series of space-memories. Time and the patterns in which its passing becomes visible provide the context through which to view JJ's experiences in the landscape. Just as music becomes the medium of expression for cultural memory and heritage in the text, the movement of the figures in the text through the landscapes of Ireland and Tír na nÓg become 'vehicle[s] of expression for a relation with the world' (Trigg 5) on both sides of the time-skin. Through physical bodily experience, a reciprocity is created between the two time-spaces.

It is important, then, that JJ physically passes through the time-skin and into Tír na nÓg. His passage is not represented as a dream, but as a physical and temporal experience. Aengus and the other inhabitants of Tír na nÓg do not age because time does not pass; physical and temporal experience are fundamentally linked. If the body 'become[s] constitutive of the world' in physical and temporal contexts, then 'the world itself is possible only through the experience of embodiment' (Trigg 11). The parallel worlds of Tír na nÓg and of Ireland are constituted by and through the physical and temporal experiences of their inhabitants, because 'we experience time in and through place' (7). The movement of the body is not reconstituted with each new place the body enters into, nor is it restored to its original state. Our movement in and through place is an ongoing temporal, physical and existential experience which does not end and begin with the leaving and entering of a place. In that temporal context, 'moving through place means tracing an arc of time' (7). If we conceive of our selfhood as constituting a personal continuity in the past, and a sense of emplacement in the present, then the construction of identity is implicated in, and influenced by, our experience of time in place. So, the 'felt temporal experience of a given day is inextricably bound with the movements of the body' so that the temporal boundaries or limits of that day 'can diminish or expand in time according to the level of spatial activity' (7). The lived experience of figures like JJ and Aengus is linked to a temporal engagement with place. Thompson attempts a recovery, a rapprochement between the stories and landscapes of mythic Ireland and its modern counterpart, where remembering becomes a connective act that restores the balance between remembered heritage and lived experience.

Siobhan Dowd: Physicality, temporality and Myth

Imagining also functions as a connective act where it influences the engagement between the domestic and the mythic, or between myth and fantasy. Farah Mendlesohn argues that there are essentially four categories within the fantastic itself and that these categories are determined 'by the means through which the fantastic enters the narrated world' (xiv). In the portal-quest the reader is 'invited through into the fantastic'; in the intrusion fantasy 'the fantastic enters the fictional world'; in the liminal fantasy 'the magic hovers in the corners of our eye'; and in the immersive fantasy 'we are allowed no escape' (xiv). The texts considered here are all various combinations of the portal-quest and the intrusion fantasy, with child figures and mythological figures alike moving across the borders between Ireland and Tir na nÓg, usually through portals that are established in the landscape. Fantasy then, and particularly these categories of fantasy, provides the authors considered here with a structure through which they can explore the connections between modern Ireland and its mythological pasts. All, that is, except Siobhan Dowd, whose novel *Bog Child* features elements of both the immersive and the liminal fantasies. This text uses the fantasy genre to explore something beyond the connections between reality and fantasy or between the domestic and the mythic; it uses the liminal and immersive aspects of fantasy to articulate the lived relations between memory, time, landscape and the human body. It is set apart from the other texts considered because of its preoccupation with mythopoeia, the making of myths. If myths are 'either composite productions … or, where they have been molded [*sic*] into mythopoesis by an individual artist, they rest on a long tradition' (Slochower 19), they offer communities and individuals analogies to their experiences of existence. In Dowd's text, her central character Fergus occupies the role of the individual artist as he uses mythopoesis to help him explain the events of his dreams. Situated in the late twentieth century, *Bog Child* articulates a concern in Irish children's literature with the connections between myth and mythmaking.

Like the other texts examined in this chapter, *Bog Child* is concerned with landscape and with the ways in which figures move through it. Landscapes are at once 'geographic and historical, natural and cultural, experienced and represented' (Carroll 2) sacred and profane. They present, in all these dimensions and more, a 'spatial interface between human culture and physical terrain' (2). Meaningful sites within them, such as the Third Valley where Pidge and Brigit confront the Morrigan, the Singing Stone that takes Kay back into Ireland's past, the clearing where Cori meets the Tir Runians, the souterrain where JJ discovers the time leak and the cut in the bog where Mel is found in Dowd's text, are Alison Landsberg's experiential sites, points at which the individual can access the wider narratives of culture, history and mythology (33). These lost images or cultural memories 'lie in the unconscious strata' of the landscape itself in 'dark, rarely disturbed layers that have accumulated ... through the shedding of innumerable lives since the beginning of life' (Hawkes 4). Physical landscape is formed by a series of processes in time, just as metaphysical landscape is formed by 'the layering of events, myths, memories and associations' (Tilley 3) over time, generation after generation. There is an effective reciprocity then between the landscape that remembers and the figure within it that lives and discovers, a reciprocity that generates meaning, in physical and metaphysical dimensions. The experiences of the child figures in these texts are the products of this varied and multilayered reciprocity.

Experiences such as these, which constitute a continuous and recurring series of engagements with landscape, are especially relevant to Siobhan Dowd's treatment of landscape in *Bog Child*, and to her protagonist Fergus's particular relationship to the mountain, and to the bog at its summit.[35] Set in the 1980s in a fictional Northern Irish town, the novel unfolds over the course of a summer and depicts the effect on one family of the recovery of a small body from a bog. If an attempt to comprehend landscapes in 'their nuanced diversity and complexity' is to also to 'enter into ... experiences through their metaphorical textual mediation' (Tilley 25), then Fergus's dreams, and the imaginative narrative he accesses through his discovery of the bog child Mel's body, can be defined as such a metaphorical textual mediation: he engages with the physical landscape by moving through it, up and down the mountain, but he also enters into the metaphysical dimension of that landscape through his dreams, and by seeing the landscape through Mel's eyes. The higher Fergus goes, the more he sees, as verticality is ensured by the polarity of the mountain and the valley (Bachelard *Space* 17). His movements up the mountain 'bear the mark of ascension to a more tranquil solitude' (17) and into a state of imaginative reverie. Dowd uses this state to engage with the idea of communal memory and with the concept that different times or even eras can be connected through the landscapes in which they unfold. The emphasis within her text and in Fergus's narrative is not on national myth (the Cycles of Irish mythology do not feature in this work) but on the power of myth to explain the world – the human urge to tell stories. In the telling of the tale we are all one blood, and all our memories converge (Le Guin *Dancing* 30). In *Bog Child*, it is myth itself which comes to the fore, through the landscapes that Dowd depicts. Her narrative is an engagement with, and a movement beyond, boundaries and borders, in a landscape that should be defined by its contemporary social context, but in which time and myth are transcended by imagination.

It is significant, then, that Fergus first dreams of Mel at the site of her discovery, in the bog at the summit of the mountain, as he sleeps above the cut where her body is still partially encased. His movement into an imaginative reverie, an exploration that occurs outside of ordinary time, signifies the depth of his emplacement in the landscape of the bog; as he dreams, he is reaching out into the metaphysical landscape (Bachelard *Reverie* 2-3). In his dream, Mel is called 'the child that time forgot' (Dowd 15). She becomes, as the narrative unfolds, and Fergus continues to dream her back into life, a manifestation of sacred, mythic time in the mountain bog: time that does not pass, time that can be endlessly repeated. Mel does not grow, and she does not appear to change. Time cannot be measured against her progress out of childhood and towards adulthood. In the house she shares with her family, dust 'from the day before blows out of the east door every morning 'and the dead in the shadows at the back curve of the house [breath] again' (15). In this intimate, domestic space, the patterns of life, death, memory and reimagination are recapitulated within the daily existence of the family. The routines of their lives become, in a domestic sense, exemplary models so that each day in the house speaks to the days that have already passed, and the days that are to come. In calling her 'the child that time forgot' (15), Mel's father is implying that her life is lived outside of the ordinary, profane time of the family; he is emplacing her in sacred, or even spiritual, time.

In the darkness of their house at night, Mel's family sleep in a broken line, an image that becomes synonymous with the permeable border between Northern Ireland and the Republic of Ireland in the landscape of Fergus's present. Her mother is at the wall, then her father. A veil floats between her parents and herself; she is next in the broken line, followed by a gap, and then her brother Brennor, then another gap, and finally, the smaller children. In Fergus's dream Mel's voice tells us that 'wherever a gap was, it stood for a child that had died' (Dowd 36). The gaps in the line are meaningful, precisely because they are empty. They stand for something that was there once and is now gone. They are memory-spaces within the lived experience of the family's life. What was lost can be retrieved or recovered by moving into the gaps, by pursuing the memory, and by understanding the image. They 'dream as a family' (36): the gaps in the line work to produce meaning. Dowd uses this image of Mel's family to explore how the physical body can signify memory, and how the act of remembering and the passing of time can be focused through physicality. The history of the world unfolds through genealogies in that each generation 'has its own time, its own age, the durations, flow, and even orientation of which' (Vernant 120) may differ from all those that have gone before, or that will come after. As these times and ages pass, it is the landscape that endures. Fergus's connection with Mel can be described in terms of the phenomenon the second section of the text is named for: second sight. It is the faculty of 'seeing an otherwise invisible object' a vision of 'something far distant in space or time' (Brown and Burdett 90). Fergus's dreams of Mel constitute experiences of second sight within the text, a sight which is looking backwards, into the past. Dowd uses the physical landscape of Drumleash, and the metaphysical landscape Fergus perceives in his dreams, to establish a connection between him and the bog child he discovers, a connection that transcends profane time, and is perpetuated in sacred time. That connection is experienced through vision, and by looking into the landscape, and into the past it remembers.

A hierophany is any manifestation of the sacred that 'fixes the limits and establishes the order of the world' (Eliade *Sacred and Profane* 33): orientation is made possible in the world through the 'revelation of an absolute reality' (21). This potential for orientation can also be attributed to manifestations of or encounters with the mythic. A hierophany effects a 'break in the homogeneity of space', and in this break the world is constituted and reconstituted: a hierophany can be equated to 'a founding of the world' (21). The moment of Mel's discovery constitutes a hierophany in the mountain bog, and this break, in the earth and in time and in memory, becomes a fixed point, 'the central axis for all future orientation' (21) around which Fergus's life revolves from that moment on. In this place, Fergus brings Mel up out of the ground and imagines her back in to life. In mythic time, memory is recovered, and heritage is reimagined, and the cut becomes a focal point in the micro-landscape within which Mel is found. The liminal energy which radiates from the cut exerts a constant draw on Fergus; he returns to it again and again, repeating his journeys up and down the mountain as though re-enacting the moment of the discovery. If the 'manifestation of the sacred ontologically founds the world' (21) and the energies exhibited by edges like the cut in the bog contribute to 'the augmentation of becoming' (Casey 'Edge of Landscape' 104), then the place where Fergus finds Mel is charged with creative and imaginative energy.

Fergus's dreams of Mel may be understood as manifestations of an attempt to recover her narrative out of the past. But this recovery can never be completed, because an evocation of the past does not restore what is lost and gone (Vernant 120). Because Fergus cannot remember Mel, he dreams of her, and within the text, his dreams take on the function of memories. His dreams do not reconstruct or abolish time. They do not unite Fergus with Mel. However, these dreams remove the barrier that separates his present from Mel's, creating a bridge 'from the world of the living to the beyond' (121). Through dreams, memory and imagination evoke representations of the past. Recollection, or anamnesis, represents 'a radical transformation of temporal experience' and profane time, constituted by 'an indefinite succession of constantly renewed cycles' (121), is concluded, only by the process of recollection. But Fergus cannot recollect Mel; he can only dream of her as the cycle of his movements up and down the mountain which endlessly recapitulates his imagined memories of Mel cannot be concluded. To remember is to enable 'the end to join up with the beginning', and to win 'deliverance from becoming and from death' (129) by accessing sacred time. The contrary experience of oblivion is 'intimately linked with human time' (129), with profane time. But Fergus cannot remember, he can only dream, and so he engages more and more deeply with a landscape that seems to foster a reciprocity between his dreams and his daily life.

This reciprocity between his dreams, his life and the landscape in which he moves becomes all the more meaningful when Fergus's imaginative relationship with Mel is considered in terms of the *aisling* or 'vision-poem' (Moody, Martin and Byrne 542), precisely because the *aisling* stages a conversation between a poet and a woman who stands for Ireland. The *aisling* form, which is arguably a traditional Irish fantasy form, constructs a poem as 'an interview between the poet and a spéir-bhean (literally, 'sky-woman') who is Ireland' (O'Rourke Murphy and McKillop 39), just as Fergus engages in an imaginative dream dialogue with Mel. The similarities to Fergus's engagement with Mel are clear but it is the way in which Dowd subverts the *aisling* form that creates meaning within the text's dream sequences. Mel may indeed stand for Ireland, precisely because her body, like the sovereignty of the nation and the state of the border, is a contested object. Yet Mel is not a 'sky-woman'. She comes from the earth. And if Mel stands for Ireland, the fact that she is confused with a child only serves to subvert the form even further; in the *aisling*, Ireland is traditionally ciphered through a beautiful or elderly woman. But the idea that in British colonial tradition, colonized nations and their native populations were regularly made subaltern and infantilized enriches Dowd's representation of Mel even further. It contains both ancient and more modern representations of the construction of Ireland as a woman.[36] Mel stands for a new nation with an ancient history. Fergus's relationship to his Spéir Bhean is fundamentally different to the usual relationship the *aisling* poem is built on. He is not interrogating a female cipher of Ireland but attempting to reach a fellow participant in a conversation. Because of this his *aisling* becomes, rather than an interview, a dream conversation with a figure who comes to embody the connections between the past, the present and the future as expressed through the enduring nature of myth and landscape.

Fergus's engagement with the mountain, and the bog at its summit, is given meaning by virtue of the fact that it is a repetition of Mel's imagined engagement with that landscape. Through his dreams, Fergus comes to know the myth of Mel's existence, and of her sacrifice. Myths 'tell how … a reality came into existence', so a myth, then, is the narrative of a sacred reality as 'it relates an event that took place in primordial Time' (Eliade 5). Mel's narrative is a myth that tells how her 'fragment of reality' (5) came into existence. While her myth does not provide Fergus 'with an explanation of the World' (13) it gives him a way to see the world, and a way to be in the world. By dreaming her story, by recollecting the myth, and by re-enacting her movements up and down the mountain with his own, Fergus creates what Eliade calls 'an ideology of repetition' (xiii). Within this repeating pattern of coming and going, his movements are imbued with the potential capacity 'of reproducing a primordial act, of repeating a mythical example' (3). In moving away from the present and towards the past, Fergus is 'only separating from the visible world' (121) in an imaginative reverie. So, his reverie 'lingers … in the patinas of time and history, in the dreams of another place and another time' (Davidson, Park and Shields 30). Fergus dreams of Mel in mythic time: her reality has always existed, even as Fergus is dreaming her into life. Sacred time, then, is 'primordial, mythical time made present' (30): Fergus's discovery of Mel's body is the hierophany that founds the world all over again.

The perception of landscape vistas draws the eye ever outward, farther and farther from the near-space in which they are at first ensconced and recognised' (Casey *Getting Back into Place* 103). In order to perceive a landscape, we must recognize its edge: there must be a horizon that the eye can apprehend. The past, the present and the future are the temporal edges we seek in order to create a sense of continuity in time. We cannot look at or move in landscapes 'without an awareness of the farther bounds of our vision and motion' (106). But a vista is not only a view of a physical landscape: it is also a mental view, encompassing stretches of time or remembered events.[37] It is also a view of the future, and of things that may be achieved or reached in that future. Fergus sees back into the past, into Mel's present, as Mel sees forward into the future, into Fergus's present. Their second sight allows them to engage with these past, and future, presents. The narrative pattern Dowd creates is marked by recurring and recapitulated images seen through the phenomenon of second sight: images of an imagined past that echo in the present. Rur, a prominent figure in Mel's community, and Owain, a soldier on the border post that Fergus engages with, are both observed looking to the horizon, as though they are attempting to see into the future, or to understand their place in the present. Owain looks 'out across the emptiness' (Dowd 126) of the landscape he is ostensibly supposed to be guarding and feels no connection to it. He stands alone as a sentinel in that landscape and yet he wonders, in a manner which foreshadows his eventual death, if his absence from his post would be noticed. Within these recurring changing images is the conceit that the past is as close as the imagination can draw it.

Fergus's movements up and down the mountain lessen that temporal distance between the present and the past even more.[38] Journeys translate place into temporal terms and Fergus's movements tell 'a story of place' (Casey *Getting Back into Place* 274). On his runs he does more than merely return to the same place, time after time. Physical movements facilitate his imaginative reveries. Imagination and memory are constantly engaging with borders in Dowd's text, and with edges, and the relationship between imagination, memory and landscape is governed by the temporal edges of the past, the present and the future. Imagination 'takes us forwards into what might be', and memory 'brings us back … to what has been' (xvi). We experience 'what already is in place (xvi). Memory is drawn to the edge of the past, imagination to the edge of the future and the present, as experienced in place, is bordered and defined by both. If imagination projects us 'out beyond ourselves' and memory 'takes us back behind ourselves', then 'place subtends and enfolds us, lying perpetually under and around us' (xvi). In the 'ecology of affect' (Davidson et al. 26) that Dowd creates in the text, place supports projection out into the future, return into the past and emplacement in the present. If time is an artefact, a human construct and 'a linear time of our own making' (Casey *Getting Back into Place* 8) then we are bound to time and time is bound to us. Time itself 'has an obscure reality' in that it 'is conceived as taking place in the mind' (10). If time is a mental construct which we use to order our existence in the world, then the potential exists for the imagination to break free of the 'double-binding' (8) connection to place and time, and to access a mythical experience that exists outside of or beyond the temporal edges of the past, the present and the future. Fergus's dreams of Mel, experienced during his runs up and down the mountain, access such mythical experiences.

When Fergus first envisions Mel's death, he is not dreaming. He is imagining the scene. He sees the execution party leading her up the hillside with 'a terrible clarity' (Dowd 243), a clarity that has already been associated with looking into the landscape in the text. In this moment, Fergus's gaze into the landscape vista is a gaze into time. As he looks again at this imaginative scene, he is simultaneously remembering and imagining, precisely because a vista is a mental view of both remembered and anticipated things. In his dream, the only rite of sacrifice that is specifically articulated within the narrative unfolds. At the head of the lough, the execution party allows Mel to stop, to look at the 'hills cascad[ing] downwards' (311) out of the past, and into the future. In an image that recalls the day Fergus discovered her in the bog, a skylark rises up, climbing an 'invisible staircase' (311) evoking the imaginary line of sight Owain followed in the forest, while the narrative recalls Yeats's 'ancient winding stair' (*The Winding Stair and Other Poems* 4) and Kay's spiral journey in *The Singing Stone*. This moment of imaginative vision is the fulcrum around which the narrative turns, as Fergus experiences a myth-like perception of the landscape. He uses his dreams of Mel to orient himself in a landscape that is simultaneously familiar and potentially treacherous, marking the passage of time through his engagement with that landscape, creating a sense of continuity in time by reaching back into the past. We can expect to find meaning at 'the centre of clusters of meaningful symbols' (Frye *Anatomy of Criticism* 73). If 'reality is conferred through participation in the symbolism of the Centre' then that centre is a sacred zone, 'the zone of absolute reality' (Eliade *Sacred and Profane* 21). The road to the centre is necessarily a difficult one, precisely because it is a rite of passage 'from the profane to the sacred, from the ephemeral and illusory to reality and eternity from life to death' (18). Mel is the meaning that resides at the heart of these landscapes. Her body is at the centre of meaning in the landscape Fergus moves through, just as his dreams of her become the metaphysical centre around which his interior life turns. The track Fergus follows up the mountain leads to Mel, to the centre of meaning in the landscape, just as his dreams lead to an imaginative communion with her. Attaining the centre becomes 'a consecration': the profane existence of before, 'gives place to a new life that is real, enduring, and effective' (Eliade *Sacred and Profane* 162).

In Dowd's text, images of a mythological heritage are produced through an imaginative dialogue between Fergus and the landscapes he moves through. In 'narrative, events are given meaning through their configuration into whole' (Ricoeur *Time and Narrative* 24). The images Fergus replays in his mind as he runs are given meaning in the same way: by replaying them, he is, in fact, reimagining them, giving them meaning by configuring them into a whole. Mel's forgotten life is reimagined and recapitulated by Fergus, within his own life, and emplaced in the landscape that she once walked. These are images of an imaginative heritage that Fergus uses to emplace himself even more deeply into the landscape he knows he must eventually leave if the pattern of his life is to progress. The spools on Mel's fingertips are redolent of the spirals at Newgrange, in the Boyne Valley and, intertextually, evocative of the spirals on the pebble Kay finds in *The Singing Stone*. The backstone of the left-hand recess in Newgrange is 'dominated by three fine and large counter-clockwise-unwinding spirals of different sizes' (Ingalls Garnett 66). The use of spirals instead of circles within the structure points to the significance of direction and polarity. As a 'representational device' (44), a spiral can be read from the inside out or from the outside in: as a symbol which implies movement when it is interpreted, it 'can indicate polarity or direction of rotation' (67). Just as Kay's physical movement through the Irish landscape in *The Singing Stone* follows a spiral pattern that creates meaning, the spirals associated with Mel lead Fergus nearer to the enlightenment promised in his dreams. In the context of Mel's life, death, and re-emergence from the bog, the 'breathing' spirals, which can be reversed by 'rolling up the free tail of the spiral in the other direction' (67), evokes the movement between life and death. These symbols were connected to the movement of the stars and the planets and influenced by time as 'measured out by the invincible revolution of the heavens' (69). But 'reflection reverses the direction of that revolution' (69): reflection turns time back on itself. On the 'plane of reflection … the celestial clock is stopped' (69). Spirals, then, in the specific context of Irish culture, are images connected to the initiation of sacred time. The spirals carved into the right-recess roofstone at Newgrange would have been reflected and reversed in the mirroring basin beneath them, a basin that is now shattered. By reading, reflecting and reimagining the spirals, sacred time is initiated. Repetition of celestial and mythical paradigms plays a fundamental role in the way in which we perceive and engage with the world. The spools on Mel's fingertips are the archetypal images that connect Mel's existence to Fergus's if only in terms of a shared humanity: the spools on his own fingertips carry the narrative of his life within them. These spools echo Bachelard's poetic image (*Poetics of Reverie* 1) in that they connect Fergus to a primordial beauty '*that takes a lifetime to understand*' (emphasis in original) (Dowd 243).

Conclusion: Knowing, forgetting and remembering in the landscape

In these narratives, the central child figures experience movements into myth, movements back to myth and movements beyond myth, in landscapes that contain and articulate experiences and perceptions of Ireland and its cultural heritage. Cultural heritage and lived experience are connected in these landscapes and within them, meaning derives 'from the moment of intersection between … two elements', and 'all that follows in the wake of the intersection' (Casey *Getting Back into Place* 13). A particular variation of the larger pattern of reimagination perceivable in Irish children's literature occurs in these texts, where the landscapes of Ireland form the physical and metaphysical ground that joins together the elements of that pattern, that is, the mythical, historical and cultural narratives that are re-experienced and recapitulated through imaginative action. These landscapes form the foundation of this particular variation of the pattern. Through the centrality of landscapes in these texts, the pattern of reimagination connects key moments in each narrative that might otherwise seem separated by time and space. Moments of reimagination are articulated in time-places. These are specific sites in these landscapes: The Third Valley where Pidge and Brigit confront the Morrigan, Fintan's tower where memories become reality, Skellig Michel where Cori is able to access the past, Eagle Hill where JJ plays the fiddle for the Dagda and the bog where Fergus finds Mel's body. In each of these texts there is a movement between hidden and buried sites and high mountains, hills and vantage points. And in each text, these movements seem to correspond to an inner emotional journey of development for the central protagonists. Movement between low and high places is connected to revelation, both in the landscapes of Ireland and of Tir na nÓg; these are the places where hierophanies occur, where the sacred and the mythic become manifest.

These low and high places are highlighted as focal points in the narrative pattern, each creating a centre in the landscape where the past, the present and the future converge. The child figures in these narratives all go further into, and even further back into, these landscapes to experience reimagined seminal moments in the cultural, mythical and historical pasts of the nation. Landscape is the medium through which these experiences of childhood are articulated and through which images of cultural heritage are transmitted and reimagined. In a repeating pattern, the images that constitute a pattern change and evolve but are connected by the recurrence of central elements. There can be variations in the pattern, but different elements speak and contribute to the whole. To look at the patterns of reimagination in these texts is to recognize a series of connections between landscape, narrative, experiences of childhood and cultural heritage where each element is reimagined in order to preserve and produce meaning. These narrative patterns echo the ways in which these modern authors reach back into myth for inspiration, 'narrative devices that establish a relationship between the fantasy world and our own while at the same time separating the two' (Attebery 66).

There is another narrative pattern evident here, one of going back into the past to seek knowledge or to retrieve knowledge that was lost and of bringing it back to a present that can be enriched or rebalanced by it. Like the physical journeys undertaken in a geographic space, these metaphysical journeys undertaken in an imaginative space follow the pattern of going and returning – going into the imaginative landscape and returning out of it into the real world. The child figures at the centre of the texts considered here realize the existence of a parallel world, and in doing so engage with the cultural and mythological heritage these worlds contain. The myths that were formal narratives at the beginning of the century have become malleable, even more so than in the literature produced for children between the 1930s and the 1970s. If we can conceive of mythology 'as traditional narrative that allows people to discuss (not explain) preternatural topics' (Sullivan 78), we will be closer to understanding the general function of mythology in society, both now and in the near and distant past. This is also part of understanding the relationship between mythology and fantasy because fantasy narratives also concern themselves with the preternatural (78). In the period examined in this chapter, figures from myth and folklore can operate increasingly outside their own narratives as authors engage with the possibilities of postmodernity; myths and folk tales are taken apart, expanded out and merged with domestic stories of life and childhood in Ireland. Where once these myths were retold for children, now they operate within new stories produced for children. Figures from these myths become, in this new wave of retelling, characters just like any others – characters in a narrative carrying the weight and connotations of their mythic history behind them. They remain Ong's 'heavy figures' (69) characters who are memorable by virtue of their capacity to commit momentous deeds, and their history of doing such. Now, however, figures who were once fixed points in oral memory are given a new voice with which to engage with contemporary culture.

These narratives present and transmit images and moments of cultural heritage through representations of landscapes that are simultaneously situated in the physical reality of a knowable geographical space, the island of Ireland, and yet dispersed within the imaginative reality of a mythic space that is continually changing, constantly moving, continuously being renewed. The pasts, presents and futures of Ireland, in real and imaginative terms, are narrated within these spaces, through narratives that promote interactions with the meaning-making potential inherent in landscape – with the stories that tell these spaces. Within the larger pattern of imagination, reimagination and re-telling so prevalent in Irish children's literature, there is a recurring sequence of engagement and reconciliation to be found, if one knows where to look – if one can see how the child figures in these narratives move through the landscapes of Ireland. The acts of going and returning, of crossing over borders and crossing back again, are intrinsic elements in this sequence; by accessing these pasts, mythological, historical, cultural or even geographical, through the traditional narratives embedded in these landscapes, the child figures in these texts are afforded the opportunity to reconcile and reimagine the images of Ireland they are presented with.

The manner in which the child figures in these texts operate in the landscape of a physical and mythic Ireland is influenced by an awareness of mythical narratives and national history; this awareness is essential to their ability to progress through the environments they find themselves in. Pidge and Brigit are able to recognize the figures from Irish mythology they encounter but they do not necessarily realize the significance of their presence in the landscape of Tir na nÓg. Kay is actively searching for the knowledge that will restore her to her true identity and it is her knowledge of Irish mythology that allows her to negotiate her way across a violent landscape. Cori's engagement with the Faery world occurs because of her openness to learn about her own heritage. In JJ's case it is his lack of knowledge that nearly proves to be his undoing; unlike Seamus in Patricia Lynch's *The Turf-Cutter's Donkey*, he does not recognize the legendary dog Bran, nor does he appreciate the mythic significance of the tale of Diarmuid and Grainne. By contrast, Fergus crosses borders, historical and emotional, moving into a space that is simultaneously imaginative and dreamlike in order to resolve his own personal conflict and to gain a perspective, through the primordial past, on the state of the present. By examining these texts, it is possible to mark the convergence of themes that are central to the texts that have featured across this analysis – myth, identity, time and place – and this convergence occurs in the landscapes of Ireland. Towards the end of the twentieth century, and the start of the twenty-first, as the physical and cultural landscape of Ireland changes, these texts demonstrate how that landscape retains and preserves the myths that have unfolded within it.

CONCLUSION: DARRAGH MARTIN, PEADAR Ó'GUILÍN

The memory of the nation

At a lecture addressing ideas of nationhood and memory, delivered at the Sorbonne on 11 March 1882, Ernest Renan posited that a nation could be defined by its 'possession in common of a rich legacy of memories' (18). If this is true, how are these memories to be used in pursuit of national definition? Is it enough for the citizens of a nation to simply enjoy the material possession of the cultural and mythological memories that constitute their heritage, or must they be able to access and continue to make meaning from them? That is, should they be able to retell the stories associated with memory and legacy, and ultimately reimagine those stories into the contemporary context of their lives and their society? In examining the ways in which Irish mythological culture is retrieved, retold, remembered and reimagined in literature produced for children between 1892 and 2016, this analysis has been addressing those questions. The texts in this body of work share a common set of archetypal symbols (Frye *Anatomy of Criticism* 105) that articulate the presence of myth in Irish culture – landscape, identity, time and, metatextually, myth itself. Thus, they enable an engagement and an interaction with mythological narratives in support of understanding national and individual memory. Archetypal symbols like these function as communicable units. And because narrative is a ritual act of symbolic communication, the symbols connect one text to another across what consequently becomes a body of work (105). By using the archetypal symbols that resonate within the narratives of the cycles of Irish mythology, these texts repeat the paradigmatic gestures associated with those narratives (Eliade *Myth and Reality* 35) and through this repetition, reactualize the present time of those myths (Ricoeur *Time and Narrative* 106). The texts that have been considered here use these symbols to retrieve, retell, remember and reimagine Ireland's mythological heritage for a young audience.

If 'myth is a story one tells oneself in order to orient oneself in the world' (Assmann *Cultural Memory* 76), then myth is also a story that a culture or society tells itself for the same purpose. If a myth 'makes normative claims and possesses a formative power' (76), then a nation's mythology becomes a valuable inherited orientation point, a locus of heritage for each new generation. The changing ways in which authors writing for children engage with myth across the twentieth century in Ireland suggests this; as has been demonstrated, initially myths are retold or expanded for children, then they are increasingly interwoven into new stories until eventually child figures interact with mythological figures and events that are recreated or reimagined completely.[1] The myths examined here demonstrate themselves to be what Astrid Erll calls 'stories about a common past, which offer orientation in the present and hope for the future' (34). They might feature what she calls 'elements of an absolute past, of mythical time' but they might also 'deal with a relative past, with history' (34). In an Irish context at least, the evolution of engagement with mythology in literature produced for children bears out Erll's observation. The nation's myths, particularly in their various recuperations for a young audience, connect quotidian and mythical time, the profane and the sacred, the past and the future.

During the Celtic Revival, Standish O'Grady, Eleanor Hull and Augusta Gregory sought to retrieve Irish myths out of the nation's past and make them relevant again to the nation's cultural discourse. Both before and after the War of Independence, Alice Dease, Violet Russell, Ella Young, James Stephens and Padraic Colum repurposed and retold myths and folklore for a child readership in an effort to promote an awareness of their cultural heritage. In the middle of the twentieth century Patricia Lynch, Una Kelly, Eilís Dillon and J. S. Andrews used myth to highlight the need to remember and engage with the past in order to fully participate in the present. By the end of the twentieth and the beginning of the twenty-first centuries, Pat O'Shea, Orla Melling, Jim O'Leary, Kate Thompson and Siobhan Dowd reimagine myth as mythic experience for their characters, who must move into sacred time in order to access their mythological and cultural heritage. Myth is a weighted paradigm for considerations of belonging, selfhood, nationhood and civic responsibility, and each of the authors considered here use myth as a medium through which to engage with, and, perhaps more importantly, articulate the reciprocity between the pressing issues of their particular moment in time. These texts, and others that are similarly concerned with articulating issues of time, landscape and identity through myth, constitute a poetics of memory where what was once lost or removed or distanced from children's cultural discourse is retrieved, repurposed, remembered and reimagined as the ways in which authors, child figures and child readers engage with Irish mythology evolve. The texts examined here share a common ancestry; they inherit a body of narratives, characters, themes and motifs from the Cycles of Irish mythology. They converge on and resonate within centres of myth, landscape, time and identity. Because we can trace this inheritance from myths retold in the Celtic Revival to myths reimagined in the twenty-first century, these texts are signs of a lineage that connects Irish children's literature to the original iterations of Irish mythology.[2]

Mythology gives a society a structure through which to engage with the world, and through which to order its experiences in that world since time beyond memory. Myth constitutes an attempt at 'causal explanation, prediction, control … and every aspect of life is permeated by myth' (Donald 191). And landscape is embedded in Irish myth. Landscape is fundamental to Irish mythology, providing a unifying theme across centuries of retellings. In many ways, the landscapes of Ireland that are represented in the texts considered here function like Mikhail Bakhtin's idyll. Within the idyll, everyday life is grafted to a place to such an extent that 'idyllic life and its events are inseparable from this concrete, spatial corner of the world' (Bakhtin *Dialogic Imagination* 225) where generations upon generations have lived and where future generations will live. Within the chronotope, this 'spatial world is limited and sufficient unto itself' (225) and not necessarily linked to other places. But within this delineated space 'a sequence of generations is localized [sic] that is potentially without limit' (225). This unity of life is defined by a unity of place, a unity which is in turn defined by emplacement of life in a single place, as experienced by each generation. In the idyll, life is inseparable from place. Bakhtin argues that this unity of place weakens the temporal boundaries between individual lives and the collective life of the community, or 'the life of the various generations who [have] also lived in that same place' (225), just as folklore creates a link between the individual and the community. The same phases of life, childhood and old age, are experienced in the same places, 'the same grove, the same stream … the same house' (225), under the same conditions. This blurring of temporal boundaries creates the 'cyclic rhythmicalness [sic] of time' (225) that is characteristic of the idyll. This cyclical rhythm is also manifested in the landscapes depicted in these texts and is experienced by the child figures who are emplaced in them. Thus, this unity of place and life also applies to the narratives of cultural heritage that are generated and interpreted by each generation that encounters them; as stories are retold, characters, events and places that are familiar return to be reimagined. It is the act of reimagination which renews and revitalizes the unity between life and place, and which facilitates the blurring of the temporal boundaries between the mythic past and the lived present the child figures in these texts experience.

This unity between life and place is also experienced in relation to selfhood, given that place and time are the pillars between which identity is experienced (Trigg xiii). Through feeling at home or displaced in a landscape and perceiving a sense of continuity in time or being able to remember a past experience in a particular place, we construct a sense of self. This is because memory allows for the concept of the identical self, 'the person existing continuously through time' (Warnock 59). For nations, communities and individuals, memory is intrinsic to identity (McBride 1), and because much of a nation's memory is contained in its heritage, it follows that the two are connected; cultural and mythological heritage influences national and individual identity. Irish literature produced for children that concerns itself with mythological and cultural heritage operates within the nexus of place and time, offering child figures and child readers a discursive space within which to construct, experience and interrogate selfhood. This is because these texts, and the mythological narratives they engage with, do not present place and time as static realities or fixed points. Place always encompasses the memory of place, and time, whether sacred or profane, is always subjective. There is a lived relation between identity, place, memory and time (Trigg xxv). In each of the texts examined here, this relation is lived through mythic experiences and through movements into the past. The child figures at the centre of each of these stories live through mythic experiences that are both physical and existential in nature. This matters because if the body constitutes the way we move into the world, and memory constitutes the way we perceive ourselves over time in the world, then the physical and the metaphysical, how we move and how we see, together constitute our being in the world. The body and the memory work together in the creation of the identity, and so the mythic experiences examined here may be understood as creative events; through the physical and metaphysical aspects, they allow the child figures in these texts to construct and reconstruct their identities.

Thus, the physicality of child bodies plays a central role in experiences of emplacement in these texts. The body is the centre of experience (Trigg 17) and because experience is a key component in creating a sense of continuity in time, then the ability of the body to retain memory becomes fundamentally important to the construction of identity. If, as Trigg maintains, 'our bodily identity is shaped through being touched by the past' (xviii) then our bodily identity is also shaped by the landscape through and within which elements of that past are retained. Place becomes crucial to our sense of self; many of the central characters in the texts examined here either gain or augment a sense of self through engagement with the landscapes of Ireland and Tir na nÓg. The body becomes constitutive of the world and the world itself is possible only through the related experience of embodiment (13). This idea becomes especially powerful when we consider the movements of child figures between Ireland and Tir na nÓg, with each movement embodying those particular spaces, and making them possible. Myth enlarges ordinary or quotidian time and space (Ricoeur *Time and Narrative* 105) so that the connection between spaces like Ireland and Tir na nÓg is augmented when myth is retold and reimagined, especially into narratives centred on childhood experience such as those considered here.

As have I demonstrated, the act of retelling is akin to a ritual, specifically a narrative ritual. Each time a story or a myth is retold, it not only commemorates the retellings that have gone before but also looks forward to the possibility that the myth might be retold again in the future. In a retelling, the past, the present and the future exist together in one narrative moment. This is because rituals access sacred time and sacred time is 'a mythical time, not to be found in the historical past, an original time' (Eliade *Sacred and Profane* 72). Ricoeur suggests that there is a reciprocal connection between myth and ritual because it is through the intercession of ritual that mythic time is revealed to be the source of world time and human time (106). Rituals allow us to access a time that is broader and deeper than ordinary profane time. As such, rituals represent the reactualization of sacred events that took place in a mythical past (Eliade 68); rituals allow us to remake the reality of events that have already happened before. Participation in rituals implies emerging from ordinary temporal duration or profane time and reintegrating into the mythical time 'reactualized [sic] by the ritual itself' (71). I have argued that retelling has the same capacity for reactualization in that a re-telling of a myth reactualizes the reality of that myth. This means that we can access sacred time through the retelling of myths, where sacred time is 'primordial mythical time made present' (68). And because sacred time is 'indefinitely repeatable' (72) through the retelling and reimagining of myths, the reality of those myths is infinitely recoverable. The passing of profane or ordinary time is made possible by the eternal presence of the mythical event (89). Ritual and ritual acts bring mythic time and the profane sphere together (105). This means that the retelling and reimagining of mythological narratives in Irish children's literature, which function as ritual acts, constitute nothing less than the meeting of the mythic and the domestic in childhood experience.

The narratives contained in the Irish mythological cycles are permeated with themes of landscape, time and identity. The lives of individual figures such as Cuchulainn and Fionn Mac Cumhaill are used to articulate the connections between these themes and to emplace temporal and existential experiences firmly in the landscapes of Ireland and Tir na nÓg. Since the Celtic Revival, Irish authors producing literature for children have looked to the cycles of Irish mythology for inspiration and for mythological narratives that provide the means to interrogate the realities of Irish culture and society. From retrieving these myths to repurposing them, remembering these myths to reimagining them, authors writing for children have drawn upon a reciprocity between the concerns narrated by Irish mythology and the ways in which childhood experiences can be used to interrogate issues of selfhood, nationhood and belonging. This movement from retelling to reimagining, where the former restores myths into children's cultural discourse and the latter expands and integrates them into contemporary experiences of childhood, demonstrates the meaning-making potential of the cultural heritage that informs Irish children's literature. These are texts that retrieve, retell, remember and reimagine Irish mythology and communicate cultural heritage.

Two texts that articulate, in very different ways, the evolution of this pattern and the depth of contemporary engagement with mythology in Irish children's literature in the early twenty-first century are Darragh Martin's The *Keeper* (2013) and Peader Ó'Guilín's *The Call* (2016). The former explicitly acknowledges children's hands at work in the retelling and the reimagination of an ancient story, while the latter reimagines elements of Irish mythology and folklore into a vision of a dystopian and violent future. These texts serve as crucial exemplars of my conclusion, enabling a demonstration of the continued presence of the cycles of Irish mythology within modern Irish literature for children.

Martin's *The Keeper* (2013) is one of the returning stories in the chronotope of Irish children's literature in that it features a familiar mythological character (in this case, The Morrigan) who is reimagined into a new narrative. Martin's text is deliberately permeated with references to Irish mythology and cultural heritage. One character, Cathleen Houlihan is clearly a reference to W. B. Yeats and Augusta Gregory's seminal play about the state of the Irish nation, *Cathleen Ni Houlihan* (1902). Angus Óg makes an appearance as a teacher on the school boat *Eachtra* that will eventually bear Oisin to a confrontation with the Morrigan. Cathad is 'a cheery druid with long white hair that trail[s] along the forest floor' (159) who tells the children about *dinnseanchas*, 'the lore of placenames' (Martin 159), and teaches them how to communicate with the animals in the forest. He evokes Cathbad, the druid who prophesises Cuchulainn's warrior fate. No explicit allusion is made to the position these figures hold in Irish culture, folklore and mythology;

they are merely present in the narrative as signs to be read by readers who have the knowledge to interpret them. Just like Oisin, Martin's readers are asked to look further than the names that are presented to them on the page.

Oisin Keane is a young boy who becomes the Keeper of the Book of Magic and finds himself embroiled in a quest to keep the Book and its power out of the hands of The Morrigan. It is never articulated precisely why Oisin has been chosen by the Book, although the narrative hints that his grandmother has more of a connection to Tir na nÓg and its culture than Oisin realizes. Shortly after Oisin discovers the book in his grandmother's house, he finds a moment to examine it more carefully. It reminds him of the Book of Kells, which he visited with his class from school. No matter how he looks at it, he still can't read the writing on the book's pages. On the first page is a picture of a creature he does not recognize, 'something with the head of a deer, bird feathers and a coil-up tail like a snake' (7). Here again are references to education and recognition and the gap that exists between the two for children who function in the fantasy narratives produced in the latter half of the twentieth century. Though Oisin has seen the Book of Kells with his class in school, he is still no closer to understanding the wider significance of that text or the one in his hands. The narrative does not reveal the name of the creature he does not recognize; is this an assumption on the part of Martin's narrator that the implied child reader will recognize what Oisin does not? Or that this is a gap in their cultural and mythological knowledge as well? Just as Bran comes to life on the edge of the moonlit bog in *The Turf-Cutter's Donkey*, the mysterious picture in the Book of Magic opens its mouth so that its green tongue can change into letters in front of Oisin's eyes, until he's looking at an inscription. This time, however, the transformation does not result in recognition. Oisin still does not know what the creature is, and its identity is never revealed to the reader. Gaps exist, not only in knowledge but also in experience and Martin's narrative exploits this to make a particular point about cultural and mythological heritage; both can be reimagined but sometimes what is lost cannot be retrieved. It can only be recreated. The inscription the mysterious creature creates reads, 'For Oisin Keane, the Keeper of the Book of Magic' (7). In reading this, Oisin is placed in a position of power and responsibility, at least in relation to the Book itself and its safety, without knowledge. Oisin, like JJ in *The New Policeman* who does not remember the story of Oisin in Tir na nÓg, does not know the significance of his own name. He will have to journey into Tir na nÓg in order to gain the knowledge that will allow him to save his sister.

The scope of Oisin's knowledge or rather the lack of it is exposed when, having seen numerous ravens at certain points in Dublin city – in Eason's bookshop on O'Connell Street, on Daniel O'Connell's statue, on the steps of the Ha'penny Bridge and in the Powerscourt Centre – his grandmother asks him and his brother and sister if 'any of you have heard of the Morrigan?' (10). The ravens symbolize the protrusion of the mythic into the urban space. The rural spaces that define mythic experiences in the works of Patricia Lynch, Eilís Dillon, Pat O'Shea and Kate Thompson are structured by physical and geographical monuments of cultural heritage such as the bog, the lost island, the standing stones and the souterrain.

In Martin's work, the city of Dublin resonates with the potential for hierophanies to erupt; the environment Oisin is so familiar with now begins to function as a heterotopia.

His grandmother continues to question them, and it becomes apparent that none of them have heard of the Morrigan. She asks, in a moment reminiscent of the way in which Patricia Lynch's Leprechaun questions the nature of Eileen's education, 'Don't they teach you the old Celtic stories in school?' (10). Oisin's brother Stephen declares that 'they're all about silly swans turning into children or old guys falling off horses' (10), unwittingly mentioning his brother's namesake and the story that he should have a knowledge of. The children's father believes that 'Irish will be obsolete in a few years' (10). Martin is deliberately using this interaction to question the ways in which Irish cultural heritage and mythology is disseminated within the educational system. Oisin's granny's declaration that 'they never teach you anything useful at school … of course you haven't heard of the Morrigan' (10) sets up a direct opposition between her beliefs and knowledge of old Ireland and the ways in which the children have been unable or willing to engage with their heritage. Just as the children are about to board a train (that will eventually bring them to Tir na nÓg, though they have no way of knowing this beforehand), Granny Keane cautions Oisin to remember his name. Again, this guidance points to the gaps that exist between contemporary childhood experience and mythological heritage in Martin's text; of course Oisin remembers his name but he does not yet know the significance of it. He must learn before he can remember.

In a scene that recalls Pidge and Bridget's meeting with the Great Irish Elk in *The Hounds of the Morrigan*, Oisin finds himself in the presence of another elk. This encounter occurs in a forest filled with shadows that adversely affect the children's emotions, signalling the presence of the Morrigan in the environment. Oisin is on his own and running from the shadows he is afraid will influence his actions towards the Book when he literally crashes into the huge animal. This is the animal 'that Oisin hadn't believed was real' (168). Just as for Cu in *Cuchulain and the Leprechaun*, it takes direct experience to connect Oisin to the reality of the myth. The elk speaks to Oisin in the language Cathad has taught him and says, 'The Enchanted Forest welcomes you Oisin the gentle … you would do well to remember your name' (186). These are the same words his grandmother spoke to him before he found himself in Tir na nÓg and Oisin knows that he has 'been named after one of the old heroes of the Fianna, Oisin the gentle' (168), but he has no idea what this might mean. Again, just like Cu, he does not realize the significance of his namesake's myth. But crucially, Oisin does not repeat the story of his namesake. He returns to Ireland out of Tir na nÓg, changed yes, but not compromised. He is at once capable of remembering his experiences in Tir na nÓg and of incorporating them into life in the Ireland of his childhood. In this, his experience resonates within that of the myth; Oisin is credited with being the narrator of the Fenian cycle of Irish mythology (Berresford 189). The novel progresses and Oisin, his brother and his little sister are forcibly transported to Tir na nÓg where they and their new friends eventually confront The Morrigan in her latest manifestation. It is during this final confrontation that the Book undergoes a profound transformation.

The inscription on the inside cover changes to read 'for everyone, the Keepers of the Book of Magic' (Martin 234). In response to The Morrigan's attack, the Book grows, filling the cavern where the children are fighting her and her forces. Oisin tells the Goddess that 'the Book isn't good or evil, it's how you read it that matters' (234), hinting at the ability of readers to not only interact with texts but also to contribute to the meanings they produce. The children begin to write on the Book, and it continues to change. Some of its illustrations come to life and begin to fight The Morrigan's army. Eventually, the Goddess is defeated, and the children leave the cavern with the Book intact. As the novel draws to a conclusion, it is the Book's appearance that becomes even more significant. It returns to its normal size, and it bears the marks of the battle fought with The Morrigan across its pages. As well as being a repository of magic, the book becomes a physical record of the goddess's defeat. Each of the children involved in the battle against The Morrigan have written on the book; 'Caoimhe's smudges with ashgrass, Antimony's orange ink, tiny inscriptions in silver that Lysander had left at the corners' (256). The Book has incorporated the children's spells into its contents, suggesting that the children are not only the Keepers of the Book now, they are also its co-authors, actively involved in both its preservation and its reimagination back into Irish culture in a way that unites both Ireland and Tir na nÓg. In this way, *The Keeper*, like many of the texts considered here, stages a dialogue between tradition and modernity, and between the culture of Ireland and the concept of Tir na nÓg. Its central character, Oisin, moves from a position of very limited knowledge regarding Irish mythology through both domestic and mythic experiences into a place of communion with his own heritage. In a wider sense, the scene discussed above where the child readers of the Book of Magic are initiated as its keepers speaks back to the aims of the Celtic Revival – to recuperate Irish mythological heritage back into cultural discourse and to empower a new generation of readers to engage with heritage.

The Call by Peadar Ó'Guilín is, in the context of the texts examined here and their engagement with mythology through patterns of retrieval, retelling, remembering and reimagining, a radical narrative. The text not only reimagines key elements of Irish mythology, it also destabilizes those elements and offers readers of Irish children's literature a new lens through which to interpret Irish cultural heritage. Set in a dystopian Ireland, *The Call* follows a group of teenagers waiting to be 'called' into the other realm of the Sídhe, who, in this particular narrative, are a displaced and violent race. Once the teenagers have been called into this other realm, known as the Grey Land, they become prey in a dangerous hunt instigated by the Sídhe, which only a handful survive. In the Ireland of *The Call*, 'everything is old and everybody is old too' (Ó'Guilín 13). There is no renewal, there is no regeneration as each new generation is decimated by the Sídhe onslaught. Now Irish culture and mythology are a matter of survival and not an inheritance.

Ireland itself has been cut off from the rest of the world by the Faerie host; a curtain of mist, redolent of the Celtic tropes associated with the Irish landscape, isolates the island from even its nearest neighbours. In keeping with Ó'Guilín's project of subversion, here the mist that has been associated at various points in the history of Irish children's literature with perception and awareness is instead a sign of insulation and suppression. The mist that surrounds Ireland is not a protective phenomenon; it is meant to isolate the nation from the outside world. The Sídhe are intent on seeking revenge against the Irish people for consigning them to the dimension they now inhabit, a strange and warped version of Tir na nÓg where the landscape and atmosphere reflect the suffering of the Sídhe over generations. Heritage and mythological knowledge have been weaponized; the teenagers in Ó'Guilín's narrative speak the Sídhe language because knowing how their enemy communicates might one day save them. The central protagonist in *The Call*, Nessa, a young girl who battles the effects of polio in order to prepare for her Call, has a working knowledge of *The Book of the Invasions* and other texts from the canon of Irish mythology. As Ó'Guilín's narrator observes, 'Never has a generation of Irish children been so aware of its own folklore, especially as it pertains to the enemy' (Ó'Guilín 216–17).

Like *The Keeper*, Ó'Guilín's text makes both explicit and implicit references to Irish mythology. The presence of the Dagda as the driving malevolent force behind the Sídhe invasion speaks back against retellings of his myth that portray him as a god associated with nature, plenty and fertility. Antoinette, one of the teenagers who experiences the Call, surveys what looks like a field of cabbages, but these are human heads 'hundreds and hundreds of them laid out in a grid' (48). Their bodies cannot be seen but some of them speak to Antoinette as she runs through them to escape her fairy hunters. This evokes the narrative of the Seven Maines, the sons of Maeve and Ailill, and the arrangement of their heads in a field following a battle fought in honour of their mother. Pidge and Bridget encounter them in *The Hounds of the Morrigan* and the seven men are restored to themselves in order to defeat the goddess of war at the text's conclusion. This field becomes symbolic of O'Guilin's sustained project of subversion and defamiliarization.

Antoinette wakes in the Grey Land to see 'silver spirals turn[ing] sluggishly in the sky, brighter than the stars but weaker than the moon' (42). Spirals have always been associated with the Tuatha Dé Danann but here these familiar symbols that usually speak to the movement into sacred time are juxtaposed against an antagonistic landscape that works towards the downfall of the teenager attempting to move through it. Antoinette's first obstacle is a carpet of slicegrass which 'tears at the skin of any who walk on it' (42). The landscape does not support her movement through it in any way. She spits 'from the bitter taste of the air' (43). The visceral nature of her bodily reactions to the landscape collapse the traditional pastoral vision of Tir na nÓg, usually a space where child protagonists who cross over from Ireland achieve personal and emotional growth and gain a knowledge of cultural heritage and mythology that informs their lives once they return. Here, in the Grey Land, Antoinette and the others who are Called can only hope to survive. There is no return from the Grey Land, only escape. For perhaps the first time in Irish literature produced for children, Ireland and Tir na nÓg, here the Many-Coloured Land and the Grey Land, are set up in opposition to each other, instead of existing in a symbiotic relationship.

A conversation between Conor, a teenager whose pursuit of survival has comprised his morality utterly, and Ó'Guilín's Dagda demonstrates the extent to which his reimagination of Irish mythology destabilizes the traditional vision of the gods of the Tuatha Dé Danann. In the Grey Land, the Dagda wears 'a crown of gleaming bone over shining hair [and] his face seems to glow, like that of a god' (264). When he reveals his identity to Conor, he states, 'I am named Dagda' (264). Conor's response indicates that despite his extensive survival education, he still does not understand the race that he is dealing with. He asks, 'after the god? The one with the Cauldron?' (264). He does not imagine that he is speaking to one of the gods of the Tuatha Dé Danann. The Cauldron to which he refers, in most retellings known as the Cauldron of Plenty, is here associated with monstrous rebirth instead of fertility; 'we put in our dead and they crawl forth eager for battle again' (266). As the Dagda informs Conor, 'All of these people here ... have lived here since the beginning' (266). The Tuatha Dé Danann have been renewing themselves since the time of *The Book of the Invasions*, preparing for a moment in time when they can re-emerge into the Ireland out of which they were banished. Ella Young's Dagda from her *Celtic Wonder Tales* is a kingly yet rustic figure, exchanging witticisms with his son Angus Óg. He wears his divinity on his ragged sleeve and is intimately connected to the Irish landscape around him and to nature and the passing of the season. Almost a hundred years later, Kate Thompson's Dagda is still as deeply connected to the landscape of Tir na Óg yet caught and suspended in a cyclical review of his grief for his lost people. Neither of these figures look forward to the warrior king Ó'Guilín reimagines for his subversive narrative.

It is significant therefore, that *The Call* was published in 2016, the centenary year of the 1916 Rising, marking as it does the breadth of evolution of Irish children's literature from that point in the early twentieth century to the present day. Ó'Guilín subverts and defamiliarizes the essential components and figures of Irish mythology. Tir na nÓg is no longer an idyllic parallel version of Ireland; the Grey Land is a violent and hellish space, deeply affective in that it fuels the anger of the Sídhe race that must abide there. The Dagda, normally a benign if not benevolent force in Irish mythology, and in the narratives into which he is reimagined such as Pat O'Shea's *The Hounds of the Morrigan* (1985) and Kate Thompson's *The New Policeman* (2008), is here the leader of a race intent on violently regaining the land from which they have been banished. A novel published in 2016 that functions on the premise that the cultural well-being of the children of the nation, and therefore the future well-being of the nation itself, is under threat, asks to be read against Pádraic Pearse's declaration in the 1916 Proclamation that all the children of the nation would be cherished equally.[3] This is how far the reimagination of Irish mythology has come, reaching a point where authors like Ó'Guilín feel confident enough to destabilize traditional mythological narratives in order to initiate new dialogues about the experience of nationhood, in both a personal and a national sense. Commemoration and remembering are two parts of the same ritual. An event or an individual cannot be commemorated without being remembered. But commemoration also offers an opportunity to look towards the future, even as the past is brought to mind. In this way, *The Call*, like the other texts examined here, both commemorates the mythology that it engages with and projects it forwards into a future where it will be reimagined again.

This analysis has engaged with and attempted to articulate acts of retrieval, particularly in relation to the mythological pasts of Ireland. John Gillis warns that identities, which are sustained by remembering and memories, change over time and cautions against referring to both 'as if they had the status of material objects … memory as something to be retrieved' (3) and identity as something that can be both lost and found. Memory and identity are not fixed objects but rather 'representations or constructions of reality' (3), subjective rather than objective. Through myths that are retold and reimagined these representations and constructions of reality can be retrieved, precisely because the ways in which these myths are retold and reimagined also change over time and with each passing generation. Myth is 'an apparently universal consequence of elaborated language development' (Egan 33) which supports the concept of myth functioning as a means to allow a people or a culture to discuss things that by their nature necessarily reside outside the scope of ordinary experience (Sullivan 78). Mythic language is needed to describe and articulate extraordinary experience. The consequences of mythic thinking occur wherever people develop language, 'whether in oral societies … or … [in] children throughout the world as they grow into language-using environments' (33). The stories children tell and retell to each other constitute a storytelling community, precisely because their language refers to and represents the world and their experience in it (Maybin 3). Cultural memory and communal or national identity or at least the stories that constitute them can then be retrieved from the pasts of Ireland. While identity is connected to a recovery of the past, this recovery must always be ongoing because identities are the names we give to 'the different ways we are positioned by, and position ourselves within, the narratives of the past' (Hall 'Cultural Identity' 225). As decades pass and generational memory fades, 'looking back and remembering has to confront … problems of representation' specifically in terms of its 'relationship to temporality and memory' (Huyssen 1). This is because the forms memory takes are subject to change, and because memory is connected to representation. All representation, 'language, narrative, image', is based on memory (1). The past does not simply abide in memory; 'it must be articulated to become memory' (1). Memory, then, is the story of the past or the past articulated into story. The myths that influence the literature produced for children in the period considered here (1892–2016) articulate the past for new generations of readers, providing access to cultural memory that moves beyond generational limits.

In oral cultures, knowledge is stored in forms subject to constant repetition (Ong 140). In this context, narrative becomes fundamentally important to an oral culture because it can contain 'a great deal of lore in relatively substantial … forms that are … durable' (141). Aspects of the culture of Irish children's literature are still oral in nature, given the primacy of storytelling within it, and given the emphasis placed on the retrieval, retelling, remembering and reimagining of mythological narratives. Oral tradition functions without the residue written words create (Ong 11). In other words, without the tangible record print culture provides. So, when a traditional oral story, myth, folktale, legend or fairy tale is not being told or re-old, 'all that exists of it is the potential in certain human beings to tell it' (11). Oral stories reside simultaneously then in the collective memory of a community, and in the memories of individuals within that community. They only exist in the moment of their telling, and, in the context of the texts examined here, in the moment they are recognized and remembered by the child figures and readers who engage with them. Retelling and reimagining traditional and mythological narratives effectively brings them back into existence. This is perhaps why so many of the child figures in these texts experience moments of mythic apprehension where a new paradigm of reality is revealed to them; as they experience these stories, they move into sacred time, and into the myths themselves. In this way, these texts, from the early nineteenth century to the beginning of the twenty-first, become part of what Ong calls 'a line of continuity outside the mind' (39), moving from the ancient mythological cycles in all their iterations to the production of literature for children in Ireland in the twenty-first century. This is because of the primacy of oral narratives embedded in the lives of Irish communities across the decades explored here. As Ong writes, oral cultures and societies must 'invest great energy in saying over and over again what has been learned arduously over the ages' (41). This is why, from the retellings of myths for children during the Cultural Revival to the return of mythological characters like Cuchulainn, Aengus Óg and The Morrigan in the late twentieth and early twenty-first centuries, the propensity to engage with and reimagine myths exerts such an influence over the literature produced for children in this country. The child figures in these texts, and the child readers who consume these narratives, become 'younger discoverers of something new' (41). As the texts produced in the latter half of the twentieth and the beginning of the twenty-first century illustrate, these myths are living stories, extending beyond their original iterations to become integral parts of new fantasy narratives. The aims of the Celtic Revival have come full circle; Irish mythology is being retrieved, retold, remembered and reimagined within the narrative culture of Irish children.

NOTES

Introduction

1 By 'Irish children's literature' I mean literature produced (although not exclusively) for an audience of Irish children that articulates specifically Irish themes and concerns. For a more detailed definition of Irish children's literature see Robert Dunbar's article 'Rarely Pure and Never Simple: The World of Irish Children's Literature' (September 1997), pp. 309–21.
2 See also, Jack Zipes's *Fairy Tale as Myth/Myth as Fairy Tale* (1983); Maria Tatar, *The Classic Fairy Tales* (1999); Martha Hixon, 'Folktales Retold: A Critical Overview of Stories Updated for Children (Review)' (2007), pp. 196–9; Tadesse Jaleta Jirata, 'Children as Interpreters of Culture: Producing Meanings from Folktales in Southern Ethiopia' (2011), pp. 269–92; Sophie Masson and Elizabeth Hale, 'Mosaic and Cornucopia: Fairy Tale and Myth in Contemporary Australian YA Fantasy' (2016), pp. 44–53; Veronica L. Schanoes, *Fairy Tales, Myth, and Psychoanalytic Theory: Feminism and Retelling the Tale* (2016).
3 See also Stith Thompson's *Motif-Index of Folk-Literature* (1955) and Hans-Jörg Uther's *The Types of International Folktales* (2011).
4 See 'Text of the Convention for the Safeguarding of the Intangible Cultural Heritage', UNESCO Culture Sector, accessed 9 June 2015, http://www.unesco.org/culture/ich/en/convention.
5 Structuralism takes a different viewpoint, positing that the relationship between the signifier and the sign is arbitrary and open to disruption. Critics such as Claude Lévi-Strauss (1908–2009), Roman Jakobson (1896–1982) and Jacques Lacan (1901–1981) produced seminal texts in the field including *The Savage Mind* (1962), *The Framework of Language* (1980) and *Écrits* (1966), respectively, arguing that human culture must be understood in terms of its relationship to larger structures. This analysis does not engage with those principles.

Chapter 1

1 See also Philip O'Leary, *The Prose Literature of the Gaelic Revival, 1881–1921: Ideology and Innovation* (2005), p. 9.
2 See *Imagining an Irish Past: The Celtic Revival 1840–1940* (1992), edited by T. J. Edelstein, pp. xiii–xvii; and Nancy Watson, *The Politics and Poetics of Irish Children's Literature* (2009).
3 Authors like Patrick Kennedy, William Allingham and Thomas Crofton Croker had been producing collections of myth and folklore since the early 1800s. See Patrick Kennedy's *Legendary Fictions of the Irish Celts* (1866), William Allingham's poem 'The Fairies' in *Poems* (1850) and Thomas Crofton Croker's *Fairy Legends and Traditions of the South of Ireland* (1838).

4 Taken together, representation, identity, production, consumption and regulation complete a circuit of culture, a circular process of interaction and exchange wherein meaning is produced within a particular culture. See Paul du Gay, *Doing Cultural Studies: The Story of the Sony Walkman* (1997), p. 3.
5 See also Plato, *Meno* (2011), edited by R. S. Bluck, pp. 8–16.
6 See Liselotte Dieckmann, *Hieroglyphics: The History of a Literary Symbol* (1970), pp. 1–3.
7 In *Fables of Identity: Studies in Poetic Mythology* (1963) Northrop Frye writes that 'in searching for a new language of symbols' Yeats was merely 'fulfilling the Romantic tradition from which he had started' and that 'his Romantic values consolidated into a tragic mask' as his career progressed. See pp. 226, 236. This nevertheless points towards a certain Romantic vision of the poet's purpose in Yeats's work, whether it remained unfulfilled or not.
8 Seamus Deane, *Celtic Revivals: Essays in Modern Irish Literature, 1880–1980* (1985), p. 14. Deane writes that during this one hundred-year period, Irish writers found themselves struggling to deal with the histories of the nation, and with ideologies of the past that arose out of those histories.
9 Malinowski dedicates his 1926 work to Frazer, citing the anthropologist as both an inspiration and a guiding force in his research. For an account of Yeats's early engagement with Frazer see Warwick Gould, 'Frazer, Yeats, and the Reconsecration of Folklore' (1990), pp. 121–37. For an analysis of the influence of the various editions of Frazer's *The Golden Bough* (1890) on Yeats's later work, see pp. 122–53.
10 See Thomas Carlyle, 'The Hero as Divinity' (1840), pp. 8–50.
11 This seems to be a reference to Lugh's hound Failinis.
12 Lugh is a god of the Tuatha Dé Danaan, renowned for his warrior's strength and skill, and is Cuchulainn's father. See Patricia Monaghan's *The Encyclopaedia of Celtic Mythology and Folklore* (2014), pp. 297–8.
13 See Standish O'Grady, *Warder* (10 December 1892), p. 5.
14 Hull also published *The Boys' Cuchulain; Heroic Legends of Ireland* in 1910 with T. Y. Crowell and Company in New York for an American audience. The emphasis on Cuchulain's childhood remains, with chapters such as 'How Cuchulain Got His Name' and 'How Cuchulain Took Arms'.
15 See 'The Boyhood of Cuculain', in *The Coming of Cuculain* (1894).

Chapter 2

1 James Stephens is an exceptional case here and this will be discussed later in the chapter.
2 The Ulster Cycle is traditionally set around the first century CE, with the tales it contains unfolding primarily in the province of Ulster. It is a collection of heroic tales chronicling the lives of Conor Mac Ness and the hero Cuchulainn. The cycle reflects a warrior society and is written mainly in prose with the centrepiece being the *Táin Bó Cúailnge*, the saga of the Brown Bull of Cooley which sees Cuchulainn pitted against Queen Maeve of Munster and her army. The cycle marks some of the earliest narrative appearances of The Morrígan, during which she encounters Cuchulainn in numerous different guises. Some of the characters from the Mythological Cycle reappear, and though Cuchulainn in particular displays godlike qualities, the characters in the

Ulster Cycle are mortal, and associated with a specific time and place. Cormac Mac Art is a major figure in the Fenian Cycle, also known as the Ossianic Cycle after its narrator Oisín. Put in chronological order, the Fenian Cycle is the third Cycle, coming between the Ulster and the Historical Cycles. It chronicles the exploits of the hero Fionn Mac Cumhaill and his band of warriors, the Fianna.

3   Versions of the Cuchulainn myth such as those retold by O'Grady, Hull and Gregory – and later Rosemary Sutcliff's 1954 retelling, *The Hound of Ulster* – usually relate the story of how the hero, once known as Setanta, received his warrior's name by killing the hound of Cullen. These versions also include episodes from the *Tain*, that aspect of the Ulster Cycle that relates Cuchulainn's encounters with Queen Maeve of Connaught, and her desire for the Brown Bull of Cooley.

4   In her retelling Dease used a variation on the standard spelling of Cuchulainn – Cuchulin. This can be viewed as an attempt to distance her vision of the hero and his actions from contemporary images circulating within the cultural discourses of the Revival. Robert Joyce Dwyer uses the form Cuhullin in his ballad *Blanid* from 1879. In this earlier version, Cuhullin's expedition to the Isle of Man is actually a rescue mission – Blanid is waiting to be liberated. Curoi Mac Daire is painted as a treacherous man, and his death occurs as a direct consequence of his own actions. Cuhullin and Blanid are lovers who are tragically parted when Blanid is killed by Curoi's minstrel. Cuhullin is the archetypal hero whose intentions and deeds are noble. See Robert Joyce Dwyer, *Blanid* (1879). It is significant then that Dease chose such a unique spelling of Cuchulainn; Cuchulin remains recognizable, retaining a link to Joyce's hero yet clearly creating a distinction between Dease's hero and the Cuculain/Cuchulain of the O'Grady, Hull and Gregory retellings.

5   Na Fianna Éireann was originally founded in 1902 by Bulmer Hobson, a leading member of the Irish Volunteers and the Irish Republican Brotherhood. It was reconstituted in 1909 with involvement from Countess Constance Markievicz, the revolutionary nationalist and socialist. The organization aimed to prepare boys and girls to fight for Irish freedom by providing them with an Irish nationalist education and military training. The organization used the *Fianna Handbook* (1914) to emphasize the qualities of self-reliance, discipline, loyalty and trust, qualities also associated with Fionn Mac Cumhaillll's Fianna and the Red Branch Knights of Ulster. Between 1910 and 1916, columns for children and young people appeared in a number of nationalist publications: the republican newspaper *Irish Freedom* (1910–14), the Fianna articles in the *Irish Volunteer* newspaper (1914–16), the *Fianna Handbook* (1914) and the nationalist paper for boys, *Fianna* (1915–16).

6   The Champion's Share or the Hero's Portion is the largest and choicest cut of meat, served to the most celebrated and courageous hero at feasts and gatherings.

7   There is an issue with this translation. The Fin Glas river, which runs through County Kerry, is named for its clear water. Fin Glas translates roughly as Clear Stream. This issue highlights the precarious position of Revival writers such as Dease and others such as W. B. Yeats and Augusta Gregory, who were operating with little or no working knowledge of the Irish language, and yet striving to reimagine some of its most seminal narratives.

8   Maud Joynt's 1925 collection *The Golden Legends of the Gael* contained strong depictions of female characters such as Maeve, Deirdre, Grainne and Niamh of the Golden Hair, arguably influenced by the author's feminist ideals.

9   See Pat O'Shea's *The Hounds of the Morrigan* (1984) and Kate Thompson's *The New Policeman* (2005), discussed in Chapter 4, pp. 148–56, 166–76.

10 'Evoke' Definition, Oxford English Dictionary, accessed 7 November 2016, https://en.oxforddictionaries.com/definition/evoke.
11 'Evoking ... generates an enriched sense of the everyday, informing the current moment with a vivid consciousness of the past and its meanings. Actions and thoughts of the past and present are identified with each other through evocation, brought into reactive proximity where both may be transformed.' Luigi Fassi, Lucy Gallun and Jakob Schillinger, *Time Out of Joint: Recall and Evocation in Recent Art* (2009), p. 31.
12 See also Pamela Shurmer-Smith and Kevin Hannam, *Worlds of Desire, Realms of Power: A Cultural Geography* (1994), p. 59.
13 See Chapter 1, p. 41.
14 See Patrick Weston Joyce, *The Wonders of Ireland and Other Papers on Irish Subjects* (1911).
15 See Lebor Gabála Érenn, *The Book of the Taking of Ireland* (1938).
16 Violet Russell, née North married George William Russell (Æ) in 1898, and thus became involved in the artistic and intellectual scene in Dublin within which her husband was an influential figure. Their home in Rathgar became a meeting point for all those invested in the artistic and national future of the country. See Henry Boylan, *A Dictionary of Irish Biography* (1998), p. 384.
17 A similar event to this occurs in Patricia Lynch's *The Turf-Cutter's Donkey* from 1934, when two children, Seamus and Eileen, are present in a forest when a member of the Fianna sounds a horn that recalls their past, and the pasts of Ireland. Paired with Russell's narrative, Lynch's text, written less than thirty years later, becomes a depiction of another moment when the horn of the Fianna is sounded in a different landscape, and in a different time, part of a rhythmic pattern in Irish children's literature where familiar moments and images are reimagined into new stories. See Chapter 3, pp. 101–13.
18 'noetic, adj. 1 and n', Oxford English Dictionary, accessed 12 May 2017, http://www.oed.com/view/Entry/127626?rskey=5VL0ch&result=1#eid.
19 This idea of time passing differently is common in narratives, which engage with the faery realm or Tir na nÓg. In Patricia Lynch's *The Turf-Cutter's Donkey* (1934) when Seamus and Eileen journey into the past through the bog, only a night has passed in the Ireland they have left behind when they return. In Pat O'Shea's *The Hounds of the Morrigan* (1985) though Pidge and Bridget, the central child characters, spend many days and nights in the faery realm, or the Other Ireland, no time has passed in their native Galway when they arrive back home. In Kate Thompson's *The New Policeman* (2005) the traditional temporal disparity between Ireland and Tir na nÓg is problematized, precisely due to the connection between the two spaces.
20 Maria Tatar writes extensively on the relationship between fairy tales and their perceived or assigned audiences. The works of Basile and Perrault were designated by their authors as old wives' tales, told by governesses and grandmothers to children. Tatar goes on to note that fairy tales still 'permeate mass media for children and adults' (1999, xi); these tales are still associated with a child audience and have been for centuries. Charles Dickens propounded fairy tales as 'a kind of holy scripture' (xi) for children. Indeed, Bruno Bettelheim wrote that 'through the centuries (if not millennia) during which, in their re-telling, fairy tales became ever more refined, they came to convey at the same time overt and covert meanings' (*Uses of Enchantment* 5) communicating those meanings to both child and adult readers.

21 John Wilson Foster suggests that T. P. G. might be the Irish parliamentarian Thomas Patrick Gill.
22 T. P. G.'s Note to the 1906 reprint (Dublin: M.H. Gill), v.
23 Stephens may have taken the title of this episode from 'The Boyhood Deeds of Fionn', a medieval narrative belonging to the Fenian Cycle, the most important manuscript version of which is the Laud 610, first edited by German scholar and philologist Kuno Meyer in 1881.
24 See the works of such writers as P. W. Joyce (this chapter, p. 84), Eleanor Hull (Chapter 1, pp. 50-4), Augusta Gregory (Chapter 1, pp. 47-50) and Edmund Leamy (this chapter, pp. 82-5).
25 This theme is also woven throughout Susan Cooper's *The Dark Is Rising Sequence*; *Under Sea, Over Stone* (1965), *The Dark Is Rising* (1973), *Greenwitch* (1974), *The Grey King* (1975) and *Silver on the Tree* (1977). Will Stanton, one of the central protagonists, must go through various trials in order to be educated about and be connected to his mythological heritage.
26 This is distinct from what might be termed the King's Son's 'true' name, a common trope in fantasy writing where the knowledge of an archetypal or iconographic designator gives one individual power over another. An example would be Ursula Le Guin's *A Wizard of Earthsea* (1968) where Sparrowhawk's true name is Ged.
27 Charles Squire writes in his 1905 work on Celtic myth that

> dispossessed of upper earth, the gods had, however, to seek for new homes ... One section of them chose to shake the dust of Ireland off its disinherited feet, and seek refuge in a paradise over-seas, situate in some unknown, and, except for favoured mortals, unknowable island of the west, the counterpart in Gaelic myth of the British [Avalon] ... But there were others – indeed the most part – of the gods who refused to expatriate themselves. For these residences had to be found, and the Dagda, their new king, proceeded to assign each of those who stayed in Ireland a *sidh*. (133, 135)

See Charles Squire's *Celtic Myth and Legend, Poetry and Romance* (1905).
28 See previous discussion of the symbolism of myth in Standish O'Grady's work in Chapter 1 and in relation to Ella Young's *Celtic Wonder Tales* in Chapter 2.

Chapter 3

1 See R. W. Dudley Edwards and Mary O'Dowd's *Sources for Modern Irish History 1534-1641* (2003), pp. 133-4.
2 'FOUR COURTS RUINS'. *Weekly Irish Times* (1921-41), 8 July 1922, pp. 10. ProQuest, http://elib.tcd.ie/login?url=https://search.proquest.com/docview/522051301?accountid=14404.
3 See 'FOUR COURTS RECORDS'. *The Irish Times* (1921-current file), 3 July 1922, p. 2. ProQuest, http://elib.tcd.ie/login?url=https://search.proquest.com/docview/520388510?accountid=14404.
4 Collections such as those from Young, Dease, Russell, Stephens, Colum and others are examined in Chapter 2.
5 A Child's Book, *Irish Press*, 18 March 1937.

6 See M. West, 'Kings, heroes and warriors: aspects of children's literature in Ireland in the era of emergent nationalism' (1994), pp. 165–84.
7 Article 41 of *Bunracht na hÉireann* (1937) stipulates that the State recognizes the family as 'the natural primary and fundamental unit group of Society'.
8 The flat-topped mountain is a reference to Ben Bulben, which features so strongly in W. B. Yeats's poem *Under Ben Bulben* (1933). In it the poet references both the contemporary present and ancient Ireland, cautioning Irish poets and artists to 'sing whatever is well made, scorn the sort now growing up … their unremembering hearts and heads'. Elements of the poem are a warning that new generations are losing their connection to Irish culture and heritage. Eileen, one of Lynch's central characters in the text, will later speak to the importance of memory in everyday life.
9 See Mircea Eliade's *Myths, Dreams and Mysteries: The Encounter between Contemporary Faiths and Archaic Realities* (1975), 20. See also, Joseph Campbell's *The Hero with a Thousand Faces* (1993).
10 In Aboriginal culture, dreaming paths 'trace ancestors' movements across the land, connecting significant places and sacred sites'. See Anne Whiston Spirn, *The Language of Landscape* (1998), p. 119.
11 See Diarmuid Ó Giolláin, *Locating Irish Folklore: Tradition, Modernity, Identity* (2003), pp. 8–31.
12 See also, Patrick S. Dineen's Irish-English dictionary, *Foclóir Gaedhilge agus Béarla*, first published in 1904.
13 Lynch's preoccupation with colloquial dialogue and Hiberno-English syntax recalls Augusta Gregory's attempts to render the local dialect of Kiltartan into her retellings of Irish mythology.
14 Again, the image of the flat-topped mountain evokes Ben Bulben, the mountain near Sligo town which captivated W. B. Yeats, and which features strongly in Irish mythology, especially in the story of Diarmuid and Grainne.
15 See the allegory of the cave in Plato's *Republic, Book II* (2000), pp. 220–41.
16 See Yeats's *The Collected Works, Volume III: Autobiographies* (1999), p. 216.
17 For a detailed analysis of the Commission's remit see Mícheál Briody's *The Irish Folklore Commission, 1935–1970: History, Ideology* (2007).
18 The 24th October edition of *The Irish Statesman* contained a declaration from the then Minister for Education Eoin Mac Neill that 'the chief function of Irish educational policy is to conserve and develop Irish nationality' (200).
19 These included *Reading Time, Fact and Fancy, The Educational Readers, The Emerald Readers* and *Young Ireland Readers*, all published by the Educational Company of Ireland.
20 This was a series of children's books published by the Parkside Press.
21 See Bruno Bettelheim, *The Uses of Enchantment* (1976), and Maria Tatar, *The Classic Fairy Tales* (1999).
22 See Ursula Le Guin, *Dancing at the Edge of the World* (1989), p. 29.
23 In 'The Frog Prince' from the Grimms's fairy-tale collection, *Grimms' Fairy Tales or Children's and Household Tales* (1812), the princess plays with a golden ball that leads her to the pond where the frog prince of the title waits. In the Slavic folk tale 'Ivan Tsarevich and the Gray Wolf', the existence of a tree full of golden apples precipitates a quest. Golden apples also feature in the Norse myth of Idunn, the goddess of spring and rejuvenation.
24 See Miranda Green's *Animals in Celtic Life and Myth* (2002), p. 181.
25 See Eliade, *Myth and Reality* (1964), ix, 68.

26 In Eleanor Hull's *Cuchulain, the Hound of Ulster* (1909) the spear is known as the Gae Bolga, the Body Spear, and Cuchulain learns its use from the female warrior Scathach in Alba. Augusta Gregory refers to it as the Gae Bulg and attributes Cuchulain's possession of it to an episode involving two sea monsters in her *Cuchulain of Muirthemne* (1902). It is also mentioned as the Gae-bolg in Standish O'Grady's *The Triumph and the Passing of Cuchulain* (1918), and it is an essential component of the hero's armoury.
27 In one example, Patricia Lynch's *The Grey Goose of Kilnevin* (1940), the central character Betsy the goose and Sheila the child protagonist in the text meet Bridgie of the Swallows at the fair, which leads to a series of adventures.
28 In folklore, acquired knowledge of an individual's true name can allow that individual to be affected by magic. See Philip Martin, *The Writer's Guide to Fantasy and Literature: From Dragon's Lair to Hero's Quest* (2002), 134. See also K. M. Briggs, *The Fairies in English Tradition and Literature* (1967). Many fairy tales make use of this theme, such as the German fairy tale of 'Rumpelstiltskin' where the young girl at the centre of the tale frees herself from Rumpelstiltskin's power by learning his name. See Maria Tatar's *Annotated Brothers Grimm* (2004) for more on this. Also, in Ursula Le Guin's *Earthsea* quintet, and specifically in her short story 'The Rule of Names' from 1964 which is reprinted in *The Wind's Twelve Quarters* (1975), knowledge of a dragon's or human's true name is synonymous with power over them. This trope also occurs in J. R. R. Tolkien's *The Hobbit* from 1937.
29 In Irish mythological tradition, the name Hy-Brazil comes from the Irish *Ui Breasail*, meaning 'clan of Breasail'. In Old Irish, *Í*: island; *bres*: beauty, worth, great, mighty. See James McKillop's *A Dictionary of Celtic Mythology* (1998).
30 This last story in the list is also a direct reference to Padraic Colum's *The King of Ireland's Son*, published in 1916 and also fundamentally concerned with the nature of stories and storytelling.
31 H. C. Lawlor, *The Monastery of St Mochaoi of Nendrum*; Maire and Liam de Paor, *Early Christian Ireland*; D. E. Lowry, *Norsemen and Danes of Strangford Lough, An Archaeological Survey of County Down* (1966).

Chapter 4

1 These authors have been previously discussed here in Chapter 1.
2 Scott neglects to mention fantasy authors such as Alicia le Fanu (1791–1826) whose verse poem *The Sylphid Queen: A Fairy Tale in Verse* was issued in 1809, Frances Browne (1816–1879) whose text *Granny's Wonderful Chair and Its Tales of Fairy Times* was published in 1857 and the prolific Charlotte Riddell (1832–1906) whose supernatural tale *Fairy Water* appeared in 1872.
3 See *Aristotle: Parva Naturalia*, edited by W. D. Ross (1955), p. 449b.
4 See 'The Theory of Recollection', in Plato, *Phaedo*; Plato, *Plato in Twelve Volumes, Vol. 1*, translated by Harold North Fowler (1966), pp. 72e–77a.
5 In their work on medieval memory Mary Carruthers and Jan M. Ziolkwoski comment on the contemporary notion of the 'mind's eye' and that a functioning memory depended on the ability to retrieve memory images or pictures over time. They note specifically that the memory gaze is fundamentally a spatial concept (13). See 'General Introduction' in *The Medieval Craft of Memory: An Anthology of Texts and Pictures* (2002), pp. 1–31.

6. See https://www.merriam-webster.com/dictionary/reciprocity.
7. See Luigino Bruni, *Reciprocity, Altruism and the Civil Society: In Praise of Heterogeneity* (2008), p. 124, Note 5.
8. See Peter Hunt's article 'Landscapes and Journeys, Metaphors and Maps: The Distinctive Feature of English Fantasy' (1987), pp. 11–14.
9. See Chapter 3.
10. Jeremy Addis has written on the nature of the schoolbooks produced for Irish children in the early twentieth century, noting books 'which introduced Irish heroes, whether of history or of the great Gaelic myths, into the imaginative life of the young'. See 'Children's Publishing in Ireland', in *The Big Guide to Irish Children's Books*, pp. 14–19.
11. See W. M. Hennessy, 'The Ancient Irish Goddess of War' (1870), pp. 32–7.
12. See 'The Raid for the Cattle of Regamon', in *Heroic Romances of Ireland*, vol. II, translated by Arthur Herbert Leahy (1905).
13. See Táin Bó Cuailnge, *Recension 1* (1976), pp. 229–30.
14. See https://en.oxforddictionaries.com/definition/fantastic, accessed 16 June 2018.
15. See also Michel Foucault, *The Order of Things* (1971).
16. The Seven Maines are the sons of Maeve and Aillil.
17. Yeats's poem *The Old Age of Queen Maeve* was first published in *Fortnightly Review* in April 1903 and depicts Maeve as an old woman reflecting on her life and mourning her seven sons, and in his play *The Countess Cathleen* from 1908 Maeve is weeping because she has forgotten the name of her lover. O'Shea is writing here into a tradition where Maeve is associated with memory, selfhood and loss.
18. References are made to the hero light in the retellings of Cuchulainn's myth by Standish O'Grady, Eleanor Hull, Augusta Gregory and Rosemary Sutcliff, discussed in Chapter 1.
19. Christine Wilkie Stibbs defines intertextuality as 'literary allusions and … direct quotations from literary and non-literary texts' (168) and argues that child readers are just as capable of accessing a text's intertextual references and of making meaning with them. She refers to the 'intertextual processes through which children take ownership of a particular text' and posits the idea that these processes 'preclude the imperialism of the text and the author' (169), meaning that while children may not make such knowledgeable readers as adults, they are capable of operating outside of the structures of meaning imposed by the author.
20. In 1912 Margaret E. Dobbs, an Irish scholar and playwright concerned with preserving the Irish language, published an article entitled 'The Spiral and the Tuatha Dé Danann' in the Royal Society of Antiquaries of Ireland in which she included a map detailing the distribution and topography of stories associated with the Tuatha Dé Danann. In this article she observes that the spiral ornamentation and patterns that feature so strongly in Newgrange have not yet been found outside the areas influenced by tales of the mythical race.
21. In Greek mythology, the Hyperboreans were a race of mythical giants who lived far to the north of Greece. Herodotus' *Histories* (Book IV, chapters 32–36) which dates from *c.* 450 BCE mentions Hyperborea, and in turn cites Hesiod and Homer as earlier sources.
22. Nuada was the first king of the Tuatha Dé Danann tribe, who lost an arm at the battle of Mag Tuiread in a contest against the Fir Bolg for the dominion of Ireland.
23. See Eric Zuelow's *Making Ireland Irish: Tourism and National Identity since the Civil War* (2009).

24 Beltain or Beltaine usually occurs on the first day of May and signifies the beginning of summer in the Celtic calendar where tributes were normally made to the *aos si* or *daoine sídhe*, the Faery folk from Tir na nÓg. One of the earliest references to the festival is found in a manuscript known as *Sanas Chormaic* or *Cormac's Narrative*. The text is also known as *Cormac's Glossary*, primarily because it contains etymologies and explanations of over 1400 Irish words, and is attributed to Cormac mac Cuileannain, the king-bishop of Munster in 908.
25 See Chapter 3.
26 See Mark G. McLaughlin's *The Wild Geese: The Irish Brigades of France and Spain* (1980).
27 The legend features in the *Comentarios Reales de los Incas* published in 1609 and written by Inca Garcilaso de la Vega, the first published mestizo writer of Colonial Andean South America.
28 This resonates with the myth of the Fianna, explored specifically in Violet Russell's *Heroes of the Dawn*, with the Fianna asleep inside a mountain cave waiting to be called to stand for Ireland again. It also resonates with the myth of King Arthur which features in Siobhan Dowd's *Bog Child* and the idea that Arthur, and other historical Welsh figures said to be the inspiration for that myth, lies waiting to be revived. There is no sense in the Incan myth however that Manco Capac's brothers will return.
29 Anne Korff is a German artist living and working in Kinvara, where she moved in 1977. She appears as herself in Thompson's text. In other words, her character is not merely named for her. Thompson included her in the text as the result of an Auction of Promises at a charity event in Kinvara. Anne is an outsider in the text because of her position in the community but also because unlike JJ and the other characters in the narrative she is based on a real person.
30 Ethnographic traditions 'are grounded in a commitment to the first-hand experience and exploration of a particular social or cultural setting on the basis of … participant observation'. See Mary Jo Deegan, 'The Chicago School of Ethnography' (2007), pp. 11–25.
31 See David Balch, 'From Endymion in Roman Domus to Johan in Christian Catacombs: From Houses of the Living to Houses for the Dead' (2008), pp. 273–302. See also Julian Thomas, *Understanding the Neolithic* (2002), pp. 1–5.
32 Oisin's narrative is part of the Fenian or Ossianic Cycle of Irish Mythology, so named because he narrates it. Primary sources for this Cycle include J. F. Campbell's *Leabhar na Féinne* (1872) and *Duanaire Finn: The Book of the Lays of Fionn* (1908–53).
33 Judith Wasserman writes that the memorial landscape, which is both a landscape that contains a memorial and a landscape that itself remembers or carries traces of the past, 'can also be understood as a sacred place [functioning] to transit community stories and validate those actions deemed honorific in a given culture' (43). See 'To Trace the Shifting Sands: Community, Ritual, and the Memorial Landscape' (1998), pp. 42–61.
34 'Every epoch not only dreams the next, but while dreaming impels it towards wakefulness.' See Walter Benjamin, *The Arcades Project* (1999), p. 898.
35 In Christopher Tilley's work the term 'life-world' is used to describe the ways in which people interact with and perceive the world around them. See *Interpreting Landscape*, p. 26. For another definition of the term, see Edmund Husserl's *The Crisis of European Sciences and Transcendental Phenomenology* (1970).

36 See 'Contexts and Concepts' in Stephen Howe's *Ireland and Empire: Colonial Legacies in Irish History and Culture* (2000), pp. 7–20. See also David Cairns and Shaun Richards's *Writing Ireland: Colonialism, Nationalism and Culture* (1988).
37 See 'Vista Definition', Merriam-Webster, accessed 5 November 2015, http://www.merriam-webster.com/dictionary/vista.
38 Peter Hollindale uses the image of a mountain to describe a child's journey into adulthood and maturity. He terms it an irregular journey, filled with many stopping points, moments of backtracking and long periods of rest. Adulthood itself is a plateau full of undulations. In this way, Fergus's movements up and down the mountain engage with Hollindale's idea of the irregular journey as one that makes progress in a multitude of ways. See *Signs of Childness* (1997), pp. 37–8.

Conclusion

1 C. W. Sullivan III writes on three ways of incorporating mythology into fantasy narratives. Expanding involves an author using the plot of a mythic or legendary narrative as a framework for his or her own fiction. Interweaving corresponds to selecting materials for a tale or group of tales and then weaving these into a cohesive whole. Inventing involves the creation of characters, sometimes children and young people who are involved in a plot deriving its basic pattern from the traditional magic tale or hero quest. This narrative is then supported by material drawn from mythology and folklore. See C. W. Sullivan's *Welsh Celtic Myth in Modern Fantasy* (1989) pp. 13, 35, 55.
2 Writing in *Tree and Leaf* (1964), J. R. R. Tolkien proposed a lineage for modern fantasy from Old Norse legends, Anglo-Saxon tales, the Arthurian myths and of course the Celtic myths. And for Tolkien, this lineage had three aspects: 'independent evolution (or rather invention) … inheritance from a common ancestry; and diffusion at various times from one or more centres' (see *Tree and Leaf*, p. 20).
3 See Liam De Paor's *The Easter Proclamation 1916: A Comparative Analysis* (2016).

WORKS CITED

Æ. *Imaginations and Reveries*. Maunsel, 1915.
Æ. "Nationality and Imperialism." *Ideals in Ireland*, edited by Augusta Gregory, At the Unicorn, 1901.
Addis, Jeremy. 'Children's Publishing in Ireland'. *The Big Guide to Irish Children's Books*, edited by Valerie Coghlan and Celia Keenan, Irish Children's Book Trust, 1996, pp. 14–19.
Agnew, Vijay. Introduction. *Diaspora, Memory and Identity: A Search for Home*, edited by Vijay Agnew, U of Toronto P, 2005, pp. 3–18.
Alderman, Derek H., and Joshua F. J. Inwood. 'Landscapes of Memory and Socially Just Futures'. *The Wiley-Blackwell Companion to Cultural Geography*, edited by Nuala C. Johnson, Richard H. Shein and Jamie Winders, John Wiley & Sons, 2013, pp. 186–97.
Alver, Brynjulf. 'Folkloristics: The Science about Tradition and Society'. *Folklore: Critical Concepts in Literary and Cultural Studies, Volume One*, edited by Alan Dundes, Routledge, 2005, pp. 43–52.
Anderson, Benedict. *Imagined Communities: Reflections on the Origins of Nationalism*. Verso, 2006.
Anderson, J. 'Nationalist Ideology and Territory'. *Nationalism, Self-Determination and Political Geography*, edited by R. J. Johnston, D. B. Knight and E. Kofman, Croom Helm, 1988, pp. 18–39.
Andrews, J. S. *The Bell of Nendrum*. Blackstaff Press, 1969.
Anonymous. 'Review of *Old John*'. *Cork Examiner*, July 1938.
Anonymous. 'The Raid for the Cattle of Regamon'. *Heroic Romances of Ireland*, vol. II, translated by Arthur Herbert Leahy, David Nutt, 1905.
Appleyard, J. A. *Becoming a Reader: The Experience of Fiction from Childhood to Adulthood*. Cambridge UP, 1990.
Arendt, Hannah. *Between Past and Future*. Penguin, 1977.
Assmann, Aleida. 'Canon and Archive'. *A Companion to Cultural Memory Studies*, edited by Astrid Erll and Ansgar Nunning, De Gruyter, 2010, pp. 97–107.
Assmann, Jan. *Cultural Memory and Early Civilisation: Writing, Remembrance, and Political Imagination*. Cambridge UP, 1970.
Assmann, Jan. *Moses the Egyptian: The Memory of Egypt in Western Monothesism*. Harvard UP, 1997.
Attebery, Brian. *Stories about Stories: Fantasy and the Remaking of Myth*. Oxford UP, 2014.
Auden, W. H. *Prose II*, edited by Edward Mendelson, Princeton UP, 2002.
Bachelard, Gaston. *Poetics of Space*, translated by Maria Jolas, Beacon Press, 1964.
Bachelard, Gaston. *Poetics of Reverie*, translated by Daniel Russell, Orion Press, 1969.
Bakhtin, M. M. *The Dialogic Imagination: Four Essays*, edited by Michael Holquist, translated by Michael Holquist and Caryl Emerson, U of Texas P, 1981.
Bakhtin, M. M. *Rabelais and His World*, Translated by Helene Iswolsky, Indiana UP, 1984.
Bal, Mieke. *Narratology: Introduction to the Theory of Narrative*. U of Toronto P, 1997.
Bancroft, Hubert. *The Native Races, Myths and Languages, Vol. 3*. A. L. Bancroft, 1883.

Barnard, F. M., editor, translator. *Herder on Social and Political Culture*. Cambridge UP, 1969.
Basso, Kenneth H. *Wisdom Sits in Places: Landscape and Language among the Western Apache*. U of New Mexico P, 1996.
Basu, Paul. 'Cairns in the Landscape: Migrant Stones and Migrant Stories in Scotland and Its Diaspora'. *Landscapes beyond Land: Routes, Aesthetics, Narratives*, edited by Arnar Arnason, Nicholas Ellison, Jo Vergunst and Andrew Whitehouse, Berghahn Books, 2012, pp. 116–38.
Benjamin, Walter. *The Arcades Project*, edited by Rolf Tiederman, Harvard UP, 1999.
Beresford, Peter. *Celtic Myths and Legends*. Avalon, 2003.
Berger, Peter L., and Thomas Luckmann. *The Social Construction of Reality*. Penguin, 1967.
Berresford Ellis, Peter. *A Dictionary of Irish Mythology*. Little, Brown Book, 2005.
Bettelheim, Bruno. *The Uses of Enchantment*. Thames & Hudson, 1976.
Bourke, Angela. 'Foreword'. *Folklore and Modern Irish Writing*, edited by Anne Markey and Anne O'Connor, Irish Academic P, 2014, pp. 1–4.
Boyd, Ernest. *A Literary History of Ireland*. Allen Figgis, 1968.
Boyer, Pascal. 'What Are Memories For? Functions of Recall in Cognition and Culture'. *Memory in Mind and Culture*, edited by Pascal Boyer and James V. Wertsch, Cambridge UP, 2009, pp. 3–32.
Boylan, Henry. *A Dictionary of Irish Biography*. New York: Reinhart, 1998.
Brace, Catherine. 'Landscape and Identity'. *Studying Cultural Landscapes*, edited by Iain Robertson and Penny Richards, Arnold, 2003, pp. 121–40.
Briggs, K. M. *The Fairies in English Tradition and Literature*. U of Chicago P, 1967.
Briody, Mícheál. *The Irish Folklore Commission, 1935–1970: History, Ideology, Methodology*. Finnish Literature Society, 2007.
Brown, Nicola, and Carolyn Burdett. *The Victorian Supernatural*. Cambridge UP, 2004.
Brown, Terence. *A Social and Cultural History: 1922–2000*. Harper Perennial, 2004.
Bruni, Luigino. *Reciprocity, Altruism and the Civil Society: In Praise of Heterogeneity*. Routledge, 2008.
Burger, Peter. *The Theory of the Avante Garde*. U of Minnesota P, 1982.
Butler, C. *Four British Fantasists: Place and Culture in the Children's Fantasies of Penelope Lively, Alan Garner, Diana Wynne Jones, and Susan Cooper*. Children's Literature Association and Scarecrow Press, 2006.
Buttimer, Anne. 'Preface'. *Literary Landscapes of Ireland: Geographies of Irish Stories 1929–1946*, edited by Charles Travis, Edwin Mellen Press, 2009, pp. iii–v.
Cabral, Amilcar. 'National Liberation and Culture'. *Return to the Sources: Selected Speeches by Amilcar Cabral*. Africa Information Service, 1973.
Cahill, Susan. 'Far Away from the Busy World: Mairin Cregan's Children's Literature'. *The Country of the Young: Interpretations of Youth and Childhood in Irish Culture*, edited by John Countryman and Kelly Matthews, Four Courts Press, 2013, pp. 70–85.
Cairns, David, and Shaun Richards. *Writing Ireland: Colonialism, Nationalism and Culture*. Manchester UP, 1988.
Campbell, John. *Past, Space, and Self*. MIT P, 1995.
Campbell, Joseph. *The Hero with a Thousand Faces*. Fontana Press, 1993.
Carlyle, Thomas. *On Heroes, Hero-Worship, and the Heroic in History*. Chapman and Hall, 1840.
Carlyle, Thomas. *Collected Works, Vol. XIII, Past and Present*. Chapman and Hall, 1843.
Carroll, Jane. *Landscape in Children's Literature*. Routledge, 2011.

Carruthers, Mary, and Jan M. Ziolkwoski. 'Introduction'. *The Medieval Craft of Memory: An Anthology of Texts and Pictures*, edited by Carruthers and Ziolkwoski, U of Pennsylvania P, 2002, pp. 1-31.
Casey, Edward. *Remembering: A Phenomenological Study*. Indiana State UP, 1987.
Casey, Edward. *Getting Back into Place: Toward a Renewed Understanding of the Place-World*. Indiana UP, 1993.
Casey, Edward. 'The Edge of Landscape: A Study in Liminology'. *The Place of Landscape: Concepts, Contexts, Studies*, edited by Jeff Malpas, MIT P, 2011, pp. 91-110.
Cassirer, Ernest. *An Essay on Man: An Introduction to a Philosophy of Human Culture*. Yale UP, 1962.
Castle, Gregory. *Modernism and the Celtic Revival*. Cambridge UP, 2001.
Cleary, Joe. *Literature, Partition and the Nation-State: Culture and Conflict in Ireland, Israel and Palestine*. Cambridge UP, 2002.
Clifford, James, and George E. Martin. *Writing Culture: The Poetics and Politics of Ethnography: A School of American Research Advanced Seminar*. U of California P, 1986.
Clute, John, and John Grant. *Encyclopedia of Fantasy*. St. Martin's Press, 1999.
Coghlan, Valerie, and Keith O'Sullivan. 'Introduction'. *Irish Children's Literature and Culture: New Perspectives on Contemporary Writing*, edited by Coghlan and O'Sullivan, Routledge, 2011, pp. 1-6.
Colum, Padraic. 'Ella Young: A Druidess', *The Horn Book*, May 1939.
Colum, Padraic. *Storytelling New & Old*. Macmillan Company, 1961.
Colum, Padraic. *The King of Ireland's Son*. Floris Books, 1978.
Colum, Padraic. *Selected Poems*, edited by Sanford Sternlicht, Syracuse UP, 1989.
Conner, Lester. *A Yeats Dictionary: Persons and Place in the Poetry of William Butler Yeats*. Syracuse UP, 1998.
Coolahan, John. *Irish Education: Its History and Structure*. Institute of Public Administration, 1981.
Corcoran, Farrell. 'Digging up the Past'. *Place and Non-Place: The Reconfiguration of Ireland*, edited by Michel Peillon and Mary. P. Corcoran, Institute of Public Administration, 2004, pp. 93-102.
Coupe, Laurence. *Myth*. Routledge, 1997.
Cregan, Mairin. *Old John*. George Allen & Unwin, 1937.
Cregan, Mairin. 'A Child's Book', *Irish Press*, 18 March 1937.
Davidson, Tonya K., Ondine Park and Rob Shields. 'Introduction'. *Ecologies of Affect: Placing Nostalgia, Desire and Hope*, edited by Davidson, Park and Shields, Wilfrid Laurier UP, 2011, pp. 1-16.
Deane, Seamus. *Celtic Revivals: Essays in Modern Irish Literature, 1880-1980*. Faber & Faber, 1985.
Dearing, John. 'Lakes'. *Patterned Ground: Entanglements of Nature and Culture*, edited by Stephan Harrison, Steve Pile and N. J. Thrift, Reaktion Books, 2004, p. 78.
Dease, Alice. *Old Time Stories of Erin*. Browne & Noble, 1907.
De Paor, Liam. *The Easter Proclamation 1916: A Comparative Analysis*. Four Courts Press, 2016.
Deegan, Mary Jo. 'The Chicago School of Ethnography'. *The Handbook of Ethnography*, edited by Paul Atkinson et al., Sage, 2007, pp. 11-25.
Dieckmann, Liselotte. *Hieroglyphics: The History of a Literary Symbol*. Washington UP, 1970.
Dillon, Eilís. *The Lost Island*. Faber & Faber, 1952.

Dillon, Eilís. 'The Unclouded Vision'. *Books Ireland*, no. 149, April 1991, pp. 65-6.
Dillon, Eilís. 'A Writer in Cork'. *The Cork Review: Cork Writers and Writing*, 1993, pp. 35-9.
Dobbs, Margaret E. 'The Spiral and the Tuatha Dé Danann'. *Journal of the Royal Society of Antiquaries of Ireland*, vol. 2, no. 4, 1912, pp. 331-4.
Donald, Merlin. *Origins of the Modern Mind: Three Stages in the Evolution of Culture and Cognition*. Harvard UP, 1991.
Dowd, Siobhan. *Bog Child*. David Fickling, 2008.
du Gay, Paul. *Doing Cultural Studies: The Story of the Sony Walkman*. Sage, 1997.
Dudley Edwards, R. W., and Mary O'Dowd. *Sources for Modern Irish History 1534-1641*. Cambridge UP, 2003.
Duffy, Patrick J. 'Writing Ireland: Literature and Art in the Representation of Irish Place'. *The Imagining of Place: Representation and Identity in Contemporary Ireland*, edited by Brian Graham, Psychology Press, 1997, pp. 64-83.
Dwyer, Robert Joyce. *Blanid*. Roberts Brothers, 1879.
Dunbar, Robert. 'Fantasy'. *The Big Guide to Irish Children's Books*, edited by Valerie Coghlan and Celia Keenan, Children's Books Trust, 1996, pp. 40-9.
Eagleton, Terry. *Scholars and Rebels in Nineteenth Century Ireland*. Blackwell, 1999.
Edelstein, T. J, et al. 'Introduction'. *Imagining an Irish Past: The Celtic Revival 1840-1940*, edited by Edelstein, U of Chicago P, 1992, pp. xiii-xvii.
Edensor, Tim. *Industrial Ruins: Space, Aesthetics and Materiality*. Bloomsbury Academic, 2005.
Egan, Kieran. *The Educated Mind: How Cognitive Tools Shape Our Understanding*. U of Chicago P, 2007.
Eglinton, John, W. B. Yeats, A. E. and W. Larminie. *Literary Ideals in Ireland*. T. Fisher Unwin, 1899.
Eliade, Mircea. *Myth and Reality*, translated by Willard R. Trask, Allen & Unwin, 1964.
Eliade, Mircea. *Myths, Dreams and Mysteries: The Encounter between Contemporary Faiths and Archaic Realities*. Harper & Row, 1975.
Eliade, Mircea. *The Sacred and the Profane: The Nature of Religion*. Harcourt Brace Jovanovich, 1987.
Eliot, T. S. *Four Quartets*. Houghton Mifflin Harcourt, 2014.
Ellis Davidson, Hilda, and Anne Chaudhri, editors. *A Companion to the Fairy Tale*. DS Brewer, 2006.
Erll, Astrid. *Memory in Culture*. Springer, 2016.
Fassi, Luigi, Lucy Gallun and Jakob Schillinger. *Time out of Joint: Recall and Evocation in Recent Art*. Yale UP, 2009.
Ferguson, Lydia. 'Cultivating Childhoods: The Pollard Collection of Children's Books'. *The Old Library, Trinity College Dublin, 1712-2012*, edited by W. E. Vaughan, Four Courts Press, 2012, pp. 191-310.
Ferriter, Diarmuid. *The Transformation of Ireland: 1900-2000*. Profile Books, 2004.
Fimi, Dimitra. *Celtic Myth in Contemporary Children's Fantasy: Idealization, Identity, Ideology*. Palgrave Macmillan, 2017.
Fivush, R., and Patricia J. Bauer. 'The Emergence of Recollection: How We Learn to Recall Ourselves in the Past'. *The Act of Remembering: Towards an Understanding of How We Recall the Past*, edited by John. H. Mace, Wiley-Blackwell, 2011, http://onlinelibrary.wiley.com/doi/10.1002/9781444328202.ch11/references.
Fontenrose, Joseph. *The Ritual Theory of Myth*. California UP, 1971.

Forde, William. *Music in the Social and Behavioural Sciences: An Encyclopaedia.* Sage, 2014.
Foster, Michael, and Jeffery Tolbert. *The Folkloresque: Reframing Folklore in a Popular Culture World.* U of Colorado P, 2015.
Foster, R. F. *The Story of Ireland.* Clarendon Press, 1995.
Foster, R. F. *Vivid Faces: The Revolutionary Generation in Ireland 1890–1923.* Penguin, 2015.
Foucault, Michel. *The Order of Thing.* Vintage, 1971.
Foucault, Michel. 'Of Other Spaces: Utopias and Heterotopias', translated by Jay Miskowiec. *Diacritics*, vol. 16, no. 1, 1986, pp. 22–7.
Fraser, Sir James George. *The Golden Bough: A Study of Magic and Religion.* Lulu Press, 2013.
Freeland Thompson, Tok. *Ireland's Pre-Celtic Archaeological and Anthropological Heritage.* Edwin Mellen Press, 2006.
Frehan, Pádraic. *Education and Celtic Myth: National Self-Image and Schoolbooks in 20th Century Ireland.* Rodopi, 2012.
Frye, Northrop. *Anatomy of Criticism.* Princeton UP, 1957.
Frye, Northrop. *Fables of Identity: Studies in Poetic Mythology.* Harcourt Brace, 1963.
Garner, Alan. *The Voice That Thunders.* Harvill Press, 1997.
Gavan Duffy, Charles. *The Revival of Irish Literature.* T. F. Unwin, 1894.
Geertz, Clifford. *The Interpretation of Culture: Selected Essays.* Basic Books, 1973.
Gellner, Ernest. *Nations and Nationalism.* Blackwell, 2006.
Gill, Christopher, Norman Postlethwaite and Richard Seaford, editors. *Reciprocity in Ancient Greece.* Oxford UP, 1998.
Gillis, John R. *Commemoration: The Politics of National Identity.* Princeton UP, 1996.
Gillman, Derek. *The Idea of Cultural Heritage.* Cambridge UP, 2010.
Glassie, Henry. *Passing the Time in Ballymenone: Culture and History of an Ulster Community.* U of Pennsylvania P, 1983.
Goody, Jack. 'Memory in Oral Tradition'. *Memory*, edited by Patricia Fara and Karalyn Patterson, Cambridge UP, 1998, pp. 73–84.
Gould, Warwick. 'Frazer, Yeats, and the Reconsecration of Folklore'. *Sir James Frazer and the Literary Imagination: Essays in Affinity and Influence*, edited by Robert G. Fraser and Carol Pert, Springer, 1990, pp. 121–53.
Graham, Brian, editor. *In Search of Ireland: A Cultural Geography.* Routledge, 1997.
Green, Miranda. *Animals in Celtic Life and Myth.* Routledge, 2002.
Gregory, Augusta. *Cuchulain of Muirthemne.* Colin Smythe, 1970.
Griffith, Arthur. *United Irishman.* 24 January 1903.
Grimm, Jacob, and Wilheim Grimm. *Children's and Household Tales.* Grimms Brothers, 1812.
Gruffud, P. 'Remaking Wales: Nation-Building and the Geographical Imagination, 1925–50'. *Political Geography*, vol. 14, no. 3, 1995, pp. 219–39.
Hall, Stuart. 'Introduction'. *Representation: Cultural Representations and Signifying Practices*, edited by Hall, Sage, 1997, pp. 1–13.
Hall, Stuart. 'Cultural Identity and Diaspora'. *Identity: Community, Culture, Difference*, edited by Jonathan Rutherford, Lawrence & Wishart, 1990, pp. 222–37.
Hanne, Michael. *The Power of Story: Fiction and Political Change.* Berghahn Books, 1996.
Hardy, Barbara. 'Towards a Poetics of Fiction'. *NOVEL: A Forum on Fiction*, vol. 2, no. 1, autumn 1968, pp. 5–13.
Hardy, Barbara. *Tellers and Listeners: The Narrative Imagination.* A&C Black, 2014.

Harrison, Rodney. *Heritage: Critical Approaches*. Routledge, 2013.
Harth, Dietrich. 'The Invention of Cultural Memory'. *A Companion to Cultural Memory Studies*, edited by Astrid Erll and Ansgar Nunning, De Gruyter, 2010, pp. 85–96.
Hawkes, Jacquetta. *A Land*. Cresset Press, 1953.
Hay, Marnie. 'Moulding the Future: Na Fianna Éireann and Its Members, 1909–1923'. *Studies: An Irish Quarterly Review*, vol. 100, no. 400, winter 2011, pp. 441–54.
Heaney, Seamus. *Seeing Things*. Faber & Faber, 1991.
Hedges Deroy, Tanya, and D. Douglas Caulkin. 'Anthropology and the Construction of Irish Identity'. *Irelands of the Mind: Memory and Identity in Modern Irish Culture*, edited by Richard C. Allen and Stephen Regan, Cambridge Scholars, 2008, pp. 73–95.
Heilbrun, Carolyn. *Hamlet's Mother and Other Women: Feminist Essays on Literature*. Women's Press, 1991.
Hennessy, W. M. 'The Ancient Irish Goddess of War'. *Revue Celtique*, vol. 1, 1870, pp. 32–7.
Herodotus. *Histories*, translated by David Grene, U of Chicago P, 1987.
Hixon, Martha. 'Folktales Retold: A Critical Overview of Stories Updated for Children (Review)'. *The Lion and the Unicorn*, vol. 31 no. 2, 2007, pp. 196–9.
Hobbes, Thomas. *Leviathan*, edited by Richard Tuck, Cambridge UP, 1996.
Hobsbawm, Eric. 'Introduction'. *The Invention of Tradition*, edited by Hobsbawm and Terence Ranger, Cambridge UP, 1992, pp. 1–14.
Hoerl, Christoph, and Terese McCormack. 'Introduction'. *Time and Memory: Issues in Philosophy and Psychology*, edited by Hoerl and McCormack, Clarendon Press, 2001, pp. 1–36.
Hollindale, Peter. *Signs of Childness in Children's Books*. Thimble Books, 1997.
Honko, Lauri. 'The Problem of Defining Myth'. *Sacred Narrative: Readings in the Theory of Myth*, edited by Alan Dundes, U of California P, pp. 41–52.
Howe, Stephen. *Ireland and Empire: Colonial Legacies in Irish History and Culture*. Oxford UP, 2000.
Hua, Anh. '"What We All Long For": Memory, Trauma and Emotional Geographies'. *Emotion, Place and Culture*, edited by Mick Smith and Liz Bondi, Routledge, 2016, pp. 135–48.
Hull, Eleanor. *Cuchulain the Hound of Ulster*. George G. Harrap, 1909.
Hunt, Peter. 'Landscapes and Journeys, Metaphors and Maps: The Distinctive Feature of English Fantasy'. *Children's Literature Association Quarterly*, vol. 12, no. 1, 1987, pp. 11–14.
Husserl, Edmund. *The Crisis of European Sciences and Transcendental Phenomenology*. Northwestern UP, 1970.
Hutchinson, John. *Dynamics of Cultural Nationalism: The Gaelic Revival and the Creation of the Irish Nation State*. Routledge, 2012.
Huyssen, Andreas. *Twilight Memories: Marking Time in a Culture of Amnesia*. Routledge, 2012.
Ingalls Garnett, Jacqueline. *Newgrange Speaks for Itself: Forty Carved Motifs*. Trafford, 2005.
Irwin-Zareck, Iwona. *Frames of Remembrance: The Dynamics of Collective Memory*. Transaction, 1994.
Iser, Wolfgang. *The Implied Reader: Patterns of Communication in Prose Fiction from Bunyan to Beckett*. Johns Hopkins UP, 1974.
Jackson, Rosemary. *Fantasy: The Literature of Subversion*. Routledge, 2002.

Jaleta, Tadesse Jirata. 'Children as Interpreters of Culture: Producing Meanings from Folktales in Southern Ethiopia'. *Journal of Folklore Research*, vol. 48, no. 3, 2011, pp. 269-92.
James, Edward, and Farah Mendlesohn. *The Cambridge Companion to Fantasy Literature*. Cambridge UP, 2012.
Joyce, P. W. *Old Celtic Romances*. C. Kegan Paul, 1879.
Joyce, P. W. *The Wonders of Ireland and Other Papers on Irish Subjects*. Longmans, Green, 1911.
Joynt, Maud. *The Golden Legends of the Gael*. Talbot Press, 1925.
Kelly, Una. *Cuchulain and the Leprechaun*. Parkside Press, 1945.
Kennedy, Máire. 'Myths, Legends and Folktales'. *The Big Guide to Irish Children's Books*, edited by Valeria Coghlan and Celia Keenan, Irish Children's Book Trust, 1996, pp. 81-90.
Kenner, Hugh. *Joyce's Voices*. U of California P, 1978.
Kiberd, Declan. *Inventing Ireland*. Jonathan Cape, 1995.
Knell, Simon, and Michael Taylor. 'Hugh Miller: Fossils, Landscapes and Literary Geology'. *Proceedings of the Geologists Association*, vol. 117, 2006, pp. 85-98.
Knowles, Murray, and Kirsten Malmkjaer. *Language and Control in Children's Literature*. Routledge, 1996.
Knox, John. *Myth and Truth: An Essay on the Language of Faith*. U of Virginia P, 1964.
Koch, John T. *Celtic Culture: A Historical Encyclopaedia*. ABC-CLIO, 2006.
Kort, Wesley A. *Modern Fiction and Human Time: A Study in Narrative and Belief*. U of South Florida P, 1985.
Larned, W. T. *American Indian Fairy Tales*. Wise-Parslow, 1935.
Leamy, Edmund. *Irish Fairy Tales*. M. H. Gill & Sons, 1906.
Lebor Gabála Érenn. *The Book of the Taking of Ireland*, edited by R. A. Stewart Macalister, Educational Co. of Ireland, 1938.
Le Guin, Ursula. *The Language of the Night*, edited by Susan Wood, G. P. Putnam's Sons, 1979.
Le Guin, Ursula. *Dancing at the Edge of the World: Thoughts on Words, Women, Places*. Victor Gollancz, 1989.
Leerssen, Joep. 'Celticism'. *Celticism*, edited by Terence Brown, Rodopi, 1996, pp. 1-20.
Leijenhorst, Cees. 'Sense and Nonsense about Sense: Hobbes and the Aristotelians on Sense Perception and Imagination'. *The Cambridge Companion to Hobbes' Leviathan*, edited by Patricia Springborg, Cambridge UP, 2007, pp. 82-108.
Levy, Michael, and Farah Mendlesohn. *Children's Fantasy Literature: An Introduction*. Cambridge UP, 2016.
Lewis, C. S. *The Allegory of Love*. Cambridge UP, 2013.
Lloyd, David. *Irish Times: Temporalities of Modernity*. Field Day, 2008.
Lowenthal, David. *The Past Is a Foreign Country*. Cambridge UP, 1985.
Lynch, Kevin. *What Time is this Place?* MIT P, 1972.
Lynch, Patricia. *The Turf-Cutter's Donkey*. Poolbeg Press, 1988.
MacGregor, Neil. *A History of the World in 100 Objects*. Penguin, 2011.
MacRaois, Cormac. *The Battle below Giltspur*. Wolfhound, 1988.
MacRaois, Cormac. 'Old Tales for New People: Irish Mythology Retold for Children'. *The Lion and the Unicorn*, vol. 21, no. 3, 1997, pp. 330-40.
Malinowski, Bronislaw. *Myth in Primitive Psychology*. Read Books, 2011.
Marcus, Philip L. *Standish O'Grady*. Bucknell UP, 1970.

Markey, Anne, and Anne O'Connor. 'Introduction'. *Folklore and Modern Irish Writing*, edited by Markey and O'Connor, Irish Academic P, 2014, pp. 5–18.
Martin, Darragh. *The Keeper*. Little Island Press, 2013.
Martin, Philip. *The Writer's Guide to Fantasy and Literature: From Dragon's Lair to Hero's Quest*. Kalmbach, 2002.
Masson, Sophie, and Elizabeth Hale. 'Mosaic and Cornucopia: Fairy Tale and Myth in Contemporary Australian YA Fantasy'. *Bookbird: A Journal of International Children's Literature*, vol. 54, no. 3, 2016, pp. 44–53.
Matthews, Caitlín. *British and Irish Mythology: A Dictionary of Myth and Legend*. Diamond Books, 1995.
Matthews, Kelly. 'Introduction'. *The Country of the Young: Interpretations of Youth and Childhood in Irish Culture*, edited by John Countryman and Kelly Matthews, Four Courts Press, 2013, pp. 1–9.
Maybin, Janet. *Children's Voices: Talk, Knowledge and Identity*. Palgrave, 2005.
McAdams, Dan P. *Power, Intimacy, and the Life Story: Personological Inquires into Identity*. Guildford Press, 1988.
McAteer, Michael. *Standish O'Grady, AE, and Yeats: History, Politics, Culture*. Irish Academic P, 2002.
McBride, Ian. 'Introduction'. *History and Memory in Modern Ireland*, edited by McBride, Cambridge UP, 2001, pp. 1–42.
McKillop, James. *A Dictionary of Celtic Mythology*. Oxford UP, 1998.
McLaughlin, Mark G. *The Wild Geese: The Irish Brigades of France and Spain*. Osprey Press, 1980.
McMahon, Timothy G. *The Gaelic Revival and Irish Society: 1893–1910*. Syracuse UP, 2008.
Meigs, Samantha A. *The Reformations in Ireland: Tradition and Confessionalism, 1400–1690*. Springer, 1997.
Melling, Orla. *The Druid's Tune*. O'Brien Press, 1986.
Mendlesohn, Farah. *Rhetorics of Fantasy*. Wesleyan UP, 2013.
Minahan McGinn, Jeanne. 'On Longing to Be Elsewhere: The Future, the Past, and Other Exiles in Irish Literature'. *That Other World: The Supernatural and the Fantastic in Irish Literature and Its Contexts*, edited by Bruce Stewart, Colin Smythe, 1998, pp. 66–80.
Mitchell, Sally. *The New Girl: Girls' Culture in England: 1880–1915*. Columbia UP, 1995.
Moody, T. W., et al. *A New History of Ireland, Volume III: Early Modern Ireland 1534–1691*. Oxford UP, 1991.
Moran, D. P. *The Philosophy of Irish Ireland*, edited by Patrick Maume, University College Dublin P, 2006.
Mulhern, Francis. *Culture/Metaculture*. Routledge, 2000.
Murphy, Daniel. 'Foreword'. *Cuchulain of Muirthemne*, edited by Augusta Gregory, Colin Smythe, 1970, pp. 7–10.
Murphy, Rose. *Ella Young, Irish Mystic and Rebel: From Literary Dublin to the American West*. Liffey Press, 2008.
Murray, Noëleen, and Nick Shepard. 'Introduction'. *Space, Memory and Identity in the Post-Apartheid City*, edited by Murray et al., Routledge, 2007, pp. 1–18.
Myers, Lindsay. *Making the Italians: Poetics and Politics of Italian Children's Fantasy*. Lang, 2012.
Natov, Roni. *The Poetics of Childhood*. Routledge, 2014.
Ni Chuilleanáin, Eiléan. 'Folklore and Writing for Children in Twentieth-Century Ireland: Padraic Colum, Patricia Lynch, and Eilís Dillon'. *Folklore and Modern Irish*

Writing, edited by Anne Markey and Anne O'Connor, Irish Academic P, 2014, pp. 113–28.

Nicolaisen, W. F. H. 'Concepts of Time and Space in Irish Folktales'. *Celtic Folklore and Christianity: Studies in Memory of William W. Heist*, edited by Patrick K. Ford, McNally & Loftin, 1983, pp. 150–8.

Nikolajeva, Maria. *From Mythic to Linear: Time in Children's Literature*. Children's Literature Association and Scarecrow Press, 2000.

Nora, Pierre. *Realms of Memory: Rethinking the French Past, Vol. 1: Conflict and Divisions*, edited by Lawrence D. Kritzman and Arthur Goldhammer, Columbia UP, 1996.

Ó Giolláin, Diarmuid. *Locating Irish Folklore: Tradition, Modernity, Identity*. Cork UP, 2003.

O'Grady, Standish. *Cuculain and His Contemporaries, Vol. II* (1880). Lemma, 1970.

O'Grady, Standish. *The Coming of Cuculain*. Talbot Press, 1894.

Ó'Guilín, Peadar. *The Call*. David Fickling Books, 2016.

O'Leary, Jim. *The Fuchsia Stone*. Aran Books, 1993.

O'Leary, Philip. *The Prose Literature of the Gaelic Revival, 1881–1921: Ideology and Innovation*. Pennsylvania State UP, 2005.

Ong, Walter. *Orality and Literacy: Technologizing the Word*. Routledge, 1982.

Orodes, Richard, and Alfonzo Ortiz. *American Indian Myths and Legends*. Pantheon Books, 1984.

O'Rourke Murphy, Maureen and James McKillop. *An Irish Literature Reader: Poetry, Prose, Drama*. Syracuse UP, 2006.

O'Shea, Pat. *The Hounds of the Morrigan*. Puffin Books, 1987.

Oxford English Dictionary. 'Evoke Definition'. Accessed 7 November, 2016, https://en.oxforddictionaries.com/definition/evoke.

Oxford English Dictionary. 'Noetic Definition'. Accessed 12 May 2017, http://www.oed.com/view/Entry/127626?rskey=5VL0ch&result=1#eid.

Peabody, Berkley. *The Winged Word: A Study in the Technique of Ancient Greek Composition as Seen Principally through Hesiod's Works and Days*. State U of New York P, 1975.

Pearce, David. 'Cultural Nationalism and the Irish Literary Revival'. *International Journal of English Studies*, vol. 2, no. 2, 2002, pp. 1–22.

Perkins, Agnes. 'Folklore & Children's Books: Bridging the Gap'. *Children's Literature Association Quarterly*, vol. 6, no. 2, 1981, pp. 1–37.

Plato. *Phaedo*, edited by David Gallop, Oxford UP, 1999.

Plato. *Republic, Book II*, edited by G. R. F. Ferrari, Cambridge UP, 2000.

Plato. *Meno*, edited by R. S. Bluck, Cambridge UP, 2011.

Prince, Gerald. *Narratology: The Form and Functioning of Narrative*. Mouton, 1982.

Putz, Adam. *The Celtic Revival in Shakespeare's Wake: Appropriation and Cultural Politics in Ireland, 1867–1922*. Palgrave Macmillan, 2013.

Rahn, Suzanne. ' "Inishrone Is Our Island": Rediscovering the Irish Novels of Eilís Dillon'. *The Lion and the Unicorn: A Critical Journal of Children's Literature*, vol. 21, no. 3, 1997.

Renan, Ernest. *The Poetry of the Celtic Races and Other Studies*. Kenikat Press, 1970.

Renan, Ernest. 'What Is a Nation?' *Nation and Narration*, edited by Homi K. Bhabha, translated by Martin Thom, Routledge, 2013, pp. 8–22.

Rennie Short, John. *Imagined Country: Environment, Culture and Society*. Routledge, 1991.

Richards, Shaun. 'Polemics on the Irish Past: The "Return to the Source" in Irish Literary Revivals'. *History Workshop*, vol. 31, spring 1991, pp. 120–35.

Ricoeur, Paul. *Time and Narrative, Volume III*, translated by Kathleen Blarney and David Peallauer, U of C Press, 1985.
Ricoeur, Paul. *Memory, History, Forgetting*, translated by Kathleen Blamey and David Peallauer, U of C Press, 2004.
Rolleston, T. W. *Celtic Myths and Legends*. Dover, 1911.
Russell, Bertrand. *The Problems of Philosophy*. Henry Holt, 1912.
Russell, Daniel. 'Preface'. *The Poetics of Reverie*, edited by Gaston Bachelard, Orion Press, 1969, pp. i–viii.
Russell, George. 'Introduction'. *The Coming of Cuchulain*, edited by Standish O'Grady, Talbot Press, 1894.
Russell, Violet. *Heroes of the Dawn*. Maunsel, 1913.
Ryden, Kent C. *Mapping the Invisible Landscape: Folklore, Writing, and the Sense of Place*. U of Iowa P, 1993.
Sandis, Constantine. *Cultural Heritage Ethics: Between Theory and Practice*. Open Book, 2014.
Scanlan, John. *Memory: Encounters with the Strange and the Familiar*. Reaktion Books, 2013.
Schanoes, Veronica L. *Fairy Tales, Myth, and Psychoanalytic Theory: Feminism and Retelling the Tale*. Routledge, 2016.
Schleifer, Ronald. *The Genres of the Irish Literary Revival*. Pilgrim Books, 1980.
Scott, Michael. 'By Imagination We Live: Some Thoughts on Irish Children's Fantasy'. *The Lion and the Unicorn*, vol. 21, no. 3, 1997, pp. 322–9.
Seaford, Richard. 'Introduction'. *Reciprocity in Ancient Greece*, edited by Christopher Gill, Norman Postlethwaite and Richard Seaford, Oxford UP, 1998.
Share, Perry, and Mary P. Corcoran. *Ireland of the Illusions: A Sociological Chronicle 2007–2008*. IPA, 2010.
Shine Thompson, Mary. 'Introduction'. *Young Irelands: Studies in Children's Literature*, edited by Shine Thompson, Four Courts Press, 2011, pp. 9–21.
Shurmer-Smith Pamela, and Kevin Hannam. *Worlds of Desire, Realms of Power: A Cultural Geography*. Routledge, 1994.
Sigerson, George. 'Irish Literature: Its Origin, Environment, and Influence'. *The Revival of Irish Literature*, edited by Charles Gavan Duffy et al., T. Fisher & Unwin, 1894, pp. 61–114.
Slochower, Harry. *Mythopoesis: Mythic Patterns in the Literary Classics*. Wayne State UP, 1970.
Smith, Anthony D. *Ethnic Origins of Nations*. Blackwell, 1999.
Smith, Lillian. *The Unreluctant Years*. American Library Association, 1953.
Smyth, Gerry. *Space and the Irish Cultural Imagination*. Springer, 2001.
Squire, Charles. *Celtic Myth and Legend, Poetry and Romance*. Gresham, 1905.
Steedman, Carolyn. *Strange Dislocations: Childhood and the Idea of Human Interiority, 1780–1930*. Harvard UP, 1995.
Steele Boggs, Ralph. 'Folklore: Materials, Science, Art'. *Folklore Americans*, vol. III, no. 17, 1943, pp. 1–18.
Stephens, James. *Irish Fairy Tales*. Macmillan, 1920.
Stephens, James. *Letters of James Stephens*, edited by Richard J. Finnernan, Macmillan, 1974.
Stephens, John, and Robyn McCallum. *Retelling Stories, Framing Culture: Traditional Story and Metanarratives in Children's Literature*. Garland, 1998.

Stott, Jon C. 'The Poetics and Politics of Adaptation: Traditional Tales as Children's Literature'. *Children's Literature*, vol. 24, 1996, pp. 193–8.
Sullivan, C. W. III. *Welsh Celtic Myth in Modern Fantasy*. Greenwood Press, 1989.
Sweeney, Michelle, and Jack Morgan. 'Ancestral Voices: Padraic Colum and the Celtic Creature Poem'. *New Hibernia Review/Iris Éireannach Nua*, vol. 6, no. 4, 2002, pp. 120–35.
Táin Bó Cuailnge, *Recension 1*, edited and translated by Cecile O'Rahilly, Dublin Institute for Advanced Studies, 1976.
Tatar, Maria. *The Classic Fairy Tales*. Norton, 1999.
Thomas, Julian. *Understanding the Neolithic*. Routledge, 2002.
Thompson, Kate. *The New Policeman*. Bodley Head, 2005.
Thompson, Stith. *Motif-Index of Folk-Literature*. Indiana UP, 1955.
Thompson, Stith. *The Folktale*. U of California P, 1977.
Thoms, William. 'Folklore'. *The Athenaeum*, vol. 983, 1846, pp. 886–7.
Thuente, Mary Helen. '"Tradition and Innovation": Yeats and Joyce and the Irish Oral Tradition'. *Mosaic*, vol. 12, 1979, pp. 91–104.
Tilley, Christopher. *Interpreting Landscape: Geologies, Topographies, Identities: Explorations in Landscape Phenomenology*. Left Coast Press, 2010.
Toelken, Barre. *Anguish of Snails: Native American Folklore in the West*. U of Colorado P, 2003.
Tolkien, J. R. R. *Tree and Leaf*. HarperCollins UK, 2012.
Tompkins, Jane. *Sensational Designs: The Cultural Work of American Fiction, 1790–1860*. Oxford UP, 1985.
Trafzer, Clifford E. *Blue Dawn, Red Earth: New Native American Storytellers*. Doubleday, 1996.
Trigg, Dylan. *The Memory of Place: The Phenomenology of the Uncanny*. Ohio UP, 2011.
Trower, Shelley. *Rocks of Nation: The Imagination of Celtic Cornwall*. Oxford UP, 2015.
Tymoczko, Maria, and Colin A. Ireland. *Language and Tradition in Ireland: Continuities and Displacements*. U of Massachusetts P, 2003.
UNESCO. 'Text of the Convention the Safeguarding of the Intangible Heritage'. UNESCO Culture Sector. Accessed 9 June 2015, http://www.unesco.org/culture/ich/en/convention.
Uther, Hans-Jörg. *The Types of International Folktales: A Classification and Bibliography, Based on the System of Antti Aarne and Stith Thompson*. Academic Scientiarum Fennica, 2011.
Vernant, Jean-Pierre. *Myth and Thought among the Greeks*, translated by Janet Lloyd and Jeff Fort, Zone Books, 2006.
Voegelin, Eric. *Anamnesis: On the Theory of History and Politics, Volume 6*, translated by M. J. Hanak, edited by David Walsh, U of Missouri P, 2002.
Von Franz, Marie-Louise. *The Interpretation of Fairy Tales*. Shambala, 1996.
Von Maltzahn, Kraft E. *Nature a Landscape: Dwelling and Understanding*. McGill-Queen's UP, 1994.
Wall, Barbara. *The Narrator's Voice: The Dilemma of Children's Fiction*. St. Martin's Press, 1991.
Waller, Alison. 'Revisiting Childhood Landscapes: Revenants of Druid's Grove and Narnia'. *The Lion and the Unicorn*, vol. 32, no. 3, 2010, pp. 303–19.
Walsh, David. 'Introduction'. *Anamnesis: On the Theory of History and Politics, Volume 6*, edited by Eric Voeglin, U of Missouri P, 2002, pp. 1–27.
Walsh, Maeve. *A Guide to Irish Mythology*. Mercier Press, 2000.

Warner, Marina. *Once upon a Time: A Short Story of the Fairy Tale*. Oxford UP, 2014.
Warnock, Mary. *Memory*. Faber, 1987.
Wasserman, Judith. 'To Trace the Shifting Sands: Community, Ritual, and the Memorial Landscape'. *Landscape Journal*, vol. 17, no. 1, 1998, pp. 42–61.
Watson, G. J. *Irish Identity and the Literary Revival: Synge, Yeats, Joyce and O'Casey*. Catholic U of America P, 1994.
Watson, Nancy. *The Politics and Poetics of Irish Children's Literature*. Irish Academic P, 2009.
West, M. 'Kings, Heroes and Warriors: Aspects of Children's Literature in Ireland in the Era of Emergent Nationalism'. *Bulletin of the John Rylands University Library of Manchester*, vol. 76, no. 3, 1994, pp. 165–84.
Whiston Spirn, Anne. *The Language of Landscape*. Yale UP, 1998.
Whyte, Pádraic. *Irish Childhoods: Children's Fiction and Irish History*. Cambridge Scholars P, 2011.
Wilkie Stibbs, Christine. 'Intertextuality and the Child Reader'. Understanding Children's Literature, edited by Peter Hunt, Routledge, 2006, pp. 168–79.
Wilson Foster, John. *Fictions of the Irish Literary Revival: A Changeling Art*. Syracuse UP, 1993.
Wolcott, Harry F. *Ethnography: A Way of Seeing*. Alta Mira Press, 2008.
Yates, Frances. *The Art of Memory*. Routledge, 2013.
Yeats, W. B. *Fairy and Folktales of the Irish Peasantry*. Walter Scott, 1888.
Yeats, W. B. *Irish Fairy Tales*. Fischer & Unwin, 1892.
Yeats, W. B. *The Wind among the Reeds*. London: Elkin Mathews, 1899.
Yeats, W. B. 'John Eglinton and Spiritual Art'. *Literary Ideals in Ireland*, edited by John Eglinton, T. Fisher Unwin, 1899.
Yeats, W. B. 'The Autumn of the Flesh'. *Literary Ideals in Ireland*, edited by John Eglinton, T. Fisher Unwin, 1899.
Yeats, W. B. 'Preface'. *Cuchulain of Muirthemne*, edited by Augusta Gregory, Colin Smythe, 1970.
Yeats, W. B. *The Collected Works, Volume III: Autobiographies*, edited by William H. O'Donnell and Douglas N. Archibald, Scribner, 1999.
Yeats, W. B. *The Collected Poems of W.B. Yeats*. Wordsworth Editions, 2000.
Yeats, W. B. *The Winding Stair and Other Poems*. Simon & Schuster, 2012.
Young, Ella. *Celtic Wonder Tales*. Maunsel, 1910.
Young, James O. *Cultural Appropriation and the Arts*. John Wiley & Sons, 2010.
Zipes, Jack. *Fairy Tale as Myth/Myth as Fairy Tale*. U of Kentucky P, 1983.
Zipes, Jack. *The Irresistible Fairy Tale: The Cultural and Social History of a Genre*. Princeton UP, 2012.
Zuelow, Eric. *Making Ireland Irish: Tourism and National Identity since the Civil War*. Syracuse UP, 2009.

INDEX

Aengus Óg 45, 60, 134, 141–6, 168
Aisling 150–1
anamnesis 21, 81, 119, 125, 129, 150
archetypal symbols 7, 154, 157
Assmann, Aleida 80
Assmann, Jan 22, 23, 39, 60, 82, 107, 138, 140, 157
Andrews, J. S. 1, 5, 75, 77, 110–14, 158

Bachelard, Gaston 13, 15, 53, 143, 146, 148, 154, 179
Bakhtin, Mihhail 87, 88, 89, 92, 158, 159
Bal, Mieke 8, 9, 75
Bell of Nendrum, The 110–14
Bog Child 147–54
Book of the Invasions, The 55, 66, 131, 165, 166, 172
border(s) 14, 80, 90, 117, 118, 143, 147, 148, 152, 156
Bran (Hound of Fionn) 85–90, 94, 98, 99, 126, 130, 141, 142, 144, 156, 162, 171

Call, The 164–7
Celtic (Cultural) Revival 1, 4, 5, 6, 17–21, 30, 33, 43, 45, 52, 53, 56, 60, 63, 66, 67, 76, 158, 161, 164, 168–70
Celtic Wonder Tales 52–6
child figures 2, 4, 5, 6, 8, 11, 15, 32–3, 69, 71, 75, 76, 77, 78, 80, 82, 83, 86, 94, 99, 111, 114, 115, 118, 119, 120, 121, 122, 123, 136, 147, 148, 154, 155, 156, 158, 159, 160, 168
child readers 4, 5, 8–15, 18, 21, 33, 39, 40, 44, 48, 55, 57, 59, 61–7, 72, 81, 82, 121, 158, 159, 168, 172
chronotope 87, 159, 161
citizenship 18, 28, 35, 43, 66, 72
Colum, Padraic 1, 5, 43, 44, 45, 52, 63, 64, 66–73, 79, 92, 158, 173, 175
Coming of Cuculain, The 29–33
commemoration 84, 138, 145, 166

continuity 7, 20, 22, 23, 39, 89, 90, 104, 114, 146, 151, 153, 159, 160, 168
Cooper, Susan 119, 130, 173
Cregan, Mairin 78–80
Cuchulain and the Leprechaun 94–104
Cuchulain of Muirthemne 33–5
Cuchulain the Hound of Ulster 35–9
Cuchulainn 1, 4, 17, 18, 28–39, 43, 46–52, 60, 65, 114, 125–6, 128–30, 161, 168, 170, 171, 178
cultural nationalism 17, 18, 25, 26, 48, 73, 93, 179, 180, 183, 184, 187, 190

Dagda, The 45, 53, 54, 60, 134, 144, 145, 154, 165, 166, 173
Dease, Alice 1, 5, 43–52, 63, 158, 171, 173
Dillon, Eilís 1, 5, 75, 77, 104–11, 134, 158, 162
domestic experience 2, 15, 76, 77, 78, 105, 106, 107, 112, 155, 164
domestic narrative 1, 6, 80, 82
domestic paradigm 84, 104, 128, 130, 147, 161
domestic register 82, 95
domestic space 79, 83, 85, 86, 89, 92, 110, 127, 138, 149
Dowd, Siobhan 1, 5, 57, 117, 147–54, 158, 177

Easter Rising (1916) 1, 43–5, 48, 77, 166, 171
education 3, 21, 43, 46, 48, 65, 88, 93, 94, 107, 125, 129, 136, 162, 163, 166, 171, 174
Eliade, Mircea 6, 7, 14, 15, 47, 83, 84, 100, 121, 132, 134, 139, 151, 153, 157, 160, 174, 182
emplacement 5, 14, 15, 76, 83, 119, 140, 141, 142, 142, 146, 148, 152, 159, 180
Erll, Astrid 107, 158, 179
evocation 13, 19, 53, 92, 129, 150, 172

fairy tales 2, 30, 55, 60, 62, 80, 94, 95, 97, 98, 99, 103, 104, 106, 168, 172, 174, 175
fantasy 3, 4, 13, 113, 117, 118, 120, 123, 130, 131, 133, 135, 139, 147, 150, 155, 162, 168, 169, 173, 175, 176, 178, 179
Fianna Éireann, The 43, 56, 57, 58, 59, 85, 87, 88, 89, 90, 91, 92, 94, 95, 101, 137, 141, 142, 163, 171, 172, 177
Fianna Éireann, Boys' Organization 48
Fionn Mac Cumhaill 56-61, 63-67, 85, 141, 142, 161, 171, 173, 177
folklore, folk tales 1-6, 18, 26, 44, 46, 47, 52, 65, 66, 67, 72, 73, 75-83, 83, 93, 94, 95, 97-100, 104-7, 110, 114-18, 122, 123, 130-3, 155, 158, 159, 161, 165, 168, 175, 177, 178
Frehan, Padraic 93, 94
Frye, Northrop 7, 58, 132, 153, 157, 170, 183
Fuchsia Stone, The 135-8

Garner, Alan 3, 119
Gregory, Augusta 1, 4, 17-19, 28, 33-8, 40, 45, 47, 117, 131, 158, 161, 171, 173-6, 179

hero, heroic figures, heroism, heroic idea 18, 25, 28, 30, 34, 35, 36, 38, 39, 40, 46-52, 57, 60, 61, 65, 66, 71, 88, 93, 95, 96, 100, 101, 120, 122, 125, 128, 134, 136, 143, 145, 170, 171, 174, 175, 176, 177, 178
Heroes of the Dawn 56-9
Hiberno-English 89, 95, 97, 174
hierophany 149, 150, 151
Hounds of the Morrigan, The 123-30
Hull, Eleanor 1, 4, 17-18, 28, 33, 35-8, 45, 47, 158, 170-1, 173, 175-6
Hy-Brazil 108, 175

Irish Fairy Tales 61-6
Irish Folklore Commission 75, 93, 174
Irish Mythological Cycles 170
Iser, Wolfgang 12, 13, 76, 84

Keeper, The 161-4
Kelly, Una 1, 5, 35, 75, 77, 93-104, 125, 158

King of Ireland's Son, The 66-73
Kort, Wesley 45, 46, 57, 59

liminality 14, 31, 58, 89, 115, 124, 126, 139, 147, 150
Lost Island, The 104-10
Lynch, Patricia 1, 5, 57, 75, 77, 82-92, 95, 106, 124-5, 132, 136, 141, 156, 158, 162-3, 172, 174, 175

Martin, Darragh 1, 5, 157, 161-4
Melling, Orla 1, 5, 117, 118, 130-5, 158
metaphysicality 47, 55, 89, 109, 113, 118, 132, 148, 149, 153, 154, 155, 160,
mythic experiences 4, 6, 15, 76, 77, 78, 79, 80, 81, 82, 83, 84, 85, 87, 94, 96, 98, 100, 101, 103, 104, 111, 112, 115, 119, 120, 122, 123, 124, 130, 136, 158, 160, 162, 164

narration 8, 9, 36, 38, 39, 64, 66, 73, 94, 106, 109,
narratology 8, 79, 87
national trauma 76-81
New Policeman, The 139-47
Nicolaisen, Wilhelm 94, 98, 122
Nimmo, Jenny 118, 119
noetic (processes, economy) 30, 60, 172

O'Grady, Standish 1, 4, 17-18, 28-33, 35, 37-40, 45, 47, 54, 61, 66, 117, 131, 158, 170-1, 173, 175-6, 185
Ó'Guilín, Peadar 1, 5, 157, 161, 164-6
O'Leary, Jim 1, 5, 117, 135-8, 158
Old Time Stories of Erin 46-52
Ong, Walter 23, 24, 60-5, 155, 168
oral culture 3, 5, 23-6, 30, 36, 39, 59-60, 67, 69, 70, 78, 93, 94, 95, 96, 97, 98, 101, 102, 105, 115, 167, 168
oral memory 119, 156
oral narratives 2
oral tradition 2, 35, 76, 83, 93, 107, 115, 124, 131, 168
O'Shea, Pat 1, 5, 35, 39, 117, 123-30, 158, 162, 166, 171, 172, 176

physicality 39, 147, 149, 160
profane time 45, 83, 84, 85, 89, 92, 100, 107, 134, 139, 142, 144, 147, 149, 150, 153, 158, 160, 161

reciprocity 1, 40, 77, 84, 120, 121, 123, 135, 136, 141, 142, 143, 145, 146, 148, 150, 158, 161, 176
register 67, 78, 82, 85, 86, 88, 92, 94, 95, 97, 98, 99, 102, 103, 127, 128
Renan, Ernest 19, 26, 157
reverie 6, 8, 13, 14, 15, 27, 40, 53, 54, 55, 91, 143, 148, 151, 152, 154
Ricoeur, Paul 23, 45, 74, 120, 153, 157, 160
ritual(s) 3, 7, 12, 19, 20, 23, 24, 26, 28, 34, 45, 59, 83, 84, 85, 100, 101, 103, 104, 121, 138, 140, 145, 149, 157, 160, 161, 166, 177
Russell, George (Æ) 18, 26, 29, 39, 40, 61, 172
Russell, Violet 1, 5, 43, 44, 45, 56–9, 61, 63, 131, 158, 172

sacred time 3, 22, 28, 39, 44, 47, 52, 53, 54, 83–6, 89, 90, 92, 99, 100, 107, 124, 126, 132, 134, 139, 142, 144, 145, 147, 148, 149, 150, 151, 153, 154, 155, 158, 159, 160, 165, 168, 174, 177
Seanchaí 61, 64, 67
selfhood 5, 14, 15, 17, 18, 25, 28, 44, 45, 61, 72, 82, 101, 118, 120, 127, 134, 135, 146, 158, 159, 161, 176
Sídhe, The 66, 68, 136, 144, 145, 164, 165, 166, 177
Singing Stone, The 130–5

spiral(s) 91, 132, 153, 154, 165, 176
Stephens, James 1, 5, 43, 44, 45, 61–6, 133, 158, 170, 173
storytelling 2, 8, 9, 10, 34, 52, 60, 63, 67, 68, 70, 71, 76, 78, 79, 94, 95, 96, 102, 107, 108, 109, 115, 133, 157, 175

temporality 5, 9, 10, 15, 19, 21, 22, 39, 44, 52, 57, 62, 76, 80, 83, 84, 87, 90, 91, 94, 98, 100, 101, 110, 111, 114, 118, 121, 122, 124, 129, 134, 138, 139, 143, 144, 145, 146, 147, 150, 151, 152, 159, 160, 161, 167, 172
Thompson, Kate 1, 5, 60, 117, 118, 139–47, 158, 162, 166, 169, 171, 172, 177
Tilley, Christopher 148, 177
time-slip 81, 110, 111, 113, 118, 130
Tir na nÓg 44, 60, 98, 113, 120, 121, 122, 123, 124, 125, 126, 127, 128, 129, 135, 139, 141
Trigg, Dylan 15, 120, 143, 146, 159, 160
Tuatha de Danann 30, 53, 54, 55, 56, 66, 68, 109, 130, 131, 132, 133, 134, 135, 136, 137, 144, 165, 166, 176
Turf-Cutter's Donkey, The 82–92

Vernant, Jean-Pierre 7, 119, 144, 149, 150

Warnock, Mary 120, 159

Yeats, W. B. 17–19, 24, 26–9, 33, 34, 40, 41, 60, 91, 117, 153, 161, 170, 171, 174, 176
Young, Ella 1, 5, 43, 44, 46, 52–6, 60, 63, 64, 66, 67, 166, 173

www.ingramcontent.com/pod-product-compliance
Lightning Source LLC
Chambersburg PA
CBHW070638300426
44111CB00013B/2164